TOXIC

A Compassionate Companion and
Guide to Overcoming a Traumatic
or Abusive Childhood

JACKIE POET

Copyright © 2024 Jackie Poet

All rights reserved. No part of this publication may be reproduced, distributed, or transmitted in any form or by any means, including photocopying, recording, or other electronic or mechanical methods, without the prior written permission of the publisher, except by reviewers, who may quote brief passages in a review.

ISBN: 978-1-7391941-2-3

Previously published as *Parents Can Really F*ck You Up: A Compassionate Companion and Guide to Overcoming a Traumatic, Abusive, or Unfair Childhood*

A catalogue record of this book is available from the British Library

Published by Waterfront Books Ltd, Ipswich, UK
waterfrontbooks.co.uk

Cover designed by Miblart

Disclaimer:

This book is intended to provide information and support to individuals seeking to understand and recover from childhood abuse and trauma. The contents of this book are based on the author's experiences, research, and insights, and are offered for general informational purposes only. It is not intended as, and shall not be understood or construed as, professional psychological, psychiatric, or medical advice, diagnosis, or treatment.

The author and publisher are not licensed therapists, counselors, or medical professionals. The information provided in this book should not be considered as a substitute for professional psychological, psychiatric, or medical advice, diagnosis, or treatment. Readers should always seek the advice of a qualified health provider with any questions they may have regarding their mental or emotional health.

Every individual's experience with trauma and healing is unique. While many may find the suggestions and advice in this book helpful, not all strategies or approaches may be appropriate or effective for everyone. Readers are encouraged to use their discretion and judgment in applying the information provided.

Neither the author nor the publisher shall be liable or responsible for any damages, whether direct, indirect, incidental, or consequential, arising from the use or misuse of the information in this book or for any outcomes related to the advice and strategies discussed herein.

If you are in crisis or need immediate help, please contact emergency services in your area or seek the advice of a qualified mental health professional.

A Note to the Reader

Before you read this book, we'd like to extend a gentle word of caution. Within these pages, we explore themes that might resonate deeply and evoke strong emotions, particularly for those who have experienced trauma or challenging circumstances. While our aim is to offer understanding, support, and healing, we recognize that some topics may be triggering. Please prioritize your well-being and proceed at a pace that feels right for you. Remember, you're not alone on this journey, and it's okay to seek support whenever you need it.

Contents

1	Our Future	1
2	Wrongdoing	9
3	How We Were Hurt	17
4	Why Early Damage is Destructive	43
5	Justifications for Abuse: Lies and More Lies	57
6	Goals for Our Recovery	69
7	Emotions and Emotional Processing	81
8	Thinking: From Surviving to Thriving	107
9	Foundations of Relationships	121
10	Recognizing and Overcoming Abuse	137
11	Romantic Relationships	143
12	Family Relationships	149
13	Finding Help: Counseling and Psychotherapy	161
14	Types of Therapy	167
15	Additional Means of Support	185
16	Whole Body Healing	193
17	Confronting our Parents	211
18	Beyond Recovery	227

A Word from Jackie Poet   235
Further Reading and Resources   237

1

Our Future

What Determines Our Future?

Imagine that we are going to spend the rest of our lives with just one person. They will be with us for our happiest and saddest moments. When we face our greatest difficulties and our biggest opportunities, they will be there. Forever by our side, they will never desert us.

Our imaginary companion has strong opinions about us. They doubt us. They do not believe that we deserve to succeed. They suggest that we are likely to fail in our relationships, at work, or whatever business we're in. Quick to criticize and blame us, never complimentary or encouraging, they undermine our achievements and our potential. Time spent with them will cause us to feel shame and guilt instead of optimism and gratitude.

How do we feel about our imaginary partner?

Do we want them to stay with us forever?

Will we be happier with or without them?

There are two shocking realities to this thought experiment.

Firstly, our imaginary companion is real.

Secondly, no matter how hard we try, we will never escape from them. The one person who is with us forever is us.

We wake up every morning with our own thoughts and feelings, with core beliefs about ourselves, other people, the world, and our place in it.

Our relationship with ourself determines our relationships with everyone and everything. It creates our future.

This future is undecided. It can change. We can change it.

The biggest challenge we face and our greatest problem to overcome is that wherever we choose to travel, we need a map. An accurate map. A detailed map. Borrowing from the poet Minnie Haskins, we want to "tread safely into the unknown."

Our map should alert us to dangers, while highlighting fascinating and fun places ahead.

Does such a map exist? Are we using a map already? If so, who drew it? Is it a help or a hindrance?

And where can we find the best map for us?

Maps

Imagine setting out on a journey to discover an incredible new land. Sandy beaches and rugged coastlines, mountain glaciers, lakes, forests, cities teeming with beautiful buildings, exciting and fun people: all are waiting somewhere on the road ahead. There are, however, difficult challenges that we need to overcome.

A major problem is that the map we are using is wrong. The cartographers who created it were neglectful, incompetent, or even malevolent. The map that we were given continually leads to dark, depressing, and dangerous places. Unable to navigate our way to the sunlit shores, serene lakes, or bustling town squares, we ask for help. Kindly strangers offer to read the map for us; some even want to accompany us on the journey. However, nothing that they do, or that we try, works.

The reality is that without an accurate map, we will never reach the places where we want to be. The journey itself becomes a difficult and depressing struggle.

Some people were raised in a loving, kind family. Their mental map of life is good. Their early childhood experiences taught them confidence, how to model healthy, happy relationships, and gifted them with a sense of purpose and direction. For many of us though, this did not happen.

When we were brought up by toxic parents, we are likely to be using a mental map that is at best damaged. At worst it is distressing and destructive. Our maps were drawn by people who, instead of loving and nurturing us, put their own needs first.

As we grew, we added to the map ourselves. The areas that we filled in, however, were about "surviving" rather than "thriving." Protection was our priority. Staying safe in our immediate family environment took all our energy. Continuing our metaphor, we designed a map to teach ourselves how to steer clear of problems. We learned how to avoid hurt and harm instead of ways to experience joy, love, and happiness.

To travel to destinations that we choose, we need more than a map. We also need to act. Just as physical journeys involve trains, planes, buses, time spent on foot and all manner of transport, our healing journey will require different approaches and steps at different times. Additionally, as we travel, we will have to check our progress, changing direction and adjusting schedules when necessary.

Our old map is not our destiny. We have the power to redraw it, to redefine our journey, to set a better course for our lives. This book will help us to draft a new mental map. It will help us to identify where our current map is wrong. Past patterns can be changed. Whether we are eighteen or eighty-plus, we can learn new ways of thinking and processing emotions. How to feel better about ourselves. And change our perceptions of other people. This will be challenging work. But the effort invested in building a better, brighter, and far, far happier life is worth it.

And we are traveling together.

We Are Not Alone: The World's Worst and Best-Kept Secret

We face an extraordinary and heartbreaking global problem, an iceberg of adversity hidden beneath the sea of the everyday. It's a monstrous specter that subtly haunts our society, an insidious problem of almost unimaginable proportions. The statistics are more than just shocking—they are a stark wake-up call to a crisis that the world prefers to ignore.

According to UNICEF, three-quarters of children between 2 and 4 years are subject to what is termed "violent discipline" from parents or caregivers. Around 176 million children live in families where domestic abuse takes place.

The World Health Organization (WHO) estimated that, globally in 2014, one billion children aged 2 to 17 years experienced physical, sexual, or emotional abuse, or multiple types of violence.

Figures from the WHO suggest that 1 in 5 women and 1 in 13 men report having been sexually abused as a child. The thinktank organization ChildUSA estimates that 60–70% never report their abuse.

The ACE (adverse childhood events) research study in the U.S. discovered that two-thirds of adults had experienced at least one adverse event, defined as something particularly problematic. This includes neglect, physical abuse, emotional abuse, exposure to drug or domestic abuse, or similar traumatic experiences. The UK-based charity, the National Society for the Prevention of Cruelty to Children (NSPCC), estimates that 1 in 10 children in the UK experience neglect, 1 in 14 are subjected to physical abuse and 1 in 14 children are brought up in an emotionally abusive family. Worldwide, the problem is enormous.

One in four adults on our planet today were mistreated as children.

This shocking statistic isn't abstract. It represents real experiences. Our experiences.

Multimillions of us have never told our story. Worldwide, an astonishing number of us spend our daily lives secretly suffering in silence. The consequences of this differ. Some of us fail to thrive. We don't enjoy the lives we deserve to live. Our relationships are substandard, and we are financially poorer than we should be. Or perhaps we exist in a permanent state of dysphoria. We never quite achieve our full potential, and we miss opportunities. Maybe our past is hitting us harder. Much harder. Our days are blighted by depression, anxiety, shame, and guilt.

We do not need to suffer. We deserve to succeed.

We owe it to ourselves to enjoy becoming everything we can be. And we can start now.

The first step on our journey to a contented future is to accept and understand that we are not responsible for our past.

It's not our fault.

It's Not Our Fault

We are all writing our own story. It should be our own choice whether this will be a tale of joy, wealth, happiness, and success, or one of misery and tragedy. However, we face an enormous problem that we are not responsible for: the first few chapters of our lives were written by someone else. The beginning of our book was badly crafted. Instead of preparing us for an exciting adventure, our upbringing harmed more than helped us. The actions of our parents or the circumstances of our early lives set us on a road heading in a direction that makes us miserable. We aren't making the most of life. We are missing opportunities. We aren't yet living the life that we deserve. We may surround ourselves with toxic relationships or stick with a job or lifestyle that we don't want. Some of us will experience deep distress. We are depressed, anxious, or enduring a chaotic and dysfunctional existence.

None of this is our fault. We are innocent. Guilt, blame, and shame belong elsewhere, not with us. This is true.

There is, however, a further truth that is both liberating and somewhat scary. Where we go next is up to us.

It's not our fault, but it *is* our responsibility.

It's Our Responsibility: We Are the Best People Who Can Help Us

Sometimes it feels as though we are serving a life sentence for crimes that we did not commit.

Beyond all reasonable doubt, some crimes were committed. But not by us. We may have been victims of actual crimes—physical or sexual assault, or neglect for example—or suffered the stress of years of substandard parenting. However we define our past, what we experienced was wrong.

It is unfair. We have the right to be angry. We have the right to be furious. It is normal and healthy to feel this way. For most of us, what should have happened didn't, or what should not have happened did. We ought to have been loved unconditionally, helped, supported, and encouraged to grow into the best possible human beings that we could be. It is wrong that we were raised the way we were.

All the above is correct. However, there is also another undeniable reality. No matter how frustrating, or how unjust, we are left to clear up the mess. We have to deal with the damage from our early lives.

Nobody else will do this for us.

We're not to blame for our past, but we can take charge of our future. American author Rick Warren states, "We are products of our past, but we don't have to be prisoners of it."

We are the only people who can fix us, but this does not mean that we are on our own. We are one person among millions worldwide with similar and shared experiences. We are all in this together. Like the captain of a ship, we are not alone, but we are in charge. We are responsible.

What is responsibility?

Being responsible is frequently seen as a burden. It conjures up the idea of blame. We might be responsible for meeting deadlines at work, ensuring that a particular project is completed by a specific date. It might be our responsibility to deliver goods to the right people on time. Or maybe we have responsibilities for health and safety or supporting junior colleagues. The question, "Who was responsible for this?" is asked when things go wrong. The idea of responsibility is often unattractive.

Mark Manson, author of *The Subtle Art of Not Giving a F*ck*, describes what he calls the "responsibility/fault fallacy." He suggests that many of us don't take responsibility for our problems because we think that by doing so, it means that they're our fault—that we caused them.

There is, however, frequently confusion about how we can escape our own histories. A common misunderstanding is to mix, muddle, and mash together blame and responsibility.

What is the difference between blame and responsibility?

Although society often puts blame and responsibility together, they are different. We can become much more effective when we learn the difference between the two.

We can blame our parents or dysfunctional families for what happened to us, while also taking responsibility for our future.

This is worth repeating. It is OK to both blame our parents and to take responsibility for our own life.

A simple example illustrates this. If we were hit by a drunk driver who mounted the pavement while we were walking to work, then they would be at fault. If they then sped off and escaped justice, they would still be entirely to blame. We would, though, be responsible for the rest of our lives after this incident. If we were severely injured, then we would be responsible for treating ourselves with care and compassion. We would also need to take charge of our own healing. It is unfair. Someone else was to blame, but we are responsible for making everything right.

We are not to blame for the way we were raised. Children shouldn't have to bring themselves up. Blame should rightfully be attributed to our parents or dysfunctional backgrounds.

But we are responsible for creating a fearless, free, and fulfilling future. We owe this to ourselves.

Tomorrow and Tomorrow and Tomorrow

Unlike Macbeth, who used the words "tomorrow and tomorrow and tomorrow" to express his resentment about the hopelessness of life, we have a choice. Macbeth's words were written by Shakespeare; we are now writing our own script.

We have three possible "tomorrows."
Our lives can:

- Be better.
- Be worse.
- Be about the same.

If we are already heading toward an unhappy future or one where we won't progress, we don't have to continue along that path: we can take a new route.

A quote derived from British poet Thomas Campbell (1777–1844) says that "the future casts its shadow before us." A little later in this book, we will look at core beliefs—our internal map or programming that is taking us in a particular direction. Our thoughts, beliefs, and behaviors are already moving us toward or away from fulfillment, fun, and the freedom that we deserve.

The ancient Greek philosopher Socrates believed that "the secret of change is to focus all of your energy not on fighting the old, but on building the new."

We cannot fight the past. We cannot change it. But we can discover its impact on our present and our future. By viewing our history with self-compassion, we will find out how it affects us today and how it potentially shapes tomorrow.

When we understand how our childhood made us into the adults that we are now, we are in a powerful position to make effective adjustments to our thinking and behavior.

To be free from our past, we need to face the reality of our upbringing. We need to understand what happened, why it matters and, most importantly, how to progress to an increasingly happy life.

2

Wrongdoing

CONFUSION AND CLARITY ABOUT OUR DYSFUNCTIONAL CHILDHOODS

There is a strange paradox at the center of dysfunctional families. What seems incredibly clear at first can actually be confusing.

On the surface, it appears that everybody knows what abuse is. After all, it is something that is widespread and features in our newspapers every day. Yet the situation is complex.

News media tend to focus on sexual abuse. It is good that this terrible problem is increasingly recognized. The more openly it is discussed, the more effective action can be taken to prevent it, and the greater the chances are that those of us who were sexually abused can find the support that we need. That said, the reporting of sexual abuse tends to run alongside an under-reporting of other types of abuse.

Additionally, extensive media coverage of gruesome crimes can lead to people creating a hierarchy of abuse. We then tend to downplay what happened to us. We look at dreadful things that were inflicted on others and convince ourselves that our situation wasn't really so bad. This is understandable; however, we are being unfair to ourselves.

We do not need to deny or belittle our own experience because we believe that other people have had a worse time than we have. We all need and deserve support.

Breaking the Cycle

There is also a strong moral reason why we shouldn't downplay what happened to us. When we minimize our own experience, we maximize the chance that abusers can get away with their behavior. Acknowledging and addressing our experiences not only aids our personal healing, but also plays a crucial role in the broader struggle against abuse. When we act to help ourselves, we help to make the world a better place by simultaneously taking steps to break the cycle. For good. For everybody's good.

How Abuse Was Hidden

For our recovery and growth, and to benefit wider society, it is important to clearly recognize dysfunction within families. This isn't always easy, as abuse is often disguised as something socially acceptable. Excuses acted as fog, clouding the path to truth and masking wrongdoing as "beneficial" behavior.

Physical abuse was disguised as "strict parenting," and emotional abuse became "tough love." The grooming process central to sex crimes had the ultimate and cruel aim of making us believe that what was done to us was partly our fault. When abuse was spiritual or ritual, it usually involved a number of perpetrators. This made it appear normal. In families where our parents misused drugs or alcohol, excuses were invented for what took place. Alcoholic parents blamed us for their own behavior. We were told the ridiculous lie that we were so badly behaved and caused so much stress that we "drove them to drink." Parents who manipulated us to take sides in divorce disputes pretended that they were doing this because we would be better off. "Stage parents" exploited us for money or to compensate for their own lack of success. They justified this by pretending that they were ambitious for our future.

Some of us are left questioning the reality of our situations, wondering if the actions perpetrated against us truly constitute abuse. This questioning and self-doubt inevitably leads to the question: how can we definitively distinguish between what is and isn't abuse?

How We Can Tell Whether What Happened to Us Was Abuse

Sometimes it's already very clear that what happened to us was abuse. For some of us though, especially when we've been heavily manipulated, it isn't easy to know the truth. The following thought exercise can help to clarify our own experience.

Picture a child who is the same age and same gender as we were when whatever we experienced took place. We have to be absolutely clear that this is an imaginary child, not us. We can give the child a name from the same culture and background that we belong to.

Visualize the fictitious youngster being treated in exactly the same way we were.

When we do this, what is our first instinct? Are we proud of what's taking place? Are the adults behaving in a warm, loving, and supportive way? Or do we want to intervene? Do we want to stop it from happening?

For some of us the answer is obvious. We would want to stop our imaginary child being physically assaulted.

Not all abuse is obvious though. There may also be more subtle abuse occurring. This is especially the case with some types of emotional abuse.

How is our child being spoken to? What are the underlying messages that our imaginary child is being given? How will they affect their friendships? How is their self-esteem, sense of worth, and confidence? Is their personality growing or shrinking? How do they feel each day when they wake up?

What is the impact of the events that are taking place?

How to Take an Objective View of the Impact Our Childhoods Had on Us

A second very helpful exercise involves taking our imaginary child and projecting them into an adult future. Remember that they experienced exactly the same circumstances that we did. This helps us to more clearly see the effect that our upbringing had on us.

It is easier to do this if we use a series of questions to prompt our thinking:

- How does what happened affect our imaginary child's relationships? As a result of their experiences, are they more or less likely to trust and to show empathy and compassion?
- How do they perceive love and affection? Do they equate love with pain, control, or neglect, or do they understand it as mutual respect, care, and understanding?
- Can they maintain healthy relationships? Do they know how to set and

respect boundaries, or do they tend to overstep or let others overstep? Do they even understand what boundaries are?
- Will they feel pride, and be confident and assertive? Or do they often feel unworthy or not good enough?
- Will their lives be dominated by shame and guilt?
- Do they have a great career and a healthy relationship with authority figures?
- Is their relationship with food, alcohol, legal and illegal drugs safe and sensible?
- Are they happy, with a positive body image?
- How is their emotional and mental well-being? Are they constantly anxious, depressed, or struggling with emotional processing?
- Do they believe that the world is full of opportunity, or a scary, threatening place?
- Are they a success (defined as being the best they can possibly be and living the lifestyle of their choice)?

This exercise can help us take a clear-eyed look at how our past might have shaped us. This is a key step to better understanding ourselves.

Picturing an imaginary child with our experiences helps us see how our past affects our present. It allows us to ask insightful questions from a safe distance about our relationships, emotions, work, and self-image.

Using this imagined child as a lens, we can see the effects of our upbringing more clearly. It shines a light on our past, helping us to understand where we are now. It allows us to confront any negative impacts while also acknowledging the strength that got us through tough times. It's about understanding and being kind to ourselves, both in the past and present, and setting up a better future. It shows we can grow, change, and control our own story.

Once we see how our past could influence us today, this understanding lets us face the realities of our upbringing. As we uncover our past, we move from just recognizing its impact to actually dealing with it. This leads us to the next big step: understanding the importance of facing our truths and the dangers of downplaying our experiences. Let's now look into why it's so important to fully acknowledge our personal history in our healing journey.

Why Facing Reality Works

The American Psychological Association (APA) defines minimizing as a "cognitive distortion consisting of a tendency to present events to oneself or others as insignificant or unimportant."

Understandably, many of us try to diminish the impact that our upbringing has had on us. Self-help books, courses, and well-meaning friends encourage us to think positively.

Certainly, positive thinking has its place. However, facing up to the reality of what happened is the best way to heal. American playwright August Wilson neatly summarized this with his words, "Your willingness to wrestle with your demons will cause your angels to sing." Of course, our biggest problems are a direct result of our history, rather than being some sort of innate personality flaw. That said, by facing our demons with knowledge and compassion, they will be defeated.

Sometimes we try to comfort ourselves with the idea that other people have had a much more difficult life than we have. Of course, this is always true. Some adults will have endured a childhood far more terrible than our own.

Deep down though, this way of thinking is just a trick our mind plays on us. It attempts to stop us dealing with our pain by trying to persuade us that our problems are not important. It is vital that we recognize our own hurt. We deserve to be healed and happy. We must avoid the trap of dismissing our own needs because some theoretical "other" person had it worse than us.

We will succeed more quickly when we face up to, rather than downplay, our personal history.

As we uncover the truth of our past and see how it shapes us, it's beneficial to remember that we're part of a bigger story. We're not alone, and, importantly, scientific studies back up what we've discovered about ourselves. Key insights come from the ACE study, which describes the deep impact our childhood experiences can have on our adult lives.

Now, let's explore what this groundbreaking research reveals.

THE ACE (ADVERSE CHILDHOOD EXPERIENCE) STUDY

Arguably, it wasn't until the mid-1990s that scientists began to recognize just how much damage was caused by events that happened to us as children. Up until this time, it was generally believed that children had poor memories and that our experiences when we were younger had little significance.

Researchers in the US, from the health organization Kaiser Permanente and the Centers for Disease Control and Prevention, looked at the lives of middle-aged adults to find out the impact of their adverse childhood experiences. A commanding and influential piece of research, the ACE study demonstrated for the first time the impact that distressing childhood experiences have on our adult lives. It was a major breakthrough in understanding childhood trauma. It is frequently quoted in academic textbooks and self-help literature.

The results were shocking.

Investigators found that distressing events in childhood inhibited normal brain growth and development. This led to relationship problems, difficulties with drugs, alcohol, and crime, depression and anxiety, and unhelpful ways of thinking (social, emotional, and cognitive impairment).

The likelihood of adopting what was termed "health-risk behaviors" was higher. Experiencing a dysfunctional upbringing meant that we were more likely to eat too little or too much, smoke heavily, drink, abuse drugs, hurt ourselves or engage in dangerous behavior. Naturally, this increased the chances of disease, disability, social problems and ultimately, early death.

The researchers defined the following as adverse childhood experiences:

- Physical abuse.
- Physical neglect.
- Emotional neglect.
- Emotional abuse.
- Sexual abuse.
- Domestic violence.
- Drug or alcohol abuse.
- Mental illness within the family.
- Divorce or separation.
- A member of the family being sent to prison.

The scientists discovered that ACEs are very common, yet very poorly recognized.

The more ACEs that a person has in their childhood, the greater the impact this is likely to have on their adulthood. Those of us who have had four or more ACEs are seven times more likely to have alcohol problems, twice as likely to develop cancer or heart disease, and twelve times more likely to attempt suicide.

Why More Research Is Needed

It is fantastic that the ACE study has highlighted the extent to which our dysfunctional childhoods have caused us difficulties as adults. Clearly though, much more research is urgently needed. In particular, it's overly simplistic to sum up the number of ACEs and suggest that the more we have as individuals, the greater their impact. One adverse event on its own might be every bit as traumatizing as another four events added together. As with much research, it says interesting things about the population as a whole, but only gives likelihoods and probabilities concerning us as individual people.

The ACE study is a simple snapshot. Like a photograph of a wedding or family event, it gives valuable information—who was there, what they were wearing, etc. Nevertheless, it gives an incomplete picture. There are a range of difficulties that we faced that aren't covered. The research is not comprehensive enough.

Psychologist Dr. Nicole LePera (author of *How to Do the Work*) highlights an interesting aspect of the ACE research—that it doesn't consider the range of what she calls "spiritual traumas." Dr. LePera describes spiritual trauma as "not feeling seen or heard or expressing oneself authentically," which she says results in our suffering loneliness and internalized shame. So, while the ACE study has undeniably shed light on the profound effect of our past on our present, it is essential to recognize its limitations and the need for a more nuanced understanding of our individual experiences. Dr. LePera's concept of "spiritual traumas" underscores this point, emphasizing the often overlooked yet deeply impactful aspects of our past that shape our identity.

The next chapter aims to shed light on the different types of abuse, providing a more comprehensive understanding of their nature, their impact, and the ways in which they intersect with and amplify each other.

3

How We Were Hurt

Some of us are very clear that what happened to us and the way we were treated fits neatly into one or more established categories of abuse. Frequently though, we experienced different kinds of abuse at different times, or several types simultaneously.

Every sort of harm that was done to us involved a degree of emotional abuse. As human beings, we are all thinking and feeling creatures. If we were physically or sexually abused, then this inevitably damaged our "spirit" as well as our physical body. If we were neglected, this would also have harmed our sense of self-worth and self-esteem.

There are also types of harmful parenting that are not widely recognized. Despite the fact that they are seldom acknowledged in textbooks, counseling, or psychology courses, they are nevertheless destructive.
Examples include:

- Parents who are fanatically focused on their children's success (sometimes described as "stage parents").
- Parents whose religious or political views are incredibly rigid and who drown out their children's ability to think for themselves.
- Narcissistic parents, who see their children as little more than extensions of themselves.

In this section, we'll take a closer look at the different forms that abuse can take, and how they may affect us in our adult lives.

Neglect

…what didn't happen has as much or more power over who you have become as an adult than any of those events you do remember.

—Jonice Webb PhD: *Running on Empty: Overcome Your Childhood Emotional Neglect*

Neglect is different from other sorts of abuse because it is focused on what should have happened to us but didn't, rather than what shouldn't have happened but did.

Neglect is not the same as poverty. It wasn't neglect if our parents or carers didn't have the money to provide what we needed. That said, poverty should be considered "societal neglect." In a world full of billionaires and extraordinary wealth, it is morally wrong that any child should ever go hungry.

There are several types of neglect defined below. The list is not exhaustive. It describes many of our experiences. That said, one of the best ways to recognize neglect is to acknowledge our own feelings. If we felt neglected, then we were.

Physical neglect

Physical neglect includes not providing enough food, appropriate clothes, and somewhere safe to live. Some of us may remember being unable to concentrate at school because we didn't have breakfast and we were starving.

Not ensuring children are clean and have good hygiene is also physical neglect. There was a terrible feeling of shame and isolation if we were noticeable in class for a lack of hygiene.

Children should also be supervised and feel protected. Depending on our age at the time, being home alone was physical neglect. The popular film *Home Alone* gives a fun fictional account of a boy left behind in his house when the rest of his family flies off for Christmas. No harm came to him. But the reality is different: when we were left on our own for prolonged periods at a young age, we felt lonely and abandoned.

Emotional neglect

Emotional neglect is different from emotional abuse because it is the failure to provide what is needed, rather than deliberately upsetting a child. Perhaps there was simply nobody there for us. Nobody came to comfort us when we were upset, no one played with us and taught us to laugh and have fun. Perhaps too we weren't given the opportunity to build happy relationships with other family members and we weren't given the chance to make friends. When we were kept isolated for large amounts of time, this was emotional neglect.

Educational neglect

A huge factor in how successful we are as adults is how good our education was. Few doctors, scientists, or engineers boast about their poor childhood learning experiences. When we weren't given a place in school (or properly homeschooled) or were simply allowed to routinely and frequently miss school, this was educational neglect.

Educational neglect isn't only limited to lack of school attendance, but also lack of appropriate education. When we were sent to schools that were ill-suited to us, or we were deeply unhappy and this wasn't addressed, then we experienced educational neglect.

The repercussions of educational neglect extend far beyond academic performance; they permeate every aspect of our lives. When we are deprived of an appropriate education, we're essentially denied the tools and resources necessary to navigate the world efficiently. This type of neglect can inhibit our potential for personal and professional growth, fostering feelings of inadequacy and contributing to a diminished self-image.

The emotional impact of educational neglect is profound. We may internalize the lack of support as an indicator of our worth, leading to feelings of inadequacy and self-doubt that can linger long into adulthood. It can create a negative cycle where the fear of failure prevents us from trying new things, causing stagnation in personal and professional development.

Moreover, the absence of a nurturing educational environment can disrupt our social development. Schools are not only places for academic learning but also social interaction, where we learn to work in teams, handle disagreements, and develop empathy. Educational neglect can, therefore, leave us ill-equipped to build healthy relationships, adding another layer to the detrimental impact on our adult life.

Lastly, our lack of education can result in tangible economic consequences. Without proper education, we may struggle to secure gainful employment and potentially face a lifetime of financial hardship. The struggle for economic stability further compounds the emotional stress, forming a vicious cycle that's challenging to break free from.

Medical neglect

As children, our bodies hadn't reached their adult size and shape. When we were ill, we needed good medical care to prevent long-term damage.

We were medically neglected when:

- We weren't treated when we were sick or injured.
- We weren't provided with the medicine that we needed.
- Our medical appointments were missed and/or treatment plans weren't followed.
- Necessary medical equipment, such as a wheelchair or hearing aid, wasn't provided for us.
- Nobody listened to us. Our symptoms of physical or mental illness were ignored.

Medical neglect also includes poor and inappropriate treatment, a failure to look after eyesight, or a lack of dental care.

Medical neglect may have been used as a tactic to prevent other types of abuse being discovered. Perhaps we weren't taken to the hospital or to the doctors because our injuries were clear evidence of physical abuse. Likewise, sexually transmitted diseases were not treated because they proved that we were being sexually assaulted.

As adults who experienced medical neglect as children, we may have chronic health conditions that could have been prevented with proper care. We may have difficulty trusting healthcare professionals, doctors, dentists, nurses, and therapists. Our mental health might be poor and some of us will have health-related phobias. Potentially, medical neglect might have caused us a lifetime of health problems, disabilities, and higher healthcare costs.

How all types of neglect affect our lives as adults

When we weren't looked after properly, this has consequences for us in our adult lives. Deep down, we will have learned that we weren't worth taking care of. Our self-image will have been damaged and we will carry around with us a frightened inner child.

We may struggle to fully take care of ourselves, have difficulties staying healthy, and feel isolated and alone. The way we were taught to think about ourselves makes it more difficult for us to be happy and fulfilled. Potentially we could ignore signs of ill health. We may not have achieved what we would otherwise have done, and we may struggle financially.

Emotional Abuse

Emotional abuse is different from emotional neglect because the abuser takes deliberate action, rather than failing to act. It is an action of commission, rather than omission (commission is an intentional act, in contrast to omission, which is when something should have happened but didn't).

When we were emotionally neglected, we weren't given the warmth and love that we needed to grow and flourish. Our parents simply didn't care about our feelings. They didn't comfort and reassure us when we were upset, help us to work through our anger, or hug us when we were scared.

When we were emotionally abused, we were deliberately treated in a way that would damage our sense of self-worth. The UK-based National Society for Prevention of Cruelty to Children cites the following as emotional abuse on its website:

- Humiliating or constantly criticizing a child.
- Threatening, shouting at a child, or calling them names.
- Making the child the subject of jokes or using sarcasm to hurt a child.
- Blaming and scapegoating a child.
- Making a child perform degrading acts.
- Not recognizing a child's own individuality or trying to control their lives.
- Pushing a child too hard or not recognizing their limitations.
- Exposing a child to upsetting events or situations, like domestic abuse or drug taking.
- Failing to promote a child's social development.
- Not allowing a child to have friends.
- Persistently ignoring a child.
- Being absent.
- Manipulating a child.
- Never saying anything kind, expressing positive feelings, or congratulating a child on successes.
- Never showing any emotions in interactions with a child, also known as emotional neglect.

Like all abuse, emotional abuse is about power and control. Our parents, caregivers, or those responsible for looking after us used emotional abuse to hurt and damage us as a way to assert their dominance.

Shannon Thomas, in *Healing from Hidden Abuse: A Journey Through the*

Stages of Recovery from Psychological Abuse, states "psychological abusers damage others—not out of impaired judgment—but because they enjoy the control they gain from abusing people."

Physical Abuse

And all of the time I tell myself that I have escaped my past, not realising that I am dragging it along behind me like a set of invisible chains.

—Charlie Mitchell: *The Nipper: The Heartbreaking True Story of a Little Boy and his Violent Childhood in Working-Class Dundee*

Charlie Mitchell's book vividly describes the effects of parental violence. It is an excellent, honest, and sometimes brutal account. While not all acts of physical abuse are as dramatic as those he portrays—though many were—they are all destructive.

As with all abuse, physical abuse occurs when adults put their own needs first and are not concerned about the consequences for children. There are a number of reasons why we were hit when we were children.

- Adults needed to discharge their own anger and rage. Perhaps they simply could not cope with life's problems and needed some sort of outlet. As vulnerable children, we were available and had no way to defend ourselves.
- Powerless and weak parents felt strong and powerful when they physically abused us.
- If we were abused in some sort of ritual or school environment, then there may well have been a sexual motive behind the physical abuse. English public schools were notorious for their sadism. Many classical English authors, including George Orwell in his essay *Such, Such Were the Joys*, describe the harsh reality of their own school life.
- Many parents were beaten themselves when they were children and modeled their own behavior on how they were brought up themselves.
- Alcohol or drugs, when misused, can reduce the ability to control impulses. If we were raised in a family of alcoholics or drug users, violence was often close by.

- Some parents never really grew up. They wanted us to fulfill their emotional needs and became furious when we were unable to do so.

None of these reasons were our fault. They reflect on our parents, not us.

Whatever the causes of what happened to us, there are consequences that stay with us. We can become hypervigilant. We are always on the lookout for problems or things that might hurt us. Some of us may develop complex post-traumatic stress disorder (CPTSD) and experience flashbacks and nightmares.

Sometimes we find it hard to trust others. Physical abuse can impact how we form and maintain relationships. We might become withdrawn and isolated or, conversely, we might end up in abusive relationships as adults because it's what we've come to see as "normal." Physical abuse can severely affect our self-image. This can lead to feelings of worthlessness and a pervasive fear of rejection. It can be difficult to develop a playful, fun, and spontaneous outlook on life.

Sexual Abuse

Those of us who were sexually abused know how lonely, devastating and distressing it is. We also share the experience of others not wanting to know what happened to us and refusing to acknowledge and validate our experience.

Our abusers' first line of defense was secrecy and silence. They also took advantage of the fact that wider society often finds sexual abuse too difficult to discuss.

Here, we are open and honest about sexual abuse. This is difficult and it may be triggering, but it is right to tell the truth. If we are able to and choose to read on, then it is helpful to have support and, above all, treat ourselves with the total respect and compassion that we rightly deserve.

There are many misconceptions about sexual abuse. Newspaper reports usually describe it as a series of acts or incidents. However, the abusive act is part of a carefully planned strategy. From our perspective as a child, it might seem that our abuser ended up in our bed at two o'clock in the morning by accident, or it was simply because the opportunity was there. This was not the case.

Their crimes, and they were crimes, were thought through in advance. Sometimes our abusers had been preparing for years, even decades. There are several aspects to this.

Grooming

Many child protection courses suggest that a sex offender's first step in the grooming process is to groom adults who are close to the child that they aimed to abuse (us). These adults might have been other members of our family, schoolteachers, members of our religious community, or sports coaches. There is a stage before these people are targeted though.

Perpetrators start by grooming society. They often develop respectable or prestigious careers. Or perhaps they gain powerful positions in the local community or voluntary sector, or become famous celebrities, actors, film directors, entertainers, or TV personalities.

Sometimes, they were simply charming, outwardly kind and caring people. They may, to borrow a description from the popular press, have been "monsters." But they were frequently monsters who disguised themselves as decent human beings.

Targeting and intention

We were never, ever at fault. Nothing we did. Nothing we said. Nothing we wore. Nothing in the way we looked. And nothing in the way we behaved toward to our abusers in any way invited or justified their abuse.

They had a choice. We didn't.

It is very likely that we were specifically targeted. Perpetrators exploit the normal vulnerabilities of life. Sometimes, sex abusers targeted our mother or father and built a romantic relationship with them, and even married them to get to us. Some parents specifically brought us into the world to abuse us.

Planning

From a child's perspective, it was impossible to recognize the amount of planning and effort our abusers made preparing for their crimes. Many of their actions appeared to be normal and random everyday behavior. Usually, they were not.

Expert psychologist Dr. Anna Salter first described "seemingly unimportant decisions," or "SUDS." Many of the decisions that abusers took, that seemed casual, were deliberately designed to create opportunities to hurt us.

What is sexual abuse?

We were sexually abused as children if we were forced or manipulated into watching or taking part in sexual activity.

All sexual abuse is also emotional abuse. It is often accompanied by physical abuse. Frequently we were threatened by our abuser. They may have said that they would hurt our family, or they promised to ruin our lives if we told anyone. They were cruel and calculating people.

The people who abused us

Perpetrators can be men and women, fathers and mothers. We may have been attacked by somebody of the same sex or of the opposite sex. Fathers can sexually abuse boys and girls, and mothers can sexually abuse boys and girls. Many of us were attacked by our brothers or sisters, or grandparents, or cousins, or aunts or uncles. Perhaps by older or bigger children. Whoever did it, they were both morally and criminally wrong. We were not. We should have been safe. We should have been protected. We have no responsibility for what happened to us.

Contact and non-contact abuse

If we were raped, touched sexually, or made to touch ourselves sexually, whether we were naked or clothed, this is considered to be contact abuse.

If we were forced or coerced into witnessing or hearing sexual acts, either in real life or by watching internet pornography, this is defined as non-contact abuse. Grooming is also non-contact abuse.

Some parents used us as a way to access our friends so that they could abuse them. We were forced to be unwilling accessories in the grooming process. Instead of being children who were loved and nurtured for being us, we were exploited to gratify the abuser's depraved desires.

When any of these things happened to us, we were abused, regardless of how much understanding or awareness we had. It was still abuse when we had no idea what was going on.

My Daddy the Pedophile: A Memoir, the powerful book written by Lily Palazzi, portrays a potent picture. Familiar to many of us who were sexually abused is the enormous amount of manipulation involved in this crime. Our thoughts and feelings were distorted. Our minds were messed with. We were illegally used for someone else's gratification.

They were to blame, not us.

Blame

Instead of treating ourselves with love and compassion, we often feel an enormous amount of shame and guilt about our experiences. Of course, we have absolutely no reason to, but that doesn't stop us from feeling this deeply.

It is extremely difficult. Sometimes (and it might take time) it is helpful to recognize the truth. And the truth is that it was planned this way from the start. Our abusers always intended to pass on their responsibility for their crimes to us. By making us feel that we were at fault, they felt that they could escape justice.

There are other aspects of what happened to us that are helpful to acknowledge.

- We felt a crushing sense of isolation and loneliness as children. We believed that we were the only people in the world that this was happening to. Those who were hurting us wanted us to feel this way. Psychological isolation, along with the belief nobody would understand or believe us, was a terrible tactic to ensure that we didn't share our experiences, allowing their crimes to remain undetected.
- Understandably, we may have enjoyed the attention that our abusers gave us; the gifts, the feeling of being unique, needed, and wanted. This is natural. All children need attention, love, and support to thrive and develop. Our abusers took our normal healthy needs and used them as weapons against us. Equally, many of us were threatened with terrible consequences if we tried to escape our abuse. Sometimes, both cruel tactics were used against us.
- Our bodies often reacted the way nature designed them to. We may have had an orgasm or an erection when we were being attacked. At the time we may have felt that our own bodies were betraying us. The reality is there was nothing wrong with our bodies. They behaved in exactly the way nature built them. There was a massive betrayal, but we did not betray ourselves. The betrayal was from our attackers, not us.
- Perhaps we had strong feelings toward our abuser. We felt a special bond and wanted to show love and affection toward them. This was doubly the case if the perpetrator was one of our parents. Again, it was intended that we should feel this so that our abusers protected themselves.

This was all part of a strategy designed to manipulate, confuse, and hurt us. None of this means that we bear the tiniest fraction of blame. We were children. We did nothing wrong.

Impact

Understandably, as adults, this potentially:

- Damages our ability to trust.
- Can leave us feeling worthless.
- Disrupts our self-identity and self-worth.
- Creates relationship difficulties.
- Evokes environment-based fears or phobias.
- Makes us more vulnerable to mental health problems.
- Leads to physical health challenges.
- Triggers chronic pain or somatic symptoms.
- Interferes with professional focus and achievements.
- Sparks spiritual or existential crises.
- Compromises our ability to find faith or trust in humanity.

Sometimes our experience of sexual abuse leads us to adopt what psychologists describe as high-risk behaviors. We try to mask our emotions and avoid feeling pain by abusing drugs or having multiple unsatisfactory sexual relationships. There is nothing morally wrong with this. They are understandable strategies. The challenge is that we may cause ourselves further hurt. It is better to treat ourselves with love and compassion and look for alternative ways to experience the joy, fulfillment, and contentment that we deserve.

For those of us who identify as LGBTQ+, we have the need to process our past as well as to challenge the cruel and unnecessary prejudice that surrounds us. The Independent Inquiry into Child Sexual Abuse for England and Wales, established in 2015, states: "Most victims and survivors the Inquiry spoke to said they experienced confusion, frustration, or difficulty with understanding their own sexual orientation or gender identity as a result of the sexual abuse. For many this was made much more difficult because of the myths, stereotypes, and attitudes in society."

Understandably things can feel distressing. This is a natural and normal reaction. It is, however, helpful to know that we are not alone in our experiences. It's estimated that worldwide, multimillions of us have faced similar childhood experiences. Our resilience is a testament to our spirit. We have not only survived, but many of us thrive and reclaim our stories, redefining our futures. Our past doesn't dictate our potential. Healing is not only possible, but highly probable. Together, as a community, we can support and champion one another, reminding ourselves that recovery is not just a dream, but a journey we're all traveling on together.

Divorce, Separation, and Weaponizing

According to the US organization the Centers for Disease Control and Prevention, over 630,000 couples divorced in 2020. Eurostat (the statistical office of the European Union) states that an estimated 0.7 million divorces took place in the EU the same year. Data take time to process; however, figures for later years are likely to be broadly similar.

Penelope Leach, author of the book *Putting the Children First When You Divorce: How to Parent Together When You're Apart*, suggests that by the age of 16, more than half of children have parents who are no longer living together.

Relationship breakdowns are usually unhappy. If managed well, however, the amount of distress that is caused to children can be minimized.

Some of our parents, though, were in very acrimonious disputes with each other. This may have resulted in us becoming "weaponized." Instead of supporting us at a difficult time, one of our parents enlisted us to fight their battles.

Divide and conquer: triangulation in weaponized disputes

In the book *Borderline, Narcissistic, and Schizoid Adaptations: The Pursuit of Love, Admiration, and Safety*, Dr. Elinor Greenberg, therapist, explains how one of our parents may have used the technique of "triangulation" to keep us apart from our other parent.

In psychology, "triangulation" refers to a tactic where one person communicates with another using a third person. This creates divisions and helps them to control the narrative. The concept, originating from Family Systems Theory, was developed by Dr. Murray Bowen.

We would have been told how terrible the parent who was not with us was. Details were given about how abusive they were. Their infidelity, affairs, and how they caused financial devastation and ruined the family were shared with us. As often as possible. To maximize the damage done. Sometimes we would have been given special treats, days out, presents, sweets, or rewards to convince us that one parent was right, and the other parent was wrong. This potentially developed into parental alienation, where one parent actively tried to destroy our relationship with the other.

The immediate effects of acrimonious separation would have been to make us afraid, angry, and ashamed. We often blamed ourselves. The UK Government states, "Frequent, intense and poorly resolved conflict between parents can place children at risk of mental health issues, and behavioural, social and academic problems. It can also have a significant effect on a child's long-term outcomes."

We may personally have experienced some of the following:

- **Crumbling confidence.** In the face of constant manipulation, we often lost trust in our own memories and experiences. The abusive story created by one parent was frequently different from our experience with the other. Our mom may have told us how awful our dad was; however, we found him kind and caring. Or our dad constantly criticized our mom, while we only ever saw a loving parent. Understandably, this was very difficult for us and sometimes we started to doubt our reality. Now as adults, as a result of these experiences, we sometimes grapple with feelings of helplessness and emotional disconnect. Trusting others becomes an uphill battle, echoing our childhood experiences.
- **Stolen innocence.** Triangulation didn't just take away our trust. It robbed us of our innocence. We were exposed to ideas and behaviors that were neither age-appropriate nor appropriate in any sense. One of our parents put adult-level decisions in our young hands. "Are you sure that you really want to spend Christmas with your dad?" "Perhaps it is better if you stop seeing your mom for a while." "Maybe you shouldn't go on holiday with your dad this year."
- **Proxy campaigns.** Sometimes, the manipulating parent enlisted friends or acquaintances in a campaign to tarnish the reputation of the other parent. This involved spreading rumors and portraying the other parent in a negative light. Often, they were painted as unstable or unfit. This intensified our confusion and mistrust. When we loved our other parent, it hurt us too.
- **Broken bonds.** Our relationship with the alienated parent was often fractured beyond repair, leading us to reject half of our own identity. The pain of the association was too raw, too overwhelming to bear. We pushed away the precious bond we had with the abused parent, which

led to a cascade of short-term and long-term problems, from unresolved grief to deep-seated issues with self-esteem.
- **Frayed family ties.** Our estrangement didn't stop at the parent. It extended to our wider family network and social circles. We were stripped of the love, support, and opportunities that come from being part of an extended family. Social support structures crumbled, and potential professional opportunities slipped away unnoticed.
- **Lost connections.** The isolation often didn't end with our immediate family either. Some of us were pulled from our social circles entirely, homeschooled, restricted in our friendships, or even relocated to entirely different locales. Our social, educational, recreational, and cultural connections were severed, leaving us to grieve in solitude. The loss of the alienated parent became a private pain, a secret sorrow nurtured by the unhealthy bond formed with the abusive parent.

Abandonment Abuse

One of the cruelest and most devastating actions that a parent can take is to choose to abandon their own children. There are occasions when for legal reasons a mother or father is denied contact with their offspring. This is extremely difficult for everyone involved. It can be traumatic. When abandonment is a deliberate choice, this causes extra psychological injury. An even greater level of harm occurs when our mother or father left us behind to start a new family. Naturally, when we were the ones left behind, we felt second best. Our birthright of enjoying a contented relationship with our father or mother was stolen from us. We had the additional indignity of being replaced by someone else's children.

Understandably, abandonment left us feeling unworthy and unloved. This self-perception might cause us enduring feelings of loneliness in our adult life, stemming directly from the void left by the parent who abandoned us. It can also lead us to struggle significantly with our self-worth and identity. As survivors of abandonment abuse, we may be hyper-sensitive to rejection. We may perceive rejection where it's not intended, leading to potential misunderstandings in our relationships. We may experience "abandonment anxiety," a persistent and often irrational fear of being deserted by those we care about. When we become parents ourselves, our past experiences add a layer of complexity; we might fear repeating our parents' mistakes or overcompensating for our own loss, adding another layer of stress to our parenting journey.

Narcissistic Parents

Narcissistic parents were perplexing and painful. They were obsessed with *their* image. *Their* needs. *Their* desires. Engulfed in their universe, they failed to recognize and validate us. We were not seen as separate individuals with our own thoughts and feelings. Being raised by narcissistic parents meant that we struggled for acknowledgment and love. These were seldom granted.

Narcissistic parents neglected our well-being. Their priority was their own gratification. They might have set impossibly high standards for us, driven not by a desire to see us thrive, but to boost their standing in the eyes of others. In their pursuit of praise and admiration, they may have pushed us relentlessly, disregarding our needs, feelings, and aspirations. Our achievements were seen not as our success, but as a feather in their cap, a testament to their "stellar parenting."

Living under the gaze of a narcissistic parent, we found our value measured by our ability to meet their expectations and feed their ego. Our worth depended on our performance, appearance, or compliance. These reinforced their narrative of superiority and entitlement. For those of us who failed or refused to fit in, the consequence was disdain, neglect, or even outright rejection.

Emotional connection and support were conditional in narcissistic families. Our parents could be charming and affectionate when it suited them, only to withdraw their love when we disappointed or defied them. Their affection felt transactional. It was only given in exchange for our adoration or obedience. We did not receive the empathy and unconditional love that we should have.

It was all about them. Not us. The shortcomings of narcissistic parents were nothing to do with our own worth, but showed their impaired capacity for empathy and unconditional love. We were not invisible, insignificant, or unworthy. We were simply unseen by them because they were unable to look beyond themselves.

When we were raised by narcissistic parents, we are likely to experience frequent feelings of unworthiness.

This feeling of not being "enough" can manifest in our adult lives. We may seek validation from others. Perhaps we subconsciously avoid situations where we might be criticized or judged.

Having grown up with the unpredictability and emotional volatility of narcissistic parents, we might find ourselves becoming people-pleasers. We may even avoid close relationships altogether, fearing the emotional toll they might take. We might gravitate toward partners or friends who exhibit the same narcissistic traits, not because it's what we want, but because it's what we've known.

There is more about narcissism in Chapter 10, Recognizing and Overcoming Abuse.

Stage Parenting and Financial Exploitation: When Children Pay the Price for Parents' Ambition

> *Fame has put a wedge between Mom and me that I didn't think was possible. She wanted this. And I wanted her to have it. I wanted her to be happy. But now that I have it, I realize that she's happy and I'm not. Her happiness came at the cost of mine. I feel robbed and exploited.*
>
> —Jennette McCurdy: *I'm Glad My Mom Died*

While it is natural for parents to want children to be successful, the drive for ambition can grow way beyond what is normal and healthy.

"Stage parents" is a term originally used to describe mothers and fathers who were obsessed by the idea that their child could be a famous theater or movie star and who put enormous pressure on their son or daughter to achieve. The powerful bestseller by Jennette McCurdy (quoted above) is an excellent account of how a parent's need to have outwardly successful children impacts their offspring.

Stage parents also describes those who are desperate for their youngsters to become sports stars, models, doctors, or wealthy and well-known in any profession. It isn't so much the activity that matters, rather the all-encompassing drive for children's outward success that defines stage parenting.

What is shocking for people who didn't experience this type of upbringing is how intensely our lives were dominated by our parents' overwhelming need for us to achieve. Tennis legend Andre Agassi put this succinctly when he described his father taping ping pong bats to his hands and encouraging him to hit tennis balls hung over his crib when he was a baby. In *Open, An Autobiography*, he details how, at 7 years old, he was hitting 2500 tennis balls a day because his dad thought this would make him a winning tennis player.

When we were constantly pressured into actions that helped our parents fulfill their dreams, not ours, then we had stage parents.

A lost childhood

Erika Christakis, author of the best-selling book *The Importance of Being Little: What Young Children Really Need From Grownups*, discusses the trend to see children as commodities to invest in. Rather than being valued as wonderful little people just the way they are, parents put time, effort, and money into their offspring in the hope of future "pay-offs."

When we experienced stage parenting, we would have felt the constant need to reach goals to please other people. As well as our parents, this could have included drama teachers, film directors, sports coaches, agents etc., depending on what it was that we were expected to achieve. It would have been hard to develop a normal sense of self as we were constantly measured against other people's ideals and targets.

Stolen time, stolen friendships

When we were stage-parented, the priority was to achieve. Most, if not all, of our time would have been "invested" in some sort of training or practice. This may have been sports, drama, dance, or similar. When our parents dreamed of us being doctors or academic geniuses, it meant extra tuition, extensive study, and excess homework.

Our parents viewed us as an extension of themselves. We were a way to attract the admiration and fame that they believed they deserved. Perhaps deep down, they saw themselves as a failure. They needed our success to compensate for their own inadequacies.

Whatever the cause of their behavior, the outcome for us will have been similar. We were pressured into achieving our parents' goals and ambitions. In turn, this meant that on some level we will have seen our own needs as less important.

As adults, we might have internalized our mother's or father's voice that constantly told us that we had to be a success to be worthwhile. We may even be in a job that we intensely dislike, or have been denied the opportunity to explore who we really are and what we want out of life. We may also feel isolated and alone, as it is difficult to relate to others who didn't experience the same abusive childhood that we did.

Parents Who Abuse Drugs and Alcohol

There are debates throughout the world around what is healthy for us, relative risk, and what substances should be lawful. Both drugs and alcohol, where legal, can be used to help us to enjoy life more.

There is, though, a difference between use and abuse. Terrible harm was done to many of us by parents who abused alcohol or other drugs when we were growing up.

Nicola Barry, in her excellent book depicting family life with an alcoholic mother, writes, "To say her drinking ruined my life would be a cop out—ruled my life is more like it." (*Mother's Ruin, The Extraordinary True Story of How Alcohol Destroys a Family*).

Although our experiences differ, her words resonate with many of us.

Alcohol or drug abuse in families has multiple consequences. It is possible that, because of our parents' use of drugs or alcohol, we have seen anger and violence. Fights between family members were frequent. There is a high chance that we became involved. We were hit or hurt ourselves. We acted as peacemakers.

Our family may have experienced legal problems, preventable injuries, and accidents. It was common for us to be in cars being driven "under the influence" of drugs or alcohol.

Perhaps within our families most harm was done by the fact that drugs or alcohol were a priority. They came first. We were secondary to them. Sometimes their effects were so powerful that we weren't even third, fourth or fifth. We did not matter at all.

The potential consequences were as follows:

- We may have been neglected, and there may not have been enough money to pay household bills or buy food or clothing. Our home may have been dirty and unsafe.
- The need for alcohol or drugs may have led our parents to take part in crime to pay for their habits. Some will have ended up being hospitalized or spending time in prison.
- When drinking or drug abuse was extreme, we will have had to care for

our parents ourselves. We became untrained and unpaid carers. When we had younger brothers or sisters, we may have been forced to care for them too when our parents were intoxicated.
- There was very little chance for us to play, explore, and be creative.
- We learned that we were never good enough. Because of the chaos that resulted from our parents' addiction, our efforts were often overlooked. We felt that no matter how hard we tried, we couldn't ever truly succeed.
- We believed that caring for our own needs was selfish.
- We blamed ourselves.

Often our parents' behavior was well hidden. It became the family secret that we were unable to talk about. We would have felt different to other children, leaving us with a lasting sense of shame or guilt. If our parents were so-called "high-functioning" alcoholics, they may have maintained successful careers and (as with sexual abusers) they may have been esteemed members of the community. This left us living in two separate worlds. To the outside world, everything appeared happy and healthy. But inside our homes, life was distressing, difficult and, at times, dangerous.

Our upbringing likely complicated our perception of what a normal family should be like. It is quite possible that we have struggled with issues around trust. Our experience can make it harder when we start romantic relationships. Sometimes we can turn into perfectionists in a subconscious effort to please and to avoid the anger of our alcoholic parents. The secrecy also stopped us from having open, honest, and mature conversations. We were taught to deny the existence of problems instead of tackling them.

INSTITUTIONAL ABUSE

Families aren't always based on a traditional model of one or two parents. Some of us were brought up or spent a considerable amount of time in institutions. They became our family. Some boarding schools, residential care establishments, churches and places of worship are targeted by pedophiles because they offer easy access to children.

Additionally, we may have been part of sports teams or community organizations where abuse took place. Sports coaches sometimes use their positions of trust to manipulate and groom those whom they are supposed to support.

Often, our trauma is increased when organizations attempt to deny or minimize the abuse that took place. Frequently, rather than being open and honest and trying to repair the damage that has been done, they seek to avoid responsibility. There are several reasons for this:

- **Money.** Organizations that rely on donations and public support don't want the truth to be heard because it could be damaging financially. They put their own need for funding first.
- **To escape justice.** When institutional abuse occurs, many individuals fail to take responsibility. They know what is going on, but don't report it because they want to avoid taking action that might harm their own careers.
- **Loss of moral authority.** It messes with the message. This is especially the case with religious institutions. They preach and tell people how to live their lives. Admitting their own crimes makes it harder for them to influence and manipulate the general public.
- **Compensation.** Claiming financial compensation isn't a matter of opportunism but of seeking justice. For us, it represents an institution's acknowledgment of its failures and is a small step toward repairing the emotional scars inflicted on us. Rather than compensating us, organizations prefer to misspend their money. Lawyers are employed to delay and complicate our rightful claims. PR people are hired to deny and deflect in an attempt to bolster the organization's reputation.
- **Lack of integrity.** Organizations avoid admitting to their own failures because they are badly led and don't have the integrity to make amends for the damage they have done.

DARVO

Institutions will use exactly the same excuses that family members make to minimize the consequences of their actions. They minimize, deny, and use a technique known as DARVO.

DARVO is a sneaky way that abusers dodge blame. It's especially tough when institutions we thought were safe use this tactic. They should have been helping us to grow and feel secure, but instead, they deny their wrongs, attack us, and turn the tables. They blame us for their abusive actions. By getting to grips with what DARVO is, we can better spot it and understand how it has affected us. It's an important step in healing. The abbreviation stands for:

- **Deny.** They attempt to say that they didn't do it, or they didn't hurt us.
- **Attack.** We may be threatened with legal action, ridiculed, accused of being a liar, being mentally unstable, being drug addicts, or anything at all that attacks our credibility and makes us less likely to be believed. There have been occasions when authorities or institutions attack adults when they disclose their childhood abuse. Rather than take responsibility, they attempt to undermine their victims.
- **Reverse Victim and Offender.** Abusers often try to pretend that they are the real victims. They point out damage to their own career, marriage, reputation, etc. And then say all of this was caused by us. The reality is, though, that they are entirely responsible for their own behavior and the consequences of it. This includes all the repercussions of what they did on their own lives and the lives of the people around them. It was their fault, not ours.

How to win against DARVO (the four R's)

It is terribly wrong that, after being mistreated, attacked or abused once, there is a second attempt to hurt us by destroying our reputation. This is then followed by the insult of offenders pretending to be the victims themselves. It is just and fair to fight back against this. The technique below, abbreviated to the "4R's," can be helpful and effective.

- **Recognize.** DARVO is less effective as a tactic when we realize that it is being used against us. Although this isn't always easy, there are actions that we can take. By keeping a journal, a copy of emails, and contemporaneous notes of what is said to us, we can learn to recognize patterns. Knowledge is power, and knowing when DARVO is used as a strategy will help us to combat it.
- **Refute and refuse.** A part of the power of DARVO is that when it is used against us, we can start to feel confused or less certain about our past. We can avoid this and stay strong by sticking to our story and refusing to accept the abuser's version of events.
- **Reclaim.** We can reclaim the narrative. This means telling our story and standing by it.

Finding support through friends, professional counselors, and support groups, while treating ourselves with the utmost compassion, helps us to fight back effectively.

A prime example of a context where DARVO might be used is within institutions like boarding schools, where abuse is often masked under the guise of tradition, discipline, or authority. The British upper class's educational system is explored thoroughly in Alex Renton's book *Stiff Upper Lip: Secrets, Crimes and the Schooling of a Ruling Class*, revealing a culture of unchecked power, secrecy, and abuse. Alex Renton takes us inside prestigious boarding schools, where a culture of secrecy and bullying creates an environment in which wealthy boys flaunt their power without consequence. Alex Renton exposes the harsh reality behind the veneer of privilege. Cruelty and abuse are widespread.

In addition to the deliberate harm that we may have experienced, there is a group of learned behaviors and emotional states that often result from growing up in a boarding school. These experiences can lead to "boarding school syndrome." This is a cluster of symptoms, including anxiety, difficulty communicating, and problems maintaining intimate relationships. According to psychoanalyst and psychotherapist Professor Joy Schaverien, the core impact of boarding school syndrome is described by the acronym ABCD: A for abandonment, B for bereavement, C for captivity, and D for dissociation.

- **Abandonment.** We felt worthlessness knowing that our parents chose to send us away.
- **Bereavement.** Moving away from home, we lost childhood friendships as well as parental relationships.
- **Captivity** refers to our feelings of being trapped in an unfamiliar and sometimes hostile environment.
- **Dissociation.** Our minds disconnected from our boarding school environment to cope with the distress that we were experiencing.

For some of us, boarding schools were terrible; for all of us though, the truth is that there is no safe substitute for a real home.

Spiritual Abuse

Spiritual or religious abuse can exist as a phenomenon on its own outside of our family. Abuse from our parents and abuse from the religious community to which we belonged (or may still belong) can also be intertwined.

Spiritual abuse is widespread. It is frequently denied and covered up.

Former judge Jean-Marc Sauvé published an in-depth report stating that around 330,000 children were abused over 70 years by priests and lay members of the Catholic Church in France. A commission in Ireland found that the Catholic Church there had covered up decades of abuse. Major abuse has been discovered in countries all over the world.

In addition to fostering abuse within the institution, there are many ways in which religious communities enable parental abuse. These can make it more difficult to identify and more difficult to challenge.

- Some religions venerate parents. They promote the idea that our father and mother have to be obeyed, no matter what.
- Verses from the scriptures or holy books may be misinterpreted in extreme ways to justify treating children badly.
- Within some faiths, women are denigrated and taught to be subservient to men.
- Many religious institutions are hierarchical and emphasize deference and obedience.
- Sometimes, rigid and authoritarian thinking is encouraged.
- Questioning and challenging are actively discouraged.
- Fear, guilt, and shame are used as a way of control.
- Children are given unrealistic targets around their own behavior.
- Ideas around chastity and purity can conflict with children's emerging sexuality.
- There is a bias against outsiders and outside institutions.

Linda Kay Klein's book, *Pure: Inside the Evangelical Movement That Shamed a Generation of Young Women and How I Broke Free*, gives a detailed account of how some religious ideas are used to subjugate women. In particular, there are belief systems that are afraid of women's power and sexuality. Their teaching can bring about lifelong trauma and fear.

Sex Trafficking

Sex trafficking is widely misrepresented and misunderstood. Movies tend to show people imprisoned and held against their will. Although this does happen, frequently there is a simple misuse of power. Wealthy individuals exploit vulnerable children.

Sex trafficking is much more common than it is assumed to be. The

International Labour Organization estimated that in 2016, 25 million people were in forced labor, of whom around 5 million were sexually exploited.

We were more vulnerable to sex trafficking if we lived in poverty or traumatic circumstances. Sex traffickers target children when they are weakest: for example, when they have lost a parent, or for other reasons are lonely and isolated.

Rich and powerful people use their money to avoid justice. They use the courts and legal systems to discredit and further attack those that they have abused. If this doesn't work, they attempt to use their money to pay off victims and to buy their silence.

Gang Abuse

> *What do we know to be true about gang violence? We know we will fail if we fixate on the symptoms and not address what undergirds it.*
>
> —Greg Boyle, Director of gang intervention and rehabilitation program Homeboy Industries

Gang abuse happens when children are manipulated into crime. The reasons why we might have become involved in gang abuse include the following:

- Especially when our own upbringing was inadequate, gangs provided a sense of belonging. They became our substitute family.
- We may have felt that we needed to be protected; this is especially the case if we were raised in parts of the world where there was a great deal of violent crime.
- Gangs gave us status or the feeling of power.
- Career opportunities were extremely limited in the environment that we grew up in, so we believed that gangs offered us a future that we otherwise would not have.
- We needed money and could not seek other ways of earning it legitimately.

The American Academy of Child and Adolescent Psychiatry states that "consequences of gang membership may include exposure to drugs and alcohol, age-inappropriate sexual behavior, difficulty finding a job because of lack of education and work skills, removal from one's family, imprisonment, and even death."

In the next chapter, we look at why early damage done to us in childhood is so potent and long-lasting.

4

Why Early Damage is Destructive

To understand why what happened to us as children has a lasting impact, it is helpful to view it from what psychologists call a "developmental perspective."

Championed by experts Jean Piaget (1896–1980), Lev Vygotsky (1896–1934) and John Bowlby (1907–1990), developmental psychology describes a number of stages that we must pass through to become emotionally healthy adults. Disruptions or failures in these stages can lead to enduring difficulties throughout our lives. Their work emphasizes the uniqueness and importance of our early years.

Our childhood experiences matter. Dysfunction and distress damaged us when we were most vulnerable. A simple analogy illustrates this.

A mature oak tree with a strong, solid trunk, deep roots anchoring it to the ground, and branches stretching into the sky is unlikely to be severely affected by storms or drought. A young green sapling with shallow roots and a thin and weak stalk is much less able to withstand trouble, turbulence, and turmoil. The early harm stunts its growth. This stops it from becoming the magnificent specimen that it was meant to be.

Everything in nature is born vulnerable. Small animals need protection and nutrition. Their parents need to teach them to find food and stay safe. We are vastly more complex than the flora, fauna, and other species that we share our planet with. As well as our basic physical survival needs, we require love, encouragement, generosity, and empathy. Without these supporting behaviors we will, in psychological terminology, "fail to thrive."

In addition to the fact that we were harmed when we were most vulnerable, we were damaged more because, in psychological terms, we "lacked agency." Put simply, we were powerless.

Powerlessness

In the battles we fought, the odds were very much stacked against us. Whatever happened to us, there was nothing that we could have done to prevent it.

- **We were completely dependent on whoever was abusing us or causing our distress.** This wasn't just the very basics of food and shelter; we needed the love and support necessary for us to grow and develop.
- **Our parents or other abusers may well have been powerful people.** Abusers frequently use their positions of trust, respect, or sometimes wealth to hide their behavior.
- **Abusers are frequently experts at manipulation.** They may have used fear or even manipulative kindness and generosity to control us.
- **We lacked knowledge and awareness.** There are several reasons for this. Trapped within our own family, we had no way of knowing how other families lived. Our experience was limited to the family that we knew. Things that went on within our family were normal for us. Those who were harming and hurting us did everything possible to prevent or stop us fully understanding what was going on.
- **Denial and disbelief.** On a deeper level, our young minds were also working to protect us from the full horror of what was happening. Incidents were blocked out and became buried deep within our psyche.

For all of us now living with the legacy of traumatic childhoods, there was no way to deal with the issues we were facing at the time. There were no mechanisms that we could use to report what happened, and the chances are that we would not have been believed anyway.

Inevitably, these adverse experiences during our formative years helped shape our perception of ourselves, others, and the world around us—in other words, our "core beliefs."

Core Beliefs

> *Of all the horrid ramifications of child abuse, the self-beliefs formed by the child reap the greatest destruction.*
> —Heyward Bruce Ewart III: *Am I Bad? Recovering from Abuse*

Our core beliefs are central to how we think and feel. What's most interesting is that many of our core beliefs are hidden from us. Core beliefs are very, very deep within us. Formed at an early age, they are often not within reach of our conscious awareness. When we wake in the morning, we always know who we are. We just know it. We may rise in different countries, homes, or hotels, and if we are traveling, temporarily wonder for a few moments where we are. We may be confused about our location, but we aren't puzzled by our identity. Outside the formal disciplines of philosophy or meditation, we never really question who we are.

Core beliefs act in a very similar way. They are at the core of our being and, in the same way that we don't question our identity, we do not tend to question our core beliefs. Our minds have already accepted them as self-evidently true. Core beliefs are about:

- Ourselves.
- Other people.
- The world.

They are often rigid and inflexible, and act as a mental filter through which we see and interpret our environment. When we experienced a difficult childhood, we developed negative and unhelpful core beliefs that are buried deep in our subconscious.

How core beliefs develop: the theory theory

> *The greatest damage done by neglect, trauma or emotional loss is not the immediate pain they inflict but the long-term distortions they induce in the way a developing child will continue to interpret the world and her situation in it. All too often these ill-conditioned implicit beliefs become self-fulfilling prophecies in our lives.*
>
> —Dr. Gabor Maté: *In the Realm of Hungry Ghosts: Close Encounters with Addiction*

Throughout childhood we tried to make sense of our world. What is sometimes known as the "theory theory" proposes that when we were children, we thought like little scientists. Our tiny brains formed hypotheses. Our minds made mini models of the way life works. We used numerous "reference experiences"—memories of incidents that happened—to build an overall picture of our environment.

When our world was negative, we created negative mental maps.

To use a basic example, a young boy with a highly critical mother who lacks warmth and affection begins to develop the theory that he may be unlovable. If his first preschool teacher is disapproving, then his original views become reinforced. The longer his mother continues to find fault with him and the less love that she shows, the more convinced he becomes of his unworthiness. His core beliefs develop so that he believes he doesn't deserve love (a core belief about himself).

In turn, his expectations of life will be lowered. He decides that other people will not love him either (a core belief about other people). He will start to act in accordance with his expectations. This means that he will act as an "unlovable" child. And so an unhelpful cycle begins. A child who thinks that they will not be loved becomes less loving to those around them and therefore receives less love in return.

In addition to core beliefs being built from our experience, we also learned them directly from our parents. Clichéd phrases such as "it's a cruel world," when frequently repeated before we had a chance to make up our own minds, became part of our deeply held belief system.

Common core beliefs that we are likely to hold that result from our unhappy childhood include:

"I am not good enough"
As with all core beliefs, this is something that isn't always expressed. "I am not good enough" can just be a feeling. It's a sense we do not fit into the world. As adults this core belief can reveal itself in several ways:

- We feel like we don't deserve to be successful or that our achievements are not valid.
- We are afraid of being judged or criticized by others.
- We have difficulty connecting with other people.

"There is something wrong with me"
There are many different variations of this belief. We might believe that we are basically a bad person, a problem that can't be fixed. Sometimes we just feel wrong. We envy other people who appear to us to be normal and "right."

"I am unlovable"
When we were denied the nurturing and love that we deserved as children, instead of blaming our parents, we blamed ourselves. We didn't have the capacity to think that adults have. If our parents did not love us, we believed there was something wrong with us. Our core belief evolved so that we saw ourselves as inherently unlovable.

A belief that we are unlovable makes it very difficult to have successful adult relationships. Subconsciously, we look for people who do not really love us. We then attempt to make them love us. The child within us is more comfortable with this situation as it's what we grew up with. We have low expectations of ourselves, and other people pick this up.

"Other people will not love me"
As the above example shows, when we experience hostile and unloving parents, we decide that we are unlovable. This naturally leads to the expectation that "other people will not love me." This has a devastating impact on our lives as adults. Subconsciously, we stop looking for people who think we are great, fantastic, and who fall in love with us. We become attracted to those who have a mediocre view of us. Our belief turns into a self-fulfilling prophecy.

"I cannot trust other people"
It is easy to see why this became a core belief for us, when our early trust was broken. The problem is that our relationships, including friendships, romances, and in our working lives, need trust to make them work.

"The world is dangerous"
This is a common and understandable core belief that developed when we were children and we were hurt. It leads to ongoing anxiety, fear of change, and feeling powerless.
When we believe that the world is dangerous, we choose what is "safe" over what we truly want. We believe that we're missing out on life. We are not reaching our potential.

When this core belief is at the forefront of our lives, it is difficult to make changes and take healthy risks. We feel the need to keep our guard up all of the time. We are scared to reveal who we truly are. We become afraid of people and afraid of life.

How to make our core beliefs work for us

There are two basic strategies. Firstly, we need to minimize the harm of having negative core beliefs and start to eliminate them altogether. Secondly, we can replace them with positive core beliefs.

Recognizing our core beliefs is the first step. This can be done through self-reflection or by working with a therapist.

A helpful technique from cognitive behavioral therapy (CBT) is called the "downward arrow." We are encouraged to write down our automatic negative thoughts (ANTs) about a situation. We then ask what they mean to us. We repeat the exercise until we discover our core belief.

For example:

ANT: I will fail my driving test.
What does this ANT mean to me?
ANT: I will have to keep retaking my test and fail future tests as well.
What does this ANT mean to me?
ANT: I will spend a great deal of money and waste time trying.
What does this ANT mean about me?
ANT: It isn't worth trying.
What does this ANT mean about me?
I will never be successful (core belief).

Journaling is helpful. Writing down our thoughts and feelings regularly helps us to spot our thinking patterns.

The concept of core beliefs is central to CBT. Dr. Seth Gillihan's best-selling book, *Cognitive Behavioral Therapy Made Simple: 10 Strategies for Managing Anxiety, Depression, Anger, Panic, and Worry*, devotes a chapter to changing core beliefs. The more insight we have, the better we will be able to make effective changes.

Once we have identified our negative core beliefs, we can begin to change them. This is a process, and it will take time for us to see the results.

Here are some practical action steps to help us to do this:

- **Challenge our core beliefs.** Once we have a better understanding of our negative core beliefs, we can use evidence to challenge them. For instance, if our belief is "I'm not good enough," we should think of specific times when we were successful or praised for something.

- **Practice believable self-affirmations.** When we feel self-doubt or negativity creeping in, we can take a moment to repeat our positive core beliefs. Regularly repeating them will reinforce our new beliefs and make them part of our everyday mindset.
- **Fake it to make it.** Our new core beliefs will feel more real when we act in accordance with them.

How we know that we are heading in a positive direction

Modern cars have speedometers, GPS, odometers, etc. It is easy to measure how fast, how far, and in what direction we are traveling.

Measuring progress toward mental goals, including developing more positive core beliefs, is more difficult, however. There are some formal psychological tests. For example, the Hamilton Rating Scale for Depression (HDRS, HRSD or HAM-D) can be used to monitor how effective treatment has been for depression. Some mobile phone well-being apps also attempt to record changes.

Generally speaking, though, progress-measuring tools can be difficult to access or use, and are sometimes inaccurate. It is, then, helpful for us to have some tools that, when used together, help us to notice changes. We can:

- **Take stock of our current thoughts and emotions.** By writing and recording how we are feeling at the present moment, we can track changes. Over time we will be able to compare our old notes with new notes and see a positive difference.
- **Watch ourselves and observe how we react to difficult situations.** When our reactions are more positive and balanced, this shows that our mindset has shifted.
- **Think about how we interpret our experiences.** By considering how we interpret different events in life, it is clearer when our core beliefs are changing from negative to positive.
- **Examine our self-talk.** Being aware of the language we use when we're talking about and to ourselves can highlight when our core beliefs have shifted.
- **Notice when we start to focus on different areas of our life.** When we pay attention to the things we are giving most of our energy to, and whether those things have a negative or positive impact, we can see how our mindset has changed.

By their very nature, core beliefs are not easy to change. If we are struggling, it is helpful to remember that change is a process. It takes time. By surrounding ourselves with support and self-compassion, we can progress no matter what.

How Our Childhoods Shaped Our Brains

People raised on love see things differently than those raised on survival.

—Joy Marino

When we were very young children, our brains were busy making sense of the world. We were figuring out how everything worked and building our core beliefs. Above all, our brains wanted to keep us safe.

In healthy families, there is a balance. Children's brains keep them away from harm, while also giving them freedom to explore and learn. But for us, things were different.

When we were surrounded by risks, our developing brains had to adapt to our hostile environment. This helped to keep us safer in the short term, but created long-term disadvantages that can cause us problems later on.

Latent vulnerability

A group of leading experts, the UK Trauma Council, describes latent vulnerability as "the unseen link between childhood trauma and later mental health problems." In other words, our childhood experiences can leave us more likely to develop emotional distress or mental health disorders as adults.

The word "latent" is significant. It means that our increased susceptibility to problems remains hidden or dormant until the ongoing impact of unresolved trauma or stress impacts our mental health later on in our lives. It is similar to having an engine fault in our car that can't be spotted by a quick inspection but will lead to a breakdown several hundred miles into our journey.

Latent vulnerability can manifest in various ways, such as an increased likelihood of developing mental health disorders like anxiety or depression, difficulties in emotional processing, or challenges in forming healthy relationships.

How Our Brains May Have Developed Differently

There is strong scientific evidence that shows that a dysfunctional upbringing causes specific changes in the structure and the functioning of our brain's thinking and feeling "systems." It can be difficult to face the reality that we were harmed by situations that we had no control over. Nonetheless there are three reasons why a basic knowledge is helpful to us.

- Firstly, we will be able to better understand ourselves. In turn, this means that we will have fewer reasons to blame ourselves, and more good reasons to show ourselves compassion.
- Secondly, by knowing what damage was done to us, we're in a stronger position to make effective repairs.
- Thirdly, it will help us to see why we behave as we do now, or did behave in particular ways in the past. This gifts us with self-knowledge and self-awareness.

Here are some areas where research has shown changes in the brain as a result of childhood trauma.

Emotions and memories: the limbic system of the brain

The limbic system is a network of different parts of our brain that work together to control our emotions, to create and store our memories, and manage our reactions to fear and stress. It is made up of several important structures including the amygdala, hippocampus, hypothalamus, and anterior cingulate cortex (ACC).

In evolutionary terms, it is an "old" part of the brain. It controls the behaviors we need for survival, like fight or flight responses, and caring for our children. It is also deeply involved in our emotional experiences: "positive" emotions, like pleasure and reward, as well as "negative" emotions, like fear and anger.

For those of us who have survived childhood abuse, there can be observable changes in different parts of this system. Changes in the limbic system can potentially contribute to a range of issues later in life, including mental health disorders like depression, anxiety, and PTSD.

The brain's threat system: the amygdala and the hypothalamus

The amygdala is especially important in processing emotions, particularly fear and anxiety. In some of us who've experienced childhood abuse, the amygdala may become enlarged and more active. This could lead to increased fear responses, heightened anxiety, and challenges in managing our emotions.

When we are in a threatening situation, our amygdala sends an "alarm signal" to the hypothalamus. This activates our sympathetic nervous system, which releases adrenaline. This is what triggers our flight, fight, or freeze responses. By sending a sudden surge of adrenaline through our system, it primes us to take immediate action. It is part of our earliest evolution and helped our ancestors to escape from immediate danger from predator animals or other humans from hostile tribes.

It is a mechanism that helps us in sudden threatening situations, and so it normally only lasts for a short time—just long enough to deal with the impending danger.

If the threat doesn't go away, the hypothalamus activates the next step in the stress response, via the hypothalamic–pituitary–adrenal axis (HPA). This regulates the release of cortisol from the adrenal glands. Cortisol is a hormone that helps the body respond to more prolonged stress.

Dr. Nadine Burke Harris, an expert on ACEs and trauma, and author of *Toxic Childhood Stress: The Legacy of Early Trauma and How to Heal*, gives an excellent description of how the brain's fear center can become dysregulated. She explains that, as children in distressing and dysfunctional families, our stress response system reacted as though a dangerous animal was coming home every night. Our amygdala began to become sensitized and extra-responsive to stress. Our brains became biased toward spotting problems and difficulties, rather than having fun.

For example, when we were physically abused, we became skilled at recognizing angry faces. We learned to predict when we were about to be hurt. We hoped that by doing this we could be better prepared to deal with what was about to happen. This is an early childhood pattern that can follow us into adult life.

Over time, constant activation of this system led to what's known as "toxic stress," which harmed our developing brains. We became extra sensitive to threats in our environment (known as "hypervigilance"). We learned to live with a high state of alert (termed "hyperarousal"). As the amygdala controls fear and aggression, its heightened activity can make it difficult for us to regulate our emotions as adults. We are likely to be triggered by minor events.

An overactive stress response system can also interfere with our sleep patterns and contribute to insomnia and nightmares. Over time, we may be predisposed to physical health problems like heart disease, diabetes, headaches, immune disorders, and chronic pain, among others.

The brain's memory system: the hippocampus

It was difficult enough to be able to focus, to learn, and to achieve at school when all our mental energy was focused on our survival. When really bad things happened, they dominated our thoughts and feelings and we didn't have much room for times tables, world history, geography, or the enjoyment of art and music. But there are also specific changes within our brain that make academic success even harder.

The hippocampus is the part of our brain that is important for the formation and retrieval of memories, particularly memories related to personal experiences. It also controls spatial navigation (our "mental map" of our environment). In some of us who suffered severe childhood trauma, our hippocampus became smaller—it is thought that these brain cells are harmed by long-term exposure to stress hormones. This could impact our ability to form and recall memories and our capacity to learn. In particular, we may have trouble remembering facts or events.

Academic failure as children made us believe that we don't have the ability to succeed as adults. This is wrong. We can enjoy lifelong learning, continually acquiring new knowledge, insight, and skills.

Overgeneral memory and bias toward remembering the bad times

Sundials, used for measuring time before clocks and watches were invented, often had some sort of inscription or motto beneath them. These may have been something deep or significant written in Latin or perhaps humorous words to lighten the day. Among the most popular and clichéd expressions are the words "I count only the sunny hours."

Like a sundial, we do not remember everything equally. Our minds prioritize some memories over others.

There is evidence that suggests that being brought up in a distressing or dysfunctional family results in an "overgeneral" memory. This is a phenomenon where we struggle to remember specific details. Our recall is of broad events such as holidays, rather than clear incidents that happened. The area of the brain involved in memory recall, the hippocampus, is less active when we try to recall positive events.

Conversely, the amygdala, the brain structure which helps to process threats, is more active compared with children who did not have challenging backgrounds. This suggests that when we were harmed in our families, we developed a bias toward recalling negative events. This leaves us more vulnerable to depression as adults.

The anterior cingulate cortex (ACC)

The ACC plays a role in many tasks, like managing emotions and regulating behavior. It also helps us to focus and to control our thinking. Some of us who've been mistreated as children may show changes in the ACC, leading to challenges with managing our emotions and thinking processes.

The brain's thinking center: the prefrontal cortex

The prefrontal cortex is the brain's thinking center. It controls some of our most complex functions: making decisions, controlling our impulses, regulating our emotions, and guiding our social behavior. It is important for our "working memory" and in learning.

Research has shown that for some of us who've experienced abuse as children, our prefrontal cortex may not have developed optimally. This could potentially make it more difficult for us to concentrate, learn, and remember things, and lead to challenges with controlling our thoughts, emotions, and behavior. Because the prefrontal cortex controls decision making and impulse control, damage to it may make it more likely that we show risky behaviors, have issues with substance abuse, or trouble with the law.

Fear of missing out (FOMO) and rejection

We need to belong.

Some of our deepest fears do not arise from physical threats. What frightens many of us is the risk that we will be rejected. When we were mistreated as children, this natural and normal concern increases. Brain activity in the areas responsible for regulating negative emotions (the dorsal ACC and also the lateral prefrontal cortex) reduces.

These changes within our brains make us more sensitive to rejection and more likely to react negatively to it when we are rejected.

The brain's reward system: the VTA

Our brains are flooded with the neurotransmitter dopamine when we take part in enjoyable activities. This is why sex, eating chocolate, taking drugs, etc., give us a high. The area of our brain that controls this "reward" response is known as the ventral tegmental area (VTA).

Whatever abuse happened to us, we will have been stressed by it. Not the simple short-term stress that we quickly recover from, but higher levels of stress that occur regularly, sometimes daily, over a long period of time.

Childhood trauma harms the VTA by causing dopamine receptors to become less responsive to the effects of dopamine. In turn, this means that we need more dopamine to experience the same results that would have occurred if our VTA hadn't been damaged. In simple terms, we need more stimulation to feel pleasure. We need more chocolate, sex, alcohol, or whatever it is that our brain enjoys.

It is easy to see how needing more of something can eventually make us unwell. More and more alcohol potentially leads toward addiction, and excessive amounts of cakes, ice cream, sugary drinks, and chocolate will, given enough time, result in us becoming unhealthy. We all know this. If we know and understand the context of our behaviors, though, we can be much more optimistic about how we can make changes for a better future. We don't have to beat ourselves up about giving in to compulsive behavior or struggling with whatever the challenge is that we are facing.

Our future brain: how the damage can be repaired

Brains that grew to cope with trauma during childhood struggle to focus on enjoying an exciting and adventurous adult life. They adjusted and acclimatized to live with dysfunction. As adults from difficult or distressing backgrounds, our brains have learned to expect problems rather than anticipating pleasure and success.

It may be helpful to imagine ourselves on a ship with a fractured hull that is taking on water. Yes, the situation is difficult and problematic. However, the damage was caused by something external; it wasn't part of the boat's original design. Likewise, seen through the lens of childhood abuse, our addictions (for example) are not character defects or personality flaws—they are wounds inflicted by something outside of ourselves. This point of view can give us tremendous hope. With the right tools and equipment, boats can be repaired. We now know that the brain exhibits "neuroplasticity"—the capacity to adapt and rewire itself—into adulthood and throughout our whole lives. This means that, with the right strategies and support, our brains can change and overcome our childhood trauma.

They can be repaired too.

5

Justifications for Abuse: Lies and More Lies

> *They say that family is the place of safety. But sometimes this is the greatest lie; family is not sanctuary, it is not safety and succor. For some of us, it is the secret wound.*
>
> —Nayomi Munaweera: *What Lies Between Us*

All abuse is about power and control. So that we stayed powerless, dishonesty was used to keep us confused. This made it easier to manipulate us. There are a number of very common untruths that we may have heard regularly. Our past continues to hurt us in the present because, deep down, we believe the lies that we were told as children.

It was natural for us to trust adults. Children grow up believing that what they are told is true. Often, we had very little to compare our own experience to. We had no way of knowing good from bad parenting. We were likely to mistake our own upbringing as being a universal experience, thinking that it was just how things are.

Our early learning was centered on our parents' need to control. We were taught things about ourselves that were not correct. Ideas were given to us so that we could be handled or exploited more easily.

When we recognize the lies that we were told as being lies, we can more easily refute them. This helps us come to terms with our past. It also means that we can begin to change our unhelpful beliefs to more useful ways of thinking.

Some of the most common untruths are listed below. Some will be applicable to us personally; others will not. Most importantly, we can begin to learn to question. We are likely to have other beliefs that hold us back. Once we recognize this, we can then learn how to change our thinking, so that we can make a positive and practical difference to our lives today.

Lies That We Were Told

We made it happen

This is one of the most common excuses used by adults who hurt children. It is a lie. It's a lie that is used by every type of abuser.

There are several reasons why adult abusers blame their child victims. Some of these include:

- **They are unable to take responsibility for their own behavior.** Parents who lost their temper and hit us are entirely at fault. They could not control themselves. They pretended that something normal that we did, and that all children do, caused their rage. It is important to remember that it definitely was *their* rage; they owned it, not us. We were targets for their anger, not causes of it. In the same way, we are not responsible for their decision to take drugs or alcohol or indulge in any of the other harmful behaviors that they, as adults, chose to do.
- **To avoid the consequences of their actions.** For those of us who endured sexual abuse, the end of the grooming process is always to make sure that the abused person feels that they somehow had responsibility for what happened. By doing this, abusers hoped that it would be less likely that we reported what was happening to us or to other family members. They made us feel responsible so that they were less likely to get caught.
- **Emotional immaturity.** Psychologist Lindsay C. Gibson gives a thorough account of the characteristics of these types of parents in her book *Adult Children of Emotionally Immature Parents*. She suggests that typical traits include being self-referential, emotionally insensitive, rigid and single-minded, having low stress tolerance, little respect for differences, and also being egocentric.
- **Narcissism.** Some parents are narcissists. They have an enormous sense of entitlement; they are unable to empathize, and they are pathologically self-centered. They believe themselves to be special, unique, and worthy

of admiration. They fantasize about power and success. They don't reflect on their own behavior. And they don't recognize their own faults.

"It never happened"

There are separate sections within this book describing denial and gaslighting. They are mentioned here because frequently after abuse, our abusers try to persuade us that we somehow got it wrong and that the abuse never happened.

- **Denial.** There are two types of denial. Firstly, those who caused us harm simply refuse to admit that they did anything wrong at all. Perpetrators of physical, emotional, or sexual abuse, and abusers who harmed us in any other way, tell outright lies and say that we are making it up. The second type of denial is when someone who hurt us admits that they did so, then attempts to minimize the effects of their actions. They confess but pretend that their actions did little damage.
- **Gaslighting.** This occurs when abusers manipulate us and try to make us question our own understanding of what is going on.

"That's just your opinion" and "Now's not the time"

One technique that is used to prevent us discussing openly and honestly what happened to us is to use what are known as "thought-terminating clichés." First described by Robert Jay Lifton in his 1961 book *Thought Reform and the Psychology of Totalism*, they are used as a way to shut down discussions to prevent difficult subjects being explored and the truth being discovered.

The phrase "that is just your opinion" is an attempt to hide what really happened. It changes objective facts into subjective opinions. For example, some family members will try and disguise our own hatred of our father for hitting us when he was drunk by suggesting that it is our opinion of him that is the problem, rather than what he actually did. Uncles, aunts, brothers, and sisters who are unable to confront the truth use the "that's just your opinion" argument to shut down conversations to avoid having to confront reality.

Similarly, "now is not the time" is a statement that pushes confronting the past into some imaginary time in the future. Just as tomorrow never comes, there will never actually be a perfect time when it will be easy for everyone to come to terms with what has happened. "Now is not the right time" is simply another way of family members saying, "we are not able to deal with this."

We imagined it

One of the most ridiculous defenses regularly seen in cases where abuse comes to court is that we somehow imagined what happened to us. Certainly, our memories will not be perfect. Memory does not work like a video. It cannot be played again and again as a completely accurate record of what took place. When something traumatic happens, we remember some details better than others. There will always be some inaccuracies. Immediately after a terrible event, for example a car accident, different witnesses will remember details that don't always match perfectly. This does not mean that the accident never happened.

When we were abused, we may make mistakes. Our recall will not be perfect. Some facts, dates, times, and places can become confused. This is normal. Inaccuracies in our accounts are evidence that we are fallible human beings. What happened still happened. It is right we stick by our truth and don't doubt ourselves.

We benefited

This is a popular lie which is told frequently by parents who physically abused us. It was sometimes referred to as "being cruel to be kind." They pretend that hitting us was intended to instill discipline. This is untrue. It is a failure of parenting. Sensible and emotionally mature adults do not need to assault children.

Similarly sexual abuse is disguised as education. Abusers cruelly tell us that they were teaching us about sex so that we knew how to do it properly.

"Whatever doesn't kill you makes you stronger"

"Whatever doesn't kill you makes you stronger" is rooted in Friedrich Nietzsche's philosophy. It's often promoted in books about trauma, resilience, and personal growth.

Matthew Parris's thought-provoking work, *Fracture: Stories of How Great Lives Take Root in Trauma,* describes how some famous people achieved success while also having distressing childhoods. These stories can inspire us, but we need to be careful in how we interpret them.

One mistake frequently made in the media is called "survivorship bias." Reports focus on people who have overcome their traumas and ignore those who continue to struggle. Just because successful people have experienced trauma doesn't mean that trauma causes success. We shouldn't forget the countless others who have experienced trauma but haven't achieved the same positive outcomes. For example, some millionaires and even billionaires were raised in poverty. This does not, however, mean that a poor and impoverished upbringing is somehow a route to financial success. The number of super-rich people who are from wealthy and privileged backgrounds vastly outnumbers those from poor ones.

Depending on the source of the statistics, roughly one in four of us had a distressing, dysfunctional, or abusive childhood. If trauma really is beneficial then as a group we should dominate universities, top jobs in government and business, and overshadow others in sports and the arts. If it is true that whatever doesn't kill you makes you stronger, we should be less vulnerable than those lucky enough to be raised in happy and healthy families. We should be underrepresented in both physical and mental health services.

The ACE study has shown the negative effects of childhood trauma on later-life health and well-being. The more trauma experienced in childhood, the higher the likelihood of facing health and social problems as adults. It's estimated that a large number of adults have experienced at least one ACE, so it's not surprising that some successful people have also experienced trauma. However, their success is not directly caused by the trauma.

Trauma is not a requirement for success. A traumatic history in the lives of successful people doesn't mean it is beneficial. While we can grow stronger and more resilient after experiencing distressing challenges, it's important to note that this growth happens despite the trauma. Not because of it. Our painful experiences shape us. But it is our personal efforts to heal, learn, and grow that truly define us. Our strength and resilience come from our own efforts, therapy, self-reflection, and hard work. Recognizing this reality helps us to develop a healthier and more compassionate understanding of trauma and resilience. We should celebrate our perseverance and determination to heal and grow, rather than focusing on the trauma itself.

"I won't love you if you misbehave"

Anyone who has ever watched a nature documentary will have seen how animals will fight to the death to protect their babies. Love is not some sort of transaction. It is not a commodity to be traded in exchange for children behaving in a way that their parents want them to.

Emotionally immature parents do not understand that their love for their children should be unconditional.

The words "I won't love you if you misbehave" have nothing to do with love. They are about parental manipulation and control.

"You're not OK"

There are multiple versions of this particular lie. Many of us have a deep-rooted unworthiness story based on this deception. If we were emotionally abused, we will have heard this lie repeated again and again. We may have been subject to constant criticism, had our achievements ignored, and normal minor faults blown out of all proportion. Some of us were told that we would never amount to anything. Often global descriptions were used against us. We were useless, bad, selfish, or lazy; we were weak, ugly, or stupid.

This was untrue.

We were told these things because they made it easier to manipulate and control us.

"Because I said so"

Many of us will be familiar with the phrase "because I said so."

Good parents are happy to explain to children why rules and boundaries are necessary. They are confident in their choices. Decisions are taken for good reasons. It is easy for them to justify their insistence on always looking both ways before crossing the road because we may be seriously hurt if we step into traffic without looking.

Abusive parents cannot tolerate any questioning of their authority. This is because they use their power to dominate us, rather than to keep us safe and happy.

If we were brought up with parents who abused their authority, then this has three potential outcomes for us as adults:

- **We became subservient, believing that those in authority are always right.** We don't question or challenge any of the norms of the society in which we live and we accept the rule of law without believing that we have any right to challenge or attempt to change it.
- **We rebel.** We express our anger and frustration in ways that are harmful to us. For example, we are just not able to get on well with our boss at work or people that we perceive to have some authority over us. For some

of us, our actions become more problematic, abusing drink or drugs, or sometimes getting into trouble with the police.
- **We acknowledge and recognize the fault is in our upbringing.** This is our most positive response. We see the need for rules, regulations, and laws, while appreciating that sometimes they are wrong. Perhaps they have been written to keep powerful and privileged people in their positions of power and privilege. When we see this is the case, we use our personal influence to campaign, vote, and make changes for everyone's benefit.

Often, we move between these three positions at different times in our lives. However, the more we understand about the impact our past has on us, the more we are able to use the third strategy, which provides the most helpful outlook for our own growth and maturity, and for wider society.

We are responsible for the consequences

Frequently encountered by those of us who were sexually abused is the myth that we are responsible for the consequences of our abuser's behavior. This means that abusers blame us for what happens when their abuse is discovered.

If their relationships with other family members or friends are damaged, this is not our fault. Neither is it our fault if they lose their career or they face legal trouble.

The truth is that the abuser chose to abuse and if they had not done so, there would be nothing to disclose. When they chose to behave in the way in which they did, they took a risk, in addition to the harm they did to us. This risk included:

- Being discovered.
- Being held legally responsible for their actions.
- Causing damage to their relationships with family members and friends.
- Causing damage to their reputation.
- Losing their job or career.

This was their choice. We were not and are not responsible.

"Adults are more important than children"

This is powerful. It originates with the fifteenth-century Augustinian clergyman John Mirk, who wrote, "Children should be seen and not heard."

Historians sometimes differ in their interpretations; however, some believe that it was applied more to girls than to boys. It's a misogynistic and malevolent view that still persists in many parts of our world today.

A pernicious version of how this untruth operates is seen when an adult is accused of child abuse. There is an enormous focus on the damage to the adult's standing, the impact on their job, their family, or their mental health. In comparison, little attention is paid to the enduring harm that was done to their victim.

"Time is a healer" and "It's all in the past"

Those trying to help us often share the widespread belief that time is a healer. It is not. If it were true, all of us would be healing all of the time. With each passing day, we would move further and further away from our trauma, and closer to becoming happy and fulfilled people. We would not need to waste money on counseling or psychotherapy, or learn to think differently. We would just have to sit it out until enough time passed for us to feel OK.

There is a real danger in the "time is a healer" idea. It stops us from seeking support when we need it. It means that we continue to punish and blame ourselves because we haven't recovered from trauma that happened a long time ago. It is also a belief that can let abusers get away with their behavior. Frequently, offenders state, "But it was 30 years ago," or use expressions like "it was historic." The implication is that we should be "over it" by now. The perpetrator is abdicating responsibility. This is an attempt to suggest that not healing is a failure on the part of the victim. It isn't. The reality is that, in some circumstances, if we don't give ourselves the support that we deserve, time itself can hurt us more than it heals us. Our emotional pain can grow as we become more and more aware of what happened to us, and that it was wrong. We may also continue to rely on strategies that were useful to us as children but no longer serve us as adults.

It is unfair. We grew up in families where things happened to us that shouldn't have. The love and care we deserved wasn't given to us. Now we can look at our pasts openly, honestly, and realistically. We should tell ourselves the truth. What took place was wrong. We can give ourselves the compassion and support that we need. This will lead to us taking responsibility for our own well-being and taking action to heal.

Time is not a healer. We heal ourselves.

"But it's your family"

We are under enormous pressure to conform to commonly held assumptions about families. Traditionally, families are revered. They are given a high moral and even religious status. The reality, though, is that some dysfunctional families are not families at all. They are make-believe. They are a network of toxic relationships masquerading as an obligation.

"What happens in the family should stay in the family—it's nobody else's business"

The UK-based charity Women's Aid, when describing the myth "Domestic abuse is a private family matter, and not a social issue" on its website, states that the reality is: that "Violence and abuse against women and children incurs high costs for society: hospital treatment, medication, court proceedings, lawyers' fees, imprisonment—not to mention the psychological and physical impact on those who experience it."

Families should be happy and healthy. They are not individual fiefdoms where abuse can go undetected and unpunished.

"It was like that for me so it will be like that for you too"

Perhaps one of the stupidest things that parents say, and believe, is that because they suffered, their children should suffer too.

Good parents learn from their own upbringing. When bad things have happened to them, it makes them determined that their own children should not experience the trauma that they did.

Immature parents harbor unresolved envy. Deep down, they are jealous. Subconsciously, they do not want their kids to have an easier time than they did.

Wanting children to suffer keeps the cycle of abuse going. Trauma is then passed on from generation to generation, a phenomenon known as "intergenerational trauma." It's not a conscious decision to inflict suffering, but a cycle that stems from unresolved issues.

However, we have the power to break this cycle. Becoming aware of these damaging patterns and making a conscious effort to heal ourselves not only helps us, but also shields our children from carrying the same burdens. Instead of allowing the cycle of abuse to continue, we can choose to pave a new path—one marked by understanding, compassion, and healing.

Lies from Newspapers and the Media

We should have reported it earlier

Implicit in many newspaper reports written by those who have never experienced abuse is the idea that it could not have been that bad or that distressing, or else we would have reported it much earlier. This is wrong.

There are good reasons why it takes time to report abuse:

- **Safety.** We may have been at risk if we disclosed our abuse early on. We were trapped and had nowhere safe to escape to.
- **Recognition.** Many of us did not understand that we were being mistreated. The harm that was done to us was a normal part of our world. As adults we can perhaps see our experience as abuse; however, many of us still struggle to correctly identify and label our history.
- **Understanding.** It takes time to process what happened to us.
- **Fear of the consequences.** Abusers expend a great deal of effort trying to convince us that if something negative happens as a result of us sharing what happened, then this is our fault. This is not true. They are responsible for the abuse and the consequences of it.
- **Nobody would help us.** A common experience for many of us was simply that there was no one to tell. Adults who abuse children hide behind a cloak of respectability. They groom the adults around them. Frequently, we felt that if we did tell anyone what was happening, we would not have been believed.

In reality, disclosing abuse is often a process rather than a one-time action. We may have tried to hint at what was happening to us, hoping that adults would notice our distress, or behaved in ways we thought would show that we were distressed. Usually, our first attempts to share were ignored.

The research report by UK children's charity the NSPCC, *No One Noticed, No One Heard*, states that it took an average of seven years for young people to disclose sexual abuse. Many of us took longer than this, or haven't ever spoken about what happened to us.

"Girls shouldn't behave like that"

Control is at the center of all abuse. One way in which girls and women are controlled is by imposing rigid and nonsensical ideals on their behavior.

Women who are meek and mild and who do not express their opinions are frequently rewarded by being told they are good. Conversely, condemnation awaits those who challenge, confront, or question.

The area where some men are most afraid, and therefore most desperate to show dominance, is female sexuality. Actions taken to prevent women from being their authentic selves include rules about how they dress and denying their ability to make their own decisions. There may be restrictions on whom they are allowed to spend time with. Most commonly, women endure everyday harassment.

Oxfam, the confederation of charities which fight against global poverty, gives some interesting and helpful information on their website, on the page entitled *Ten harmful beliefs that perpetuate violence against women and girls.*

When girls are told that they "shouldn't behave like that", this is not a useful life lesson, merely a method of making it easier to control them and to silence their voice.

Misogynistic thinking damages men too. Disempowering women does not empower men. Backward attitudes hold us all back, no matter who is expressing them.

"Lies" That We Told Ourselves: How We Coped

We told "lies" to ourselves to shield us from the reality of our upbringing. The lies were subconscious, and we genuinely believed them at the time. This wasn't a moral failing. It was a necessary survival technique to protect ourselves from deep emotional hurt.

It took courage to survive then, and it takes bravery to face the truth now.

We could have stopped our abuse from happening, if only we…

If only we behaved better. If only we could be more loveable, more successful, more like our brother or sister who wasn't being hurt.

After any sort of abuse, this is frequently the lie that we mistakenly tell ourselves.

Realistically there is nothing we could have done to escape our upbringing. But our subconscious tried to convince us that there was something we could have done to make things better. The truth is that we were innocent children. It was not our fault. Adults had all the power and control and there was nothing that we could have done.

We tell ourselves this lie to protect ourselves from our own vulnerability. Our young minds preferred to feel guilty, rather than helpless. It would have been too frightening and overwhelming to admit that we were helpless, so we incorrectly convinced ourselves that it was our fault and then felt guilty about that.

Many of us still feel shame and guilt a great deal of the time. This is undeserved guilt. It is the unprocessed remains of our childhood coping strategy. As adults, we can deal with this by reparenting ourselves and gifting ourselves the enormous compassion we deserve. We can also tell ourselves that we are safe now, and begin to process emotions we weren't able to handle as children (see Chapter 6: Emotions and Emotional Processing).

We should have made better choices

We frequently punish ourselves by believing that we should have helped ourselves and made better choices as soon as we escaped from our dysfunctional family (assuming that we have done so).

Our choices may have taken us down difficult roads. These led us to unhappy places. The truth is that our decisions, on some level, were all meant to keep us happy. They were based on learned behaviors and patterns that we used as children. They were strategies to keep us safe and feeling OK about ourselves.

Up until now, we have been living the best possible lives that we could have lived.

We can learn and change though. Whatever holds us back now—poor relationships, financial insecurity, over-drinking, drugs, or simply self-defeating habits and behaviors—are a legacy of our past and a way of dealing with it. We can understand ourselves better, progress and take our journey to a happier and more fulfilling future. This is best achieved by treating ourselves with compassion and acceptance.

The faults and errors in our lives are coping strategies, not poor moral choices.

6

Goals for Our Recovery

WHY A JOURNEY OF A THOUSAND MILES DOES NOT START WITH A SINGLE STEP

There is both truth and wisdom in the quotation from Lao Tzu (the ancient Chinese philosopher), who said that a journey of a thousand miles starts with a single step. It describes how essential it is to take action to achieve our goals, and also emphasizes the way in which huge tasks can be broken down into multiple smaller pieces so that they become manageable and realistic. This is good. Realistically though, all of life's successful journeys begin firstly with intention, and secondly with planning.

WHY WE NEED TO PLAN A "RECOVERY PLUS"

This book uses the term "recovery" as it makes sense to people. It is, though, problematic, or at least too limited when applied to difficult or traumatic childhoods.

Dictionaries define recovery as getting back something that was lost or stolen, or the process by which we return to some sort of normal state of health. But, firstly, for some of us who had the most distressing families, we never actually experienced love, warmth, and support in the first place. We cannot get any of these things back because they were never there to begin with. Secondly, there is the idea of "normality." We deserve more than this. Much more.

Boats need to be solidly constructed, watertight, and have effective navigation and communication systems. Most importantly, to be seaworthy, they must have a reliable working engine. This needs to be strong enough to sail both still waters and the stormiest seas. No mariner ever wants to be stranded mid-Atlantic as a rusty, worn engine finally gives up.

But just restoring or replacing a marine engine isn't sufficient to enjoy sailing to the most beautiful destinations. And yet this limited repair approach is taken by many self-help courses, books, counselors, and psychotherapists. Instead of helping us to make and reach ambitious goals, they simply focus on fixing a deficit.

Yes, it's vital to fix the engine, but it is nowhere near enough. Detailed charts, routes, timetables, and plans are needed on a long voyage. Similarly, therapists can teach us to deal with "single issues": to manage anxiety, help us to resolve a relationship problem, or process anger, for example. There are many individual challenges that we may face, and solving specific issues is likely to be very helpful and a good first step, but on its own this isn't adequate.

We ought to have the opportunity to end up somewhere wonderful, rather than just compensating for a distressing childhood and making up lost ground. We deserve not just a repaired, functional motor, but also raised sails and a strong gleaming hull—a magnificent boat that will take us through rough seas to reach our best destination.

When it comes to mental health, for most of the world, "normality" means living a suboptimal life which is generally pretty miserable. It is frequently stressful and depressing.

Especially after our upbringings, we are entitled to want contentment, happiness, and sometimes, states of bliss. This is covered more in Chapter 18: Beyond Recovery. However, for now, it is worth considering the words of psychiatrist R.D. Laing who described the process of recovery, or at least working with a therapist, as one which leads to an "absence of ecstasy." R.D. Laing recognized that many patients were led on a healing journey that ended with a dull mediocre life, rather than one full of wonder and joy.

The best intention that we can set ourselves is not only to recover, but, as described by psychologist Abraham Maslow, to become "self-actualized." By this, he meant reaching our full potential: developing into the happiest, healthiest and, should we choose it, wealthiest person we can possibly be.

It is worth noting that Maslow used the words *self*-actualized. He didn't say society-actualized, parent-actualized, or work-actualized. Change, growth and development are about our own values. They're not dependent on the often-arbitrary measures of success that are held by consumer cultures or other people who are motivated by what they want, rather than what is healthy for us.

Starting With the End in Mind

American businessman and educator Stephen Covey wrote in *The 7 Habits of Highly Effective People*, "start with the end in mind." Stephen Covey held an MBA from Harvard University and, while the corporate and personal worlds don't always mix, he was very driven by his personal beliefs and values. And it is certainly helpful at whatever age or stage we are in life to have a general sense of direction.

As individuals who endured adverse childhood experiences, we became experts in resilience and survival. Our focus was on staying safe. Our strategy helped us survive our past. But it can limit our capacity to imagine a future where we thrive, rather than just exist. This means that the principle of "starting with the end in mind," when that is a happy and fulfilling life, can feel out of reach.

However, our goals don't have to be about grand achievements or far-fetched ambitions. Instead, they can be about envisioning a future where we are at peace with our past. Where we have a loving relationship with ourselves. Where we have nurtured our ability to trust and build healthy relationships. Where we see ourselves not just as survivors, but as individuals experiencing joy, love, and contentment.

It will not be easy, and the path will not be linear. But the rewards are a sense of self and a life that is far more enriched and authentic.

It's about embracing the possibility of expansion, of believing that we can build a life defined not by what we've experienced, but by who we want to become.

Purpose and Passion

Spanish artist Pablo Picasso suggested that the meaning of life was to find our gift and then to give it away. One of the world's most famous media personalities and generous philanthropists, Oprah Winfrey, talks about pursuing our passion, then purpose will follow. Some of the best advice around purpose, passion, and motivation is given by author John Coleman in his book *HBR Guide to Crafting Your Purpose*. He suggests that purpose is made, rather than found. It is something that we need to actively work on, rather than suddenly discover. John Coleman emphasizes that our purpose may evolve over time. It isn't necessarily one fixed goal that lasts all of our lifetime.

As people who were raised in dysfunctional families, we are likely to have experienced emotionally immature parents. They would have had a fixed mindset. It is therefore understandable that, having lived with this example, we make the mistake of thinking too narrowly. The idea of purpose evolving is particularly pertinent. It moves us away from a static way of thinking, and that opens up more possibilities.

Recognizing that our purpose can change over time is liberating. It means we aren't confined by the limitations of our past. And we don't have to bear the pressure of figuring everything out immediately. Additionally, our experiences may already have given us a depth of understanding and empathy. This resilience can be channeled into a meaningful purpose.

This purpose isn't about reaching a specific destination, but about walking a path that aligns with our values and aspirations. It's about creating a meaningful story for our lives. This embraces our past, accepts our present, and looks forward to a future where we're active contributors to our own well-being and, perhaps, even that of others.

The road may not always be straight or smooth. The act of goal setting, while immensely rewarding, can present its own set of challenges. In the next section, we will discuss common goal-setting errors and how to avoid them. By staying aware of these potential missteps, we can steer our journey effectively, aligning our aspirations with actionable steps, and progressing to a brighter future.

Common Goal-Setting Errors

When we are setting our goals there are a number of common mistakes that it's useful to be aware of and look out for.

Trying to control the behavior of others

When our parents are still in our lives, we may want them to change their behavior toward us. Or perhaps our husband, wife, partner, boyfriend or girlfriend isn't treating us the way we want to be treated. It is tempting to write our goals focused on how we want other people to be. This is perfectly understandable; however, we cannot control other people's behavior.

It is far better to state our goals in terms of action that *we* can take. This means, for example, setting clear boundaries. A simple example would be to set a goal of not tolerating being relentlessly criticized and deciding to leave people or situations when this happens, rather than attempting to control the way someone else treats us.

Setting negative goals

It works much better if we can say to ourselves "I want to feel confident and assertive at family events," rather than "I don't want to feel weak and vulnerable when I am around my relatives."

Similarly, we can set a goal of making sure that we have a supportive dialogue with ourselves. We can aim to teach our inner voice to be encouraging, rather than trying to "silence our inner critic."

Negative goals are based on a dislike of ourselves. For example, we want to lose weight because we believe that we look overweight, rather than seeing ourselves as happier and healthier when we exercise more and have a healthy shape and size. It is better to move toward well-being and joy, rather than away from ill health and unhappiness.

Setting goals that hold us back

Sometimes we can unintentionally set goals that keep us locked into our current situation. For example, we set a goal to improve our relationship with a toxic person, rather than ending it.

Setting unrealistic goals

Motivational psychologist Heidi Grant Halvorson, in her book *Nine Things Successful People Do Differently*, uses the concept of "realistic optimism." We need balance. Setting goals that are too optimistic and ultimately unachievable doesn't benefit us. It's helpful to set SMART goals (Specific, Measurable, Achievable, Realistic and Timed).

Allowing too many goals to cloud our vision

When we've spent a lifetime yearning for change, it's understandable that we might want to create an abundance of goals. But this can overwhelm, divide our attention, and limit our progress. It's helpful to identify our most important goals and address those first.

Not paying attention to our core values

As survivors of dysfunctional families, we may have grown accustomed to living by the rules and values imposed by others. When setting goals, it's easy to fall into this old pattern. Our goals are more achievable when they match our own values and beliefs.

Not revisiting and adapting our goals

We're no strangers to change—we've had to adapt to survive. Similarly, our goals may need to adapt as we grow and evolve. Regularly reviewing and adjusting our goals ensures they continue to serve our current needs and future ambitions.

Setting goals based on external expectations

Those of us from dysfunctional families often become adept at pleasing others to avoid conflict or gain acceptance. We may find ourselves setting goals based on what we think others expect of us or what societal norms dictate. But remember, our goals should reflect our own aspirations, not someone else's expectations.

Feeling Wrong Before We Feel Right: The Strange Change Paradox

Turn bad days into data, be curious not furious.
—Daniel G Amen MD

One very interesting phenomenon that we will encounter when we start on our journey to reach our goals is that, to begin with, everything just feels wrong.

Whenever we try to change something, there is an initial period when everything feels difficult and uncomfortable. It can seem that we are moving backward not forward.

To begin with, we are likely to experience less confidence and competence when we are doing things differently. That is one of the reasons that many people avoid change or give up in the early stages.

This phenomenon happens in many situations. We notice how unfit we are and feel self-conscious at the start of a new fitness program. Running is extremely hard work and we do not feel welcome in the gym. Myriads of mistakes are made while learning a new language, and it is a necessary part of the process to feel some embarrassment.

We can deal with the contradiction that is part of the change process by:

- **Accepting the opposite.** This means that we recognize that in the early stages of behaving differently, we will feel the opposite of what we want to be. We will feel less confident instead of more confident. Knowing that this is a temporary state that we are passing through will help our understanding and keep us motivated.
- **Keeping focused on the future.** While accepting and fully feeling our current discomfort, we can hold in our minds the vision of a better future.

How Our Past Holds Us Back

The past is in the past, but the strategies that we used to try to keep us safe are part of our present. We all have recurrent patterns and routine behaviors that were once helpful to us, but now harm us.

It is possible to change. It isn't easy though. Advice and guidance intended to help frequently miss a crucial step: they go directly from the problem to the solution, without looking at what is driving our behavior.

A good example comes from strategies to help those of us who drink too much alcohol. Advice usually begins by identifying the problem. This is frequently done with some sort of consumption calculator. It then goes on to suggest ways to cut down. These include switching to drinks that are weaker in alcohol, only drinking with meals, having nights off, etc.

Some of these strategies may work well. The problem is, however, that even though our behaviors may be harmful, they were all originally intended to help us to cope. What was once our survival strategy is now our symptom.

We need to ask ourselves what problems our coping methods are solving (even if they are doing so in a destructive way). Then we can look at other ways of dealing with these issues. In the above example, we might over-drink to avoid feelings of loneliness, to help us feel confident, or to blot out pain.

If we simply stop drinking without tackling the underlying problems that it masked, then we risk suddenly coming face to face with those problems. By understanding and finding ways to navigate loneliness, pessimism, and pain, we can pave the way for permanent change.

What we need is a range of helpful behaviors to replace the recurrent patterns from our past that hurt us in the present.

A toolbox of strategies

Philosopher and behavioral scientist Abraham Kaplan developed what he called "the law of the instrument." This is also known as "Maslow's Hammer" after psychologist Abraham Maslow, who is also credited with inventing the theory. Kaplan said, "Give a small boy a hammer, and he will find that everything he encounters needs pounding."

The idea is that we all rely too much on simple, tried and tested strategies. Toolboxes contain saws, screwdrivers, wrenches, pliers, etc. They have a range of instruments, each one best suited for a particular job. Likewise, we need a psychological and emotional toolbox to successfully deal with the complexity of life's challenges.

Emotionally immature and abusive parents model a limited range of behaviors. These are often maladaptive and/or over-simplistic. This means that we learned unhelpful ideas about complicated concepts, such as trust.

Trust

Everything that matters most—our deepest loving relationships, health, wealth, success, and happiness—all depend on trust. We trust our husbands, wives, or partners to remain faithful to us. Within open relationships, we expect that the boundaries we set will be kept. In a world of dating apps, hook-ups, and casual sex, at a bare minimum we need to trust those we meet not to hurt us. We trust professionals who look after our well-being—doctors, dentists, and a whole range of therapists—to give us high-quality care. We trust our employers or customers to pay us on time and banks to keep our money safe.

We also need to trust ourselves. Over 1600 years ago, Greek philosopher Aristotle stated, "the most important relationship we can all have is the one you have with yourself." Our relationships with everyone else are dependent on how we see ourselves. How effective we are in life is greatly determined by how much we can trust ourselves to achieve what we want to achieve.

To succeed, we also need to trust in the world around us. Albert Einstein famously said that "the single most important decision any of us will ever make is whether or not to believe that the universe is friendly or not." If we believe that the universe is a dark, dangerous, and unfriendly place, then we will behave very differently than if we see it as somewhere full of opportunity.

We need to be able to build trusting relationships with other people, trust ourselves, and have some trust in life itself. This can, however, present some serious challenges. As children raised in dysfunctional families, it was sensible for us to learn *not* to trust people. For our safety and survival, we knew that it was important to be hypervigilant, constantly on guard so that we could anticipate where threats were coming from and take whatever action we could to protect ourselves.

When the biggest dangers were from our own family, we learned that those closest to us were often the ones that we could trust the least of all. There was also a very real problem that was central to many of our childhood traumas: we could not escape. We may have been hit, hurt, neglected, emotionally or sexually abused; however, we were still reliant on parents or caregivers to look after our basic needs. To use a psychological term, we had no "agency." We couldn't act independently and make choices. As kids, especially very young ones, we couldn't simply say, "I've had enough," pack our bags, ring a taxi, and book into the nearest hotel.

There was, therefore, a very difficult dilemma. For our survival, we had to trust people who could not be trusted.

We had to trust our parents who may well have put us in danger or hurt us at least some of the time. This added complexity. Perhaps we could trust them to look after our physical needs, but not our emotional needs. Maybe they were outwardly very good people who gave us a good education and appeared to love us but subjected us to sexual assault.

Understandably, this would have affected our thinking, feeling, and view of the world. We are likely to hold at least some of the following core beliefs:

- The world is a dangerous place.
- Ultimately everyone will hurt and betray us.
- We must always be strong and never vulnerable.
- We must not share our innermost thoughts and feelings.
- Our relationships will always fail.

We may also have a tendency toward all-or-nothing thinking when it comes to trust. We either trust people or we don't trust them.

Of course, as adults these ideas are unhelpful. They prevent us from taking the healthy risks that are a necessary part of life.

How we can learn to be healthy risk takers

Only those who will risk going too far can possibly find out how far one can go.

—T.S. Eliot

Within self-help literature and social media there is tremendous pressure on us all to take more risks. Risk takers are seen as glamorous and attractive. Adventure holidays and extreme sports have grown exponentially. Films portray heroes risking everything in one final act, climaxing in them winning some sort of outstanding victory. Quotes, including the one above from writer T.S. Eliot, try to persuade us to take increasingly big and "riskier" risks. There is, however, a downside to risk. Its rewards have to be balanced with potential costs to us. We could experience loss, pain, damage, and personal hurt.

In order to thrive and grow, we have to take healthy risks. We need to be challenged to develop new skills, perspectives, and relationships. However, it's crucial to differentiate between healthy and unhealthy risks.

Healthy risks propel us toward our goals and personal growth.

Unhealthy risks hurt and harm us and hinder our progress.

We are all unique. What is risky for some of us is safe for others. A trained and experienced mountaineer has a lower risk on a difficult climb than a novice does. Risks are also determined by our environment. This changes with time. The same road can be safe on a sunny summer's day, while being treacherous in the icy weeks of winter. There are, however, some rough guidelines to help us tell the difference between healthy and unhealthy risks. These are not hard and fast rules, just basics to guide our thinking.

We can:

- **Consider the potential outcomes.** Healthy risks have potential benefits that outweigh the potential drawbacks. Unhealthy risks, on the other hand, can lead to negative consequences that far exceed any potential rewards.
- **Evaluate the level of potential harm.** Healthy risks involve challenges that may be uncomfortable but ultimately won't cause significant harm. Unhealthy risks can result in physical, emotional, or psychological harm to ourselves or others.
- **Assess how much control we have.** With healthy risks, we have some

degree of control over the situation and can adapt or change course if necessary. Unhealthy risks often involve situations where we have little to no control over the outcome.
- **Assess whether they align with our personal values.** Healthy risks align with our personal values and contribute to our overall well-being. Unhealthy risks may conflict with our values, leading to feelings of guilt or regret.
- **Reflect on past experiences.** We can use past experiences as a guide to determine if a risk is healthy or unhealthy. If a similar risk in the past led to positive growth and development, it may be a healthy risk to take again.

A mini strategy for taking healthy risks

When it is appropriate, we might decide to take more risks. Below are ideas for us to consider. We may:

- **Start by reflecting on our goals and values.** Consider what we want to achieve in life and what values are important to us. We can identify areas where taking risks can help us reach our goals and align with our values.
- **Start small.** We gradually build our confidence and risk-taking abilities by starting with smaller, manageable risks before tackling bigger challenges.
- **Investigate and research.** It is wise to learn as much as we can about the risk we're considering. This helps us make informed decisions and prepare for potential obstacles.
- **Seek advice and support.** We can talk to trusted friends, family, or professionals about the risks we're considering. They could offer valuable insights and support as we navigate the decision-making process.
- **Evaluate and learn.** After taking a risk, we can then reflect on the experience. What did we learn? How can we use this knowledge to make better decisions in the future? We can use each experience as an opportunity for growth.

Understanding the difference between healthy and unhealthy risks and following this mini strategy leaves us better equipped to take risks that can positively impact our lives and help us achieve our goals. We also need self-compassion, acknowledging that we are always surrounded by risks. There is no perfect or simple solution. We owe it to ourselves to be supportive and kind, whatever the outcome of our decisions.

7

Emotions and Emotional Processing

NAVIGATING THE EMOTIONAL LANDSCAPE: UNDERSTANDING OUR FEELINGS

> *Emotion is necessary for survival. Emotions tell us when we are in danger, when to run, when to fight and what is worth fighting for. Emotions are our body's way of communicating with us and driving us to do things.*
>
> —Dr. Jonice Webb, PhD, therapist specializing in emotional neglect, and author of *Running on Empty: Overcome Your Childhood Emotional Neglect* and *Running On Empty No More: Transform Your Relationships With Your Partner, Your Parents and Your Children*

During school geography lessons, many of us learned to identify towns and cities within our own country. We were taught their relative importance, how they connect together to create provinces or states, and the special features that define them. Some are industrial. Some are economic. Some are tourist centers. Some are bustling growth hubs, while others are largely historic.

It is strange that while we were educated about physical places, we weren't informed about emotional places that are an essential part of being human.

Without formal education, we learned about emotions from our immediate environment. If our parents were immature or our families were dysfunctional, our emotional education would, through no fault of our own, have been affected.

We may have been told:

- **That some emotions are good and that some are bad.** This is not true. Our emotions are there to help us. They give us information and motivation.
- **That we should not feel certain things.** That it is wrong to feel angry and a sign of weakness to feel sad. This isn't true either. There are no "wrong" or "right" emotions.
- **To shut up or not make a fuss.** This was a way to control us. Ultimately it will have led to us repressing our feelings.

We are unlikely to have been helped to understand the whole range of emotions that we can feel as people. In addition to our immediate family environment, we received our ideas about how feelings work from the lifestyles and values of the people and places where we lived.

Our wider world: societal and cultural influences on our emotional landscape

Society shapes broad narratives about gender expectations, but each of us navigates them in our own way. The examples that follow highlight common themes and may not precisely reflect our unique journey.

If we grew up in a culture that stigmatizes certain emotions, we will have learned to hide or suppress our feelings.

Society and culture have, in many ways, influenced the emotional expression and regulation of both women and men. These are some examples of how societal norms and expectations have impacted women's emotional landscapes.

- **The "emotional woman" stereotype.** Women have historically been labeled as "too emotional" or "hysterical" when expressing strong feelings, especially in professional or public settings. This stereotype discourages many women from showing genuine emotions, like anger or frustration, for fear of being dismissed or not taken seriously. As a result, they may suppress genuine reactions or try to present them in ways that are more "palatable" to avoid being deemed irrational.
- **Expectation to be nurturing and pleasant.** Society often expects women to be the nurturers, to always be pleasant, accommodating, and agreeable. When a woman shows emotions that deviate from this role—like assertiveness or directness—she might be labeled as aggressive or "bossy." This societal pressure pushes many women to bottle up feelings to avoid

confrontations or maintain harmony, even when it's detrimental to their own well-being.
- **The double bind of motherhood.** Women often receive mixed messages about motherhood. On one hand, they are expected to be ever-devoted, always happy, and unconditionally loving mothers. On the other hand, expressing fatigue, overwhelm, or regret is taboo. Mothers who express feelings of dissatisfaction or struggle with postpartum depression often face societal judgment or the accusation of being "bad mothers."
- **Sexuality and emotional expression.** Women have traditionally been caught between being labeled as "prudish" or "overly emotional" if they withhold affection, and "easy" or "desperate" if they express affection or desire openly. This societal judgment around women's sexuality often leads to internal conflicts where women feel they cannot express their genuine feelings without facing negative labels.
- **The silent strength expectation.** In many cultures, women bear a significant burden of familial and societal responsibilities. They are expected to manage multiple roles—as caregivers, professionals, and community members—with grace and resilience. This expectation to constantly showcase silent strength can deter women from expressing vulnerabilities, anxieties, or seeking help when overwhelmed.

Men too have been deeply influenced by societal norms and cultural expectations. Here are some examples of how societal norms have impacted men's emotional landscapes.

- **The "man up" mentality.** From a young age, many boys are taught to suppress their emotions with phrases like "boys don't cry" or "man up." This instills a belief that showing vulnerability or sadness is a sign of weakness. As they grow, many men feel pressured to maintain this stoic exterior leading them to bottle up emotions, which can have long-term psychological impacts.
- **Hero and provider stereotype.** Men are often seen as the "protectors" or "providers" of society, which brings an expectation to always be strong, unyielding, and fearless. This can discourage men from expressing feelings of insecurity, doubt, or fear, as they might be perceived as failing to live up to this role.
- **Limited emotional vocabulary.** In many cultures, men are not taught the language to express their feelings. They might be comfortable expressing

anger or frustration, but find it difficult to articulate feelings of sadness, loneliness, or anxiety. This lack of vocabulary can limit their ability to process and communicate more complex emotions.
- **Perception of emotional men as "less masculine."** Men who openly display emotions or engage in behaviors traditionally seen as feminine, such as nurturing or caregiving, might face ridicule or be labeled as "less manly." This societal pressure can deter men from embracing a full range of human emotions or taking on roles they might genuinely enjoy.
- **Fear of intimacy.** Due to societal expectations, men might associate emotional intimacy with femininity, and thus shun it. They may avoid deep emotional connections or discussions, fearing it might make them appear vulnerable. This can hinder the formation of genuine, meaningful relationships and lead to isolation.

As we work to understand and navigate our emotions, it's important to remember these broad cultural factors. They're not excuses; they are pieces of the puzzle that build our emotional world. Recognizing them helps us to break free from constraints on our feelings. This leads to a more honest and genuine emotional understanding.

As we progress together, we need to show ourselves compassion and understanding. Our emotions, and the way we express them, are a complex interplay of personal, familial, societal, and cultural influences. Once we understand this, we can start to untangle our feelings, heal from our past, and reclaim our emotional well-being.

Before exploring our emotions any further, it's important to address a common belief. From a young age, we are often misled into labeling our feelings as "good" or "bad."

Typically, this looks something like this:

"Good" emotions and feelings	"Bad" emotions and feelings
Happiness	Sadness
Calm	Anger
Excitement	Fear
Serenity	Anxiety
Pleasure	Frustration
Satisfaction	Dissatisfaction

But every emotion has a purpose. Let's explore this further.

The hidden value of "negative" emotions

Certainly, there is a difference in how we perceive emotions. It feels better to be calm rather than angry. We prefer to be happy rather than sad. It is also true that some emotions can become self-destructive.

However, what if we changed our perspective and started to see all emotions as helpful, rather than morally good or bad?

What if we recognized that emotions are not barriers blocking the road ahead, but the energy that we need to keep going? Just as cars need petrol or electricity, yachts are powered by wind, and rockets are blasted into space with liquid hydrogen and oxygen, we are fueled by our emotions.

Our emotions also provide us with invaluable information, much like a ship's captain receives reports about the weather and sea conditions. It would be nonsensical for us to ignore our emotions, just as it would be for the captain to ignore news about nearby storms or icebergs.

For those of us who have encountered challenges such as abuse or familial dysfunction, emotions like fear, anger, or sadness might carry heavy associations. Perhaps we were punished for expressing anger, or were taught that sadness was a sign of weakness. Yet, every emotion has a role and purpose in our lives.

Fear

For many of us raised amidst unpredictability, fear acted as our guardian. It wasn't our fault that we felt it. Fear was a natural response to the world around us. Its whispers of caution were there to protect us from harm. Today, when interpreted with kindness, fear can be a reminder to care for ourselves and make safe choices, always serving our best interests.

Anger

During times when our boundaries were repeatedly crossed or our voices went unheard, anger became our unspoken advocate. We were right to feel it. Now, anger can empower us to assert our boundaries.

Sadness

Feeling sad was not a sign of our weakness or our failing. Far from it. Sadness grew when we yearned for love, connection, and understanding. It was our heart's way of seeking solace. Now, it reminds us to connect with our inner self and reach out for the support we rightfully deserve.

Jealousy

Perhaps it echoed our desire for consistency, attention, or the love we observed others receiving. It wasn't borne out of inadequacy, but rather out of a genuine longing. Today, it can guide us to recognize and pursue our true values and desires.

Shame

The shame we felt wasn't ours to bear. It wasn't a reflection of our worth or our actions. Instead, it was the misplaced guilt and shame of our abusers, projected onto us as a means for them to avoid their own accountability. Over time, we may have unwittingly adopted these feelings as our own. Recognizing this is the first step in letting go. Now, as we grow in understanding, we can see shame for what it is: an external burden that was never truly ours. This awareness empowers us to shed these layers and reconnect with our true selves, valuing our inherent worth and rejecting the unjust labels placed on us.

We did nothing wrong in feeling these emotions. They arose as natural reactions to the world we were navigating—a world that was often confusing and challenging. These feelings were, and are, part of our human experience. Embracing them with compassion and understanding is our path forward, a journey where we reclaim our narrative and recognize our inherent strength and worth.

Anger and Why Everything That We Were Taught About Anger Is Wrong

Anger has a nasty reputation.

It is seen as universally bad. We are told that it has the potential to destroy us.

There are anger management courses. People are described as having "anger issues." Anger is considered to be the root cause of violence, destruction, and antisocial behavior. Newspapers report violent road rage incidents. Increasingly, air rage, when angry passengers have to be restrained, is becoming a phenomenon.

But there is though no such thing as a bad emotion. Every emotion makes sense. Over millions of years, our feelings have evolved to keep us safe.

And anger is every bit as normal as joy, happiness, bliss, love: the feelings that are seen as positive. It can also be healthy and helpful. This does not mean that we should welcome anger or enjoy being angry. Instead, we can see it as both a signpost and a tool to work with. When we feel anger, it seems difficult to deal with. It *is* unpleasant—but it is meant to be. Anger evolved to be uncomfortable so that it couldn't be ignored. Anger provides important messages to listen to and learn from. Rather than trying to deny our anger, we can learn to work with it to our advantage.

We can use anger as:

- **Information.** Anger lets us know when our boundaries are being broken or our safety and well-being are being threatened.
- **Motivation.** Anger is powerful. We can harness this power to give us the strength to move forward and progress.

Acknowledging anger

As people raised in dysfunctional families, experiencing both overt and hidden anger is normal and can be healthy.

Lacking anger can mean that we are struggling to be honest with ourselves and express our emotions. We may be denying the reality of what happened to us. Perhaps we have learned to suppress our thoughts and feelings. Our anger may be buried deep within us.

Psychologist Carl Jung believed that "we cannot change anything until we accept it." Certainly, when we begin to work with anger, a crucial first step is to acknowledge it. This can be challenging for two reasons.

- As children from dysfunctional families, it is likely that we were trained not to be in touch with our feelings.
- Conversely, it may be that anger is so familiar to us that we no longer notice it.

Anger as information

Mark Epstein, psychiatrist and author, who writes about Buddhism and psychotherapy, believes that "anger is a sign that something needs to change."

This may seem simplistic. Those of us who grew up in dysfunctional families are already aware that there is a huge amount that needs to change. Nevertheless, it is both meaningful and helpful to keep reminding ourselves that emotions aren't things to be suppressed. They are there to provide useful information. Anger is a flashing red warning light. It tells us there is a problem.

Aircraft are equipped with a series of warning lights. They alert the pilot to every possible sign of trouble: an engine fire, smoke inside the plane, ice on the wings, or low levels of aviation fuel. For obvious reasons, this information should not be ignored. Similarly, it would be a mistake for us to ignore our own anger when it is sending us important messages.

Unlike airline pilots, we're not always given an immediate and clear signal that says what the issue is. Our anger can be confusing and complex.

There are obvious sources of anger: for example, when somebody cuts us off on the highway. There are also deeper and longer-lasting types of anger, like a volcano smoldering in the background ready to erupt. Deep-rooted anger can be confusing because we don't always know what causes it. The origin of our emotions can be hidden from us.

It is useful to consider some of the common reasons for our anger so that that we can deal with these successfully.

- **Family history.** Frequently, we share deep and subconscious feelings rooted in our upbringing. This is normal. Our mental survival strategies as children were hidden and locked away. They now express themselves as anger.
- **Repetition compulsion.** We are trapped in a cycle where we replay our past. Someone—a boyfriend or girlfriend, colleague or boss—is exploiting us in the same way that we were exploited as children, and we are currently unable to find a way to prevent this from happening (see section on repetition compulsion in Chapter 9).
- **Transference.** Anger sometimes disguises itself and plays tricks with us, directing itself at something that isn't actually a cause but becomes a target. This phenomenon is known as "transference" and was originally described by Sigmund Freud, the founder of psychoanalysis. For example, we might have a lingering resentment toward our boss at work when we are actually angry with our own parents.

Anger as motivation

Anger helps us establish and maintain our boundaries, propelling us to stand up for ourselves when we feel mistreated or exploited. It signals to others that their actions or behavior are unacceptable. In other words, anger fosters assertiveness—an essential skill for healthy communication and relationships. Psychologists Robert Alberti and Michael Emmons, in their book *Your Perfect Right: Assertiveness and Equality in Your Life and Relationships*, discuss how healthy anger can help people assert their needs and rights in a non-aggressive manner.

Moreover, anger is a strong motivator for social justice. It can incite us to fight against social inequalities or perceived unfairness, leading to positive societal changes.

Anger can even be a tool for personal growth and self-awareness. Psychologist and anger researcher Dr. Leon F. Seltzer posits that our anger can act as a mirror, reflecting our deepest insecurities, fears, and wounds. By examining our anger, we can uncover and address these hidden aspects of our psyche.

Shame and Guilt

Shame is the lie someone told you about yourself.
—Anaïs Nin

Of all the emotions visited on us by our past, shame is one of the most toxic and destructive. For those of us raised in difficult and dysfunctional families, it is enormously common. How much shame we feel varies from person to person. It can lie dormant in the background waiting to be triggered, or perhaps it's a weight on our shoulders, a burden that we constantly carry around. At its worst, shame can ruin our lives, causing deep pain, and feelings of hopelessness and despair.

Carolyn Spring, educator and survivor, provides a compelling account of the effect of shame in her online course *Working with Shame*. She describes how, in early childhood, shame is an adaptive response that we become "stuck" in as adults.

When we can recognize, understand, and rid ourselves of shame, a far happier and healthier life awaits us. Life outside its prison walls is lighter and more fun and fulfilling than a life locked in by shame.

Psychoanalyst Carl Jung stated, "Shame is a soul-eating emotion." Philosopher Alain de Botton from the School of Life said, "If one could be granted one wish to improve the internal well-being of humanity, then it would be, with the wave of a magic wand, to do away with shame."

How shame differs from guilt

It's vital to remember, when traversing the challenging terrain of our emotions, that we are not to blame. The heavy weights of shame and guilt belong to our abusers, not us. These burdens have been passed onto us unfairly. We've been forced to carry guilt and shame that belong to others. Psychologist Erik Erikson said, "Shame is rage turned against the self." More accurately, shame is rage mistakenly turned against the self.

While both shame and guilt may intertwine in our experiences, they are distinct. Guilt typically revolves around actions—perhaps something we did or didn't do. It emerges when we believe we may have caused harm or failed in our responsibilities. Yet, it's essential to note that we often shoulder guilt for actions and circumstances that were beyond our control or that were never ours to bear in the first place.

On the other hand, shame reaches deeper and is more personal. It's about how we perceive ourselves, colored by external voices and past traumas. But remember, this internalized feeling is not a true reflection of our worth or our reality. We are deserving of love, acceptance, and understanding, always.

Why shame develops

Shame is deep-rooted and powerful. Human ancestry ensured that we all belonged to tribes. Belonging to a tribe enabled us to share the spoils of hunting, stay safe from predators, and reduced our personal vulnerability. We all desperately needed the approval of others to remain part of the tribe. In a very real sense, being seen as okay by other people was a matter of life and death. This explains why shame evolved to become so important.

As children, those of us who were physically or sexually abused struggled to rationalize the abuse. We needed the love and protection of our parents. Our minds were unable to process the enormity of what was happening. We weren't able to understand the reality that the very people who should be helping us were hurting us. So that we could maintain a sense of control, we began to blame ourselves, even though the abuse that we suffered was entirely due to our parents. Blaming ourselves left open the false belief that we could change the situation by behaving better. This gave us a sense of control, albeit an imaginary one. There was nothing that we could have done to save ourselves. Over time, we internalized the idea that what was happening to us was our fault; a deep sense of shame grew and became part of our core self. This was the only defense we had.

When we were emotionally abused, we believed that we deserved the treatment we were given. We thought that our parents were constantly criticizing us because we were bad people. The cruel, unfair, and unkind things that they said about us became internalized and shaped our identity.

We grew up with shame when our parents abused alcohol or drugs. We recognized that our parents were different and that this difference was troubling. We were afraid that their behavior would be found out and that they risked rejection from society.

There is also the possibility that we feel shame about the way we handled our abuse as children, or how we continue to handle its effects as adults. Realistically, we had no way to prevent or stop the abuse that we suffered. To compensate or feel a sense of control, we may have become violent or aggressive to our younger siblings or acted out our distress in antisocial ways. As adults, we may have abused alcohol or illegal drugs or hurt those closest to us.

We cannot change what happened to us or what we did to other people. We can, however, change our future, and looking closely at shame and how it impacts on our lives will help us do this.

The words of Anaïs Nin quoted above accurately describe reality: shame is the lie somebody told us about ourselves. None of us deserved the mistreatment that we endured. Quite the opposite. We should have been brought up in a loving, kind, protective, and safe environment. However, the reality is that we now need to take responsibility for our own futures. There is an inner child within us all who is waiting to be rescued.

We do not need to run away from shame. We can acknowledge the damage that it has done to us. We can face it, accept it, and deal with it. As adults we can become our own rescuers and live the happy fulfilled life that we deserve to live.

How then can we permanently defeat the toxic shame that haunts us now, and could potentially destroy the rest of our lives?

How to destroy toxic shame

Shame can be a heavy emotion to carry, often making us feel immobilized or stuck. On one hand, it might make us feel as though certain behaviors are an unchangeable part of who we are. At times, it might make us feel as if our actions define our entire worth, creating a belief that change is out of reach. On the other hand, the weight of shame may urge us to keep our feelings hidden, making it challenging to open up or seek support. Remember, it's okay to seek understanding and healing; we are together in this journey.

Working with an informed and empathic psychotherapist is one of the best solutions to dealing with childhood trauma. It is, though, essential to choose a skilled counselor. Many therapists are excellent and can help us to permanently change our lives for the better. But there are some very poor practitioners. Lacking both experience and insight, they can add further problems to the challenges that we already face. Advice on selecting a psychotherapist can be found in Chapter 13—Finding Help: Counseling and Psychotherapy.

Beverly Engel's book *It Wasn't Your Fault: Freeing Yourself from the Shame of Childhood Abuse with the Power of Self-Compassion* recommends mindfulness and compassion-based therapy. Researcher Kristin Neff has written extensively about compassion. In *Self-Compassion: The Proven Power of Being Kind to Yourself*, she gives a comprehensive range of techniques to help us become more compassionate to ourselves. A more detailed section focuses on self-compassion in Chapter 8.

An important point to consider when using any self-development techniques is that they have to be continually practiced. Books and articles often use words like "healing," which seem to suggest a time-limited event, rather than an ongoing process. Developing a healthy mind is similar to developing a healthy body: it takes time, effort, and constant maintenance. It is a journey rather than a destination.

Changing our story

As well as being more compassionate toward ourselves, we can begin to change the way we see ourselves and the way we view our past.

Many of us have a very narrow view of ourselves and our past. But how we see ourselves isn't necessarily the reality of who we are. It is merely a story that we tell ourselves about ourselves.

We were victims; however, we can choose to see ourselves as survivors, and acknowledge our own courage and admire our own determination to succeed. We deserve our own respect and admiration for being who we are. We can change our own internal narrative so that we recognize the pain that we have been through while being enormously proud of being fighters and survivors. We can change our internal narrative and foster a sense of pride and resilience. There are different strategies that may help.

- **Talking to an empathic and supportive psychotherapist.**
- **Journaling.** Regularly writing down our thoughts and feelings can help

us process our past, recognize our strength, and chart our journey from victim to survivor.
- **Support groups.** Joining groups where others have gone through similar experiences can be healing. There are many online groups where we can choose to be anonymous if that feels safer for us. Sharing our stories and hearing others' validates our feelings and experiences.
- **Art therapy.** Expressing ourselves through art, be it painting, drawing, or any other medium, can be therapeutic and provide a tangible representation of our growth and resilience.
- **Reading inspirational survivor stories.** Understanding how others have navigated their journey from pain to empowerment can offer both comfort and a roadmap for our own journey.

We can also literally rewrite our own history. From the perspective of a kind, caring, and compassionate adult, we can write down on paper what happened to us, clearly placing the blame where it should lie. We can acknowledge that there was nothing we could have done to control the situation, that it wasn't our fault, and we can shift that shame to where it truly belongs.

While acknowledging and dealing with the shame, we can also begin to let it go. We can believe the truth: at our core, we are good people.

Emptiness

Many of us who had dysfunctional childhoods feel a strong or overpowering sense of emptiness at some time in our lives. Perhaps even most of the time.

It is a very familiar feeling, but one that's a bit difficult to define. This is because it is a mixture of different thoughts and emotions combined. To help us to gain a more thorough understanding of emptiness and how we can tackle it, these component parts are described below.

- **Loneliness.** Often in our childhoods we were very much alone. There was no one that we could turn to for support or comfort. Frequently, the adults who should have been solving our problems were the ones creating them. Loneliness, therefore, became a normal part of our world. For many of us, this experience has become locked inside us. It is stubborn and difficult to move. Even when we have opportunities to love, be loved, and feel a sense of belonging, it remains.

- **Despair.** Despair feels pretty terrible. It is the incredibly uncomfortable feeling that we can never be happy. We have lost hope. It is a very cruel and unfair emotion, because actually the world is full of opportunities and aspirations. However, we learned to despair as children because it was far safer and less damaging to our psyche if we didn't hope, rather than hoping and seeing our hopes dashed.
- **Unworthiness.** At the heart of unworthiness is a feeling that we just don't matter. We feel insignificant and small.
- **Lack of belonging.** We somehow cannot connect to other people or even connect with events that are going on around us. We feel like a spectator of life, rather than playing an active part in it.
- **Longing.** There is a deep melancholy at the heart of emptiness. There is a void, a big empty space where we know that something should be. Often this is accompanied by a feeling of being lost. On occasions the sense of longing almost feels like grief.

Tackling feelings of emptiness

Feelings of emptiness are a symptom of the damage that was done to us as children, rather than being an isolated problem to be dealt with on its own.

Many of the skills and techniques described throughout this book will help to alleviate feelings of emptiness. It is, though, worth reinforcing some of the basics while focusing specifically on ways to combat emptiness here.

Acceptance

Acceptance is counterintuitive. When our emotions are uncomfortable or distressing, our instinct is to deny the way we feel or to fight against it.

However, by accepting our feelings, we can learn more about what we really need. British psychoanalyst Adam Phillips states, "In Freud's story our possibilities for satisfaction depend on our capacity for frustration; if we can't let ourselves feel our frustration—and, surprisingly, this is a surprisingly difficult thing to do—we can't get a sense of what it is we might be wanting, and missing, of what might really give us pleasure."

Acceptance is both recognizing the feeling of emptiness and allowing ourselves to truly feel it. This can be very difficult; however, it is a very important step on the road to recovery. It is similar to being lost on a journey. We cannot really begin to find the right route to our destination until we both recognize and accept that we were lost. Otherwise, we can end up traveling further and further from where we want to be.

Once we have recognized and accepted our situation, we can start to act.

Action

Taking action needs planning followed by commitment. For example, we could decide to begin therapy, schedule time, and book a slot in our diary to have our first counseling session.

As well as considering therapy, there are a number of things that we can do to help ourselves. This depends on how much support we need. We all have different needs and there isn't one universal solution that works for all of us. We may wish to try several techniques to see which is most effective.

Additionally, feelings of emptiness may just be part of a whole range of challenges we face that were caused by our dysfunctional childhoods. There are a range of strategies within this book to help us to take a holistic approach. The most important thing to remember is that we can move forward. We can beat a hopeless childhood with a hopeful future.

Connect

Our upbringing might not have provided us with the best examples of how to connect deeply with others, especially if our parents faced challenges in their own relationships. Despite this, we have the innate strength and capability to write our own narrative. Later in this book, we'll explore nurturing trust, sidestepping potential pitfalls, and cultivating enriching relationships.

Contribute

One of the best ways to connect and combat loneliness and emptiness is to give something to the world in which we live. Understandably, we may find the idea of giving something back problematic. It is easy to give something back if we were gifted a fantastic start in life. For many of us though, it just doesn't make sense. We can't give anything back because we were never given anything in the first place. We can't return something we never had. This isn't about self-pity, envy, or jealousy. It is realistic. The more honest and realistic we can be, the more we can help ourselves and other people.

Yet, what if we reframed our perspective? Instead of "giving back," consider it as "giving forward." We can transform our pain and experiences into strength and resilience, paving a brighter path not just for ourselves, but for others too. It's not about repaying a debt to the past, but sowing seeds for a better future. By sharing our stories, championing for change, or simply being there for someone in need, we actively dispel our feelings of emptiness and carve out a legacy of hope. Every act, no matter how small, ripples out and creates change. Through our experiences, we're uniquely positioned to be a beacon of light for others, showing that even in adversity, there's potential for growth, healing, and transformation.

Depression

Becoming depressed is a realistic and understandable response to an upsetting childhood.

From an evolutionary perspective, depression can be seen as a sensible strategy to help us survive. During periods of extreme sadness, it was helpful for primitive men and women to withdraw from their environment. It was sensible to hide away and shut down. By both metaphorically and literally staying in a dark cave, humans were able to avoid risks. They could stay safe from predators, aggressive people from other tribes, and harsh weather. Withdrawing also created time to recover. Sufficient mental and physical strength were built up to fight threats.

When we grew up in dangerous and dysfunctional families, adopting a depressed outlook and pessimistic core beliefs may have been necessary for our own survival. In an environment where we might have been physically hit, hurt, sexually assaulted, or emotionally abused, not being noticed was beneficial to us. Feelings of hopelessness protected us. The reality was that there was little we could have done to make things better. Quite the opposite. Any action that we did take could have made us more noticeable and therefore more vulnerable. Over time, our brains learned to become depressed so that we would be able to withstand the pressures of a hostile outside world.

Growing into adults, many of us carry this ability to become depressed deep within us, and it can have a devastating effect on our lives. While it's a sobering reality that our experiences taught us to resort to depression as a survival mechanism, there's a silver lining embedded in this fact. This conditioning suggests that our emotional responses can be learned and unlearned.

As adults, we're no longer bound by the constraints of our childhood environment. With the right strategies and tools, we have the ability to rewire our coping mechanisms, effectively combat depression, and pave the way toward the fulfilling, joyful lives we deserve.

Before considering the best steps that we can take to help ourselves, it is helpful to gain a more thorough understanding of depression. And to acknowledge how challenging and difficult it can be. This understanding will provide more insight. In turn we can then show ourselves more compassion. Knowledge will also help us to fight depression more effectively.

Learned helplessness

How well we solve problems matters.

When our train is canceled, we feel frustrated. Restricted railway services can cause more resentment. Generally, though, we will try to find a solution. Taxis, buses, and, for longer journeys, airplanes might provide an alternative to reach our destination. Sometimes, however, we have had enough. We give up. When there is widespread signal failure and queues for everything, it makes sense to abandon our trip and go home.

When, as children, nothing worked, when all our efforts just made the situation worse, and when we couldn't see a way out, we gave up too.

We didn't even have the luxury of going home. Home was the place where the problems were.

When our minds decided that there was nothing that we could do to escape, we entered a state first described by psychologist Martin Seligman as "learned helplessness."

One feature of learned helplessness is that we feel powerless even when there are ways out of our situation. Our belief that we are helpless stops us from seeing an escape route.

This is relevant to us as adults. The reality of our helplessness as children can persist when we have grown out of childhood. Our learned helplessness keeps us entrapped in a state of passivity, stunting our growth, and preventing us from thriving. But remember, this feeling of powerlessness is learned, not innate. And so we can unlearn it, helping us to steer steadily toward peace and self-compassion.

Building on our understanding of learned helplessness and its profound impact on our perspective, we can also recognize other feelings stemming from our experiences. This sense of helplessness in our youth often manifests as feelings of entrapment and defeat.

Entrapment and defeat

It is possible that we felt defeated and trapped by our early upbringing. Research shows that feelings of defeat and entrapment increase the likelihood that we will become depressed. The way to deal with this is to acknowledge how difficult our childhood was, while also knowing that as adults, we have options open to us that we never had as children.

Defeating depression

Navigating depression feels like crossing a stream using stepping stones. Each stone represents not just days or moments, but the care, patience, and effort we invest in ourselves. While some stones are stable, giving us moments of clarity and strength, others wobble. And we feel vulnerable. It's during these uncertain times that we might need a helping hand or some guidance to find our balance again. Overcoming depression isn't about a sudden leap to the other side or a miraculous transformation. It's about daily care, patience, and consistent effort. Every step, even the most tentative one, shows our resilience and determination. This journey is not about how quickly we can cross, but about understanding and embracing the rhythm of our own healing, knowing that each day brings its own challenges and triumphs. And through it all, we learn to navigate the waters of our emotions with growing skill and compassion.

Many of us are surprised by the physicality of depression. It feels exhausting. It is hard to get out of bed. It is a struggle to do anything at all. Finding the motivation to look for help, or to help ourselves, can be difficult.

To begin with it is helpful to:

- **Recognize and accept.** We can feel pressured to "just think positively." There is a plethora of self-help books, online programs, and podcasts persuading us to do this. But denying or suppressing our feelings makes them stronger. Psychologist Carl Jung stated, "What you resist not only persists, but will grow in size." Recognition and acceptance do not mean that we are in any way giving in. Quite the contrary. The first step to dealing with any problem is always to acknowledge that it exists. "Name it to tame it" is a phrase by author and psychiatrist Dr. Daniel Siegel. When we give a name to our feelings and correctly call them depression, we have taken our first step toward recovery.
- **Show ourselves compassion.** This isn't the same as self-pity. Self-compassion is realistic. It acknowledges the reality that we are human,

imperfect, and at times vulnerable. Aaron Beck, founder of CBT, believed that depressed people self-blame and self-criticize until they end up hating themselves. If we give ourselves a hard time for being depressed, it will just make our lives more difficult.
- **Allow time.** It is good to have goals for our recovery. The problem is that if our targets are unrealistic, we will not meet them. Then we feel more deflated and defeated, and this adds to our depression. It is better to allow time and not give ourselves unnecessary stress.

When embarking on our individual paths through the complexities of healing from depression, it's heartening to remember that progress is often made in small, consistent steps. It might begin with setting an intention to nourish our bodies—eating well or drinking an extra glass of water each day. Prioritizing sleep by creating a calm bedtime routine or ensuring the bedroom is dark and comfortable can make a difference for some of us. Engaging in light physical activity—a short walk outside or a few minutes of stretching—can be a boost to both body and spirit. These actions, while they might seem inconsequential on their own, cumulatively act as our stepping stones. Each one grounding us, reinforcing our connection to ourselves, and helping us to slowly and steadily progress.

If we can manage to take early steps in recovery, there are longer-term strategies that we can use to ensure that we become and stay well.

The long-term aim of recovery is to discover what depression is trying to tell us. We can then build enough courage to face problems and make lasting changes. It is helpful to:

- Remind ourselves that we are not to blame for our upbringing and the damage it may have done to us. But we are responsible for our future. We owe it to ourselves to give ourselves the best life possible.
- Create goals that matter to us.
- Add meaning to our lives (there is more about this in the final chapter of this book).
- Build more positive and rewarding relationships (See Chapters 9–12).
- Change our thinking. Through journaling or working with a therapist, we can learn to change our ANTS (automatic negative thoughts) into PETS (performance-enhancing thoughts).
- Integrate principles from ACT (acceptance and commitment therapy). ACT encourages us to embrace our feelings, memories, and sensations

without judgment, even those that are the most difficult and upsetting. Good information is provided in *The ACT Workbook for Depression and Shame: Overcome Thoughts of Defectiveness and Increase Well-Being Using Acceptance and Commitment Therapy* by Matthew McKay PhD, Michael Jason Greenberg PsyD, and Patrick Fanning.

We can never make ourselves fully bulletproof. Being vulnerable, at times sad, and sometimes feeling hopeless and helpless are part of life. But we can learn to accept our emotions, learn from them, and continue the lifelong process of becoming better, stronger people.

Anxiety

A degree of anxiety from time to time is healthy. It is helpful, sharpening our focus on problems or challenges ahead. Anxiety before a sports performance gets our adrenaline flowing. We then react more quickly and strongly. When we are meeting someone new who could play a big role in our lives, a potential partner or someone with significance for our career or business, it can be useful to have a little anxiety so that we are alert to opportunities. Anxiety before exams aids concentration and helps us to think fast.

There are times when anxiety literally saves our lives. It is clearly a good thing if we are too anxious to make an unnecessary car journey on dangerous roads in the snow and ice. The information that our anxiety is giving us is that the situation just isn't safe.

Anxiety, in its proper context, serves as a survival mechanism. It's the "fight or flight" response that equips us to handle threats or danger. But what happens when that alarm system, which should only sound occasionally, is blaring non-stop? For many of us who grew up in dysfunctional or abusive households, this is the reality we face.

As adults, even though we may have physically left these harmful environments, our internal alarm systems continue to operate as if we're still there. The smallest triggers can set us off—loud noises, raised voices, certain words, sudden movements, even specific smells or tastes. These reminders, sometimes called "trauma cues," plunge us back into our pasts. They evoke the same intense anxiety we felt as children.

This anxiety is not merely an uncomfortable feeling—it's a pervasive state of being. It can feel utterly overwhelming. It disrupts our sleep, our relationships, our work, our health, and our overall quality of life.

Even when it feels like anxiety has a firm grip on us, there are strategies we can employ to manage it.

- **Recognize the anxiety.** The first step is to become aware of our anxiety and to identify its triggers, its symptoms, and the situations where it tends to spike. This will allow us to anticipate and prepare for these instances, rather than being caught off guard.
- **Ground ourselves.** When we're in the throes of anxiety, our breathing becomes shallow and rapid, which only heightens our sense of panic. By consciously focusing on taking slow, deep breaths, we can help to calm our nervous system. Grounding techniques, like focusing on our physical sensations or surroundings, can also help bring us back into the present moment.
- **Seek support.** We don't have to face our anxiety alone. Connecting with others who have similar experiences can be incredibly validating and empowering. Therapy, particularly trauma-informed therapy, can also be immensely beneficial.
- **Self-care.** It's not selfish to prioritize our well-being—it's necessary. Whenever we take small steps to support ourselves, we reinforce the reality that we are worth caring for.
- **Mindfulness and meditation.** Mindfulness and meditation can help us develop a more compassionate relationship with our anxiety. Rather than seeing it as an enemy to be vanquished, we can learn to see it as a part of ourselves that is trying to protect us, albeit in a misguided way.

Managing anxiety is a process, not a destination. There will be good days and bad days, progress and setbacks. But with patience, perseverance, and compassion for ourselves, we can learn to navigate our anxiety and head toward fuller, healthier lives.

Perfectionism

Perfectionism is closely related to anxiety and often exacerbates it. High standards can drive us to achieve, but when those standards become unrealistically high, they can cause us stress and worsen our anxiety.

In her book *The Instant Mood Fix: Emergency Remedies to Beat Anxiety,*

Panic or Stress, Psychologist Dr. Olivia Remes highlights a quote from writer and philosopher, G.K. Chesterton: "Anything worth doing is worth doing badly the first time."

This is a particularly helpful way to frame situations, especially when we have some performance anxiety.

Dr. Remes suggests that we can easily waste an enormous amount of time working out the best way of achieving something when we set unrealistic standards for ourselves. By accepting that our first attempts are likely to produce poor results, we can take a more relaxed approach, which in turn means that we are more likely to take action rather than being stuck forever worrying and procrastinating.

Historian and philosopher Voltaire stated, "Don't let the perfect be the enemy of the good." It takes time and practice to develop this way of thinking and we may have to challenge our core beliefs (see section on core beliefs in Chapter 4); however, our effort will be worth it as we become less anxious and more effective.

Complex Post-Traumatic Stress Disorder (CPTSD)

CPTSD develops in response to traumatic experiences, especially ones that are ongoing or repetitive, and where it is impossible to get away. For many of us, this is an accurate description of our childhood. Certainly, it was difficult if not impossible to escape. We needed love, protection, and nurturing; instead, we experienced distressing situations. These may have been dramatic or part of a long-term disturbing pattern. Either way, our young and still-developing minds were traumatized, living lives that other children did not have to face.

Gabor Maté, author of *The Myth of Normal: Trauma, Illness and Healing in a Toxic Culture*, makes an excellent point when he says, "Trauma is not what happens to you; it is what happens inside you as a result of what happens to you." Although trauma is frequently regarded as being the result of big nasty issues such as war and natural disasters, it is equally valid to see it as something that is provoked by a distressing childhood. All children are vulnerable. What happened inside of us as a result of what happened to us potentially caused a more complex form of PTSD; hence the description "complex post-traumatic stress disorder" was developed to describe our reality.

In recent times, CPTSD has started to receive the recognition and attention it deeply warrants. The American non-profit organization the CPTSD Foundation states: "Humans require safe people, safe places, and safe things during childhood and adolescence in order for healthy brain development to take place. Many adult survivors of complex trauma, having experienced this loss of safety, had no agency over themselves or their environment during critical times in brain development for extended periods of time. This loss of agency during their early years stunted their growth, depriving them of the opportunity to create the lives they deserved, and has ultimately left many stripped of their sense of worth and sense of self."

The World Health Organization describes CPTSD in its International Classification of Diseases (ICD-11) as: "a disorder that may develop following exposure to an event or series of events of an extremely threatening or horrific nature, most commonly prolonged or repetitive events from which escape is difficult or impossible."

The WHO suggest that CPTSD has the following impact: "Complex PTSD is characterized by severe and persistent 1) problems in affect regulation; 2) beliefs about oneself as diminished, defeated, or worthless, accompanied by feelings of shame, guilt or failure related to the traumatic event; and 3) difficulties in sustaining relationships and in feeling close to others. These symptoms cause significant impairment in personal, family, social, educational, occupational or other important areas of functioning."

In other words, complex PTSD can:

- Cause us trouble managing our emotions.
- Leave us with feelings of worthlessness, shame, guilt, or a sense of failure tied to the trauma we experienced.
- Give us trouble maintaining relationships or feeling close to others.

These symptoms can have a strong impact on our personal and family life, interactions with other people, education, work, or other key parts of daily living.

How our triggers developed

Forewarned is forearmed. When we are able to predict things, we are better able to manage and control them. This works with our triggers. The more we understand what caused our triggers, and when and how we are likely to be triggered, the better we can deal with our CPTSD.

Any threatening situation that we faced would have put our bodies on full alert. Our physiology would have prepared us to either fight the threat, flee by running as fast as we possibly could away from it, or freeze to minimize the amount that we would get hurt. Our hearts would beat incredibly fast and some of our normal cognitive functions such as short-term memory would shut down, so we were fully focused on survival.

As children we were defenseless and relied on our parents to protect us—the very same people who were hurting us. And our brains were still growing. We didn't have the resources or support to understand what was happening to us. We didn't have anyone to turn to, like a counselor or therapist, who could help us make sense of our experiences. We also couldn't stop the distressing events happening around us. As a result, the stress and trauma we experienced became locked deep inside us because we weren't able to process and let go of it.

So that we could better deal with the same traumatic situation in the future, our brains stored memories associated with the events so that we could recognize the threats more easily when they came along. This is similar in some ways to the landmarks we might remember on our journey home. We know we are getting closer to where we live when we notice familiar objects, trees, street signs, buildings, road junctions, or any distinctive feature close by. None of these features is our home, but our mind connects them to it. In the same way, our triggers are memories of the trauma that we endured and remind us of it. For example, we might associate the smell of cigarettes with a parent who abused us, and each time we recognize that same smell we are triggered into remembering what happened to us.

Recognizing the role of triggers in our lives is the first step toward controlling them. Triggers can quickly take us back to past traumas, often causing distressing feelings or terrifying flashbacks. But, with the right techniques, we can change how we react to these triggers, turning them from painful reminders of our past into symbols of our strength and survival.

There are a range of strategies aimed at lessening the power of triggers. These include body-centered therapies such as yoga or tai chi, mindfulness practices, working on building healthy relationships, and embracing creativity. Using these techniques can empower us to cope with and gradually diminish the power of our triggers, leading us away from reliving trauma and toward more control, healing, and personal growth.

Flashbacks

Many of us will be familiar with the classic movie scenes depicting flashbacks. What usually happens is that a soldier is going about his or her everyday life and there is a sudden noise, perhaps a car backfiring or fireworks being set off, and suddenly they are transported back to the horrors of warfare. Their mind's eye pictures a terrible battle with guns and explosions, and they are frozen in a state of horror and fear.

Some of this is an accurate portrayal. It is, however, limited. We can experience flashbacks without any mental images or sounds. We might just feel a sense of panic, claustrophobia, being unable to escape, or total powerlessness. We don't always know what triggered these emotions although we can, as discussed, begin to recognize our triggers.

These triggers might not necessarily be dramatic. When our CPTSD was caused by our experience as children it can be triggered by many different and apparently ordinary things. This includes seeing other people or even animals in helpless situations. We may also be triggered by objects, buildings, schools, children's toys, particular makes of cars that we used to travel in, or anything in our memory connected to our childhood.

Flashbacks can be extremely unpleasant because while they are happening, our bodies react to our historic childhood trauma as though it were taking place now. We can feel overwhelmed and out of control.

We sometimes revert to an earlier way of being. The person experiencing a flashback is the child within us, rather than our adult self. This is one of the reasons why flashbacks are difficult: our inner child does not have the strength, understanding, and ability to express itself that our adult self does.

Effective strategies to manage flashbacks

There are some steps that we can take to manage flashbacks when they happen:

- **Recognize and remind.** The first step is to recognize that we are in fact having a flashback. We can aim to accept that what is happening feels unpleasant and difficult, while understanding that these emotions are part of our past and not our present. We can remind ourselves that we are safe now.
- **Talk to our inner child.** The chances are that in the past there was no

one to reassure us and help us. The helplessness remains trapped inside us. As adults we can soothe and comfort this inner child. The practical way to do this is to repeat helpful thoughts to ourselves. We can silently say, "it is OK, I hear you, I am here for you, you are safe," and similar statements. When we are not sure of exactly what to say, it is helpful to think what we would say to an actual frightened child in front of us in need of reassurance.

- **Build boundaries.** As children it felt as though what was happening to us could last for ever. As adults experiencing a flashback, we can tell ourselves that a flashback is limited and will soon be over.
- **Stop listening.** Especially when we are used to catastrophizing, our mind may want to take us to all sorts of terrible places. We do not have to follow our thoughts.
- **Kill the critic.** We can tell our inner critic that it's wrong. We can become angry with it. We do not need or deserve to feel shame or guilt.
- **Feel the fear.** It can be helpful to acknowledge and feel the fear without running away from it. We can learn to let it wash over us. The more we try to run away from it, the more power we give it.

Flashbacks remind us of our past, but they also highlight the strength we had to get through it. Next, we'll look at how to build on that strength by adapting our thinking.

8

Thinking: From Surviving to Thriving

For those of us who experienced an abusive childhood, unhelpful thinking patterns can be deeply ingrained, often amplifying anxiety and self-doubt. Learning to identify and challenge these patterns helps us to foster resilience and promotes positive and empowering thought processes.

As children living in sometimes very difficult circumstances, we did everything we could to survive. It is right that we acknowledge and respect our childhood resilience and strength.

The problem is that some of the strategies that we used to stay safe have remained active within us when they are no longer really needed. Our childhood adaptations and the changes within our brain structure that once helped us now hinder our progress. One example of this is hypervigilance.

HYPERVIGILANCE

> *After a traumatic experience, the human system of self-preservation seems to go onto permanent alert, as if the danger might return at any moment.*
>
> —Judith Lewis Herman: *Trauma and Recovery: The Aftermath of Violence—From Domestic Abuse to Political Terror*

Hypervigilance describes a state of constant alertness. Somewhere deep within our psyche, our mind is trying to protect us. It is as though a voice within us that is scared of our past keeps saying "I must not let this happen again." It continuously scans our surroundings for threats and problems. Whatever abuse or distress we experienced, our message to ourselves is the same: "I must not let this happen again, I must not let this happen again, I must not let this happen again."

It made sense when we were children to be constantly aware of what might be about to occur. In dangerous and difficult situations, being hypervigilant keeps us alive.

Military people are trained to spot threats and take immediate action to stay safe. By constantly scanning the environment, they learn to see snipers, approaching enemy planes, and other dangers. An ordinary level of vigilance would just not be good enough.

The problem is that it is a learned skill that is difficult to turn off. Some soldiers, especially those with PTSD, continue to be hypervigilant after leaving the war zones in which they have worked. They carry on being super-alert during ordinary civilian life. The mental energy and focus needed for this causes constant stress. This results in their feeling exhausted, and potentially depressed and anxious. It keeps them from being fully present and authentic in their lives. It takes away the fun and enjoyment.

When we were abused as children, we too used hypervigilance as a self-protection strategy. Our priority was to stay safe. We tried to anticipate when we would be hit or hurt. In the same way that soldiers' sensible survival strategies shielded them from harm, we stayed secure by constantly looking out for threats.

But hypervigilance is difficult to stop. Many of us find that years after leaving our abusive families, we are still constantly searching for trouble ahead. Early on we try to spot the signs that new relationships will not work. We worry about being exploited at work. It can be hard to build trusting friendships when we are suspicious of people and suspicious of life itself.

Why hypervigilance wrecks holidays and ruins relaxation

Holidays in particular are extremely difficult. Time away from the busyness of work gives us space to think. Instead of helping us to find peace, this increases our anxiety.

Without our normal day-to-day distractions, our minds stress and catastrophize. This explains the challenge many of us have in getting a good night's sleep. The stillness and silence bring distress and fear rather than comfort and calm.

One of the difficulties with hypervigilance is that we can't just stop being vigilant altogether. There are real dangers in life. Ordinary day-to-day activities—crossing roads, driving to work, cooking—all involve real risks. There are also times when it makes perfect sense to be hypervigilant. On busy underground trains and in tourist destinations, it's important to be very aware of our surroundings and keep tight hold of our money as there is a very good chance that pickpockets will be around.

We need to find a way to replace hypervigilance with realistic vigilance.

Staying safe: changing hypervigilance to carefulness and caution

There are five key elements to tackling hypervigilance.

- **Living safely.** Above all, we need to both be safe and feel safe. This means that we might have to change our environment. If we are living with an abusive partner, don't have job security, or have any genuine threats to our well-being, then changing these circumstances is a priority. There is little point in using mindfulness, relaxation, or mind–body medicine to make ourselves feel better when the risks that we face are real.
- **Recognition.** If we are safe now then it helps to recognize that hypervigilance was an important strategy to keep us safe as children, but that it is no longer helpful to us as adults. It was valuable to us at that time, and our brains are reluctant to turn it off. It isn't wrong or bad, it is simply redundant. The urge to remain hypervigilant comes from a deep desire to look after ourselves.
- **Relearning.** By working with a psychotherapist or counselor we can begin to face and process what happened to us.
- **Retraining.** We can teach our bodies to be in a state of relaxation the majority of the time. Skills for this include practicing mindfulness and learning breathing techniques.
- **Situational awareness.** To stay safe in a risky world it is necessary to develop what is known as situational awareness. This means knowing what is going on around us. We can then identify and manage real risks.

Throughout this process, we can remember to show ourselves compassion.

We are hypervigilant not through some genetic weakness or innate problem with our nervous system, but because we learned this skill as children. It was one of the very few ways in which we could try to keep safe. It wasn't a conscious choice. Our brains reacted to circumstances that were inflicted on us by other people: it wasn't our fault.

Rumination

Sometimes even the world's best satellite navigation systems (GPS) become stuck. Perhaps they have not been updated quickly enough to account for roadworks or changes in the road layout or configuration. Or maybe they are simply using out-of-date data. Instead of taking us on a straightforward route to our destination, we end up going around in a circle, so we finish our journey at the exact same spot that we started it. Obviously, at some stage we would realize there was a fault in the system and break free; however, potentially we could continue circling forever.

Our minds can also behave in this way. Our thoughts become stuck. One particular topic keeps repeating itself again, again, and again.

In the same way the faulty satellite navigation system takes us absolutely nowhere, our thinking wastes time and energy and doesn't solve our problems. It is a genuine attempt to solve them, but it doesn't help. When ruminating, we believe that if we keep thinking about something that is upsetting, we will gain insight. We think that we will understand why it happened and everything will make sense. Revisiting the past is a strategy that can work if we have a therapist who can work with us to help us to see things more clearly and to challenge our thinking. However, when we are doing it on our own repeatedly and persistently, we become trapped in an endless unhelpful loop.

The subjects of our rumination tend to be similar. We are likely to ask ourselves versions of the following questions:

- **Why me?** We may wonder why we were born into such a difficult and distressing family.
- **How could I have stopped this?** The things that happened to us were never our fault; however, we often torture ourselves by thinking that if we had done things differently, we could have been treated differently.

- **Why didn't I just…? If only…** It is common to fantasize about all of the alternative possibilities that could and should have happened if life had turned out differently.

Drop the story and focus on feelings

One of the most effective ways of successfully dealing with rumination is known as "dropping the story."

There are theories that we ruminate to avoid feeling difficult emotions. This means that although we think that we are looking for a solution, we are actually just distracting ourselves. We constantly replay details of what happened to us, rather than facing the pain of our past.

It is difficult. However, if we focus on our emotions and allow ourselves to feel anger, grief, sadness, or the underlying emotions connected to what happened to us, then our ruminations will reduce. A therapist can help us to do this.

Further techniques for defeating rumination

Understanding our triggers

We are less likely to ruminate if we recognize what is triggering us and take action to stop the rumination early on.

Inside out

Our minds do not have unlimited capacity. We simply can't focus on different things all at once. We tend to ruminate more when we haven't anything else to do. When we are bored or alone, we are much more likely to ruminate. This means that if we go out, meet with friends, or take part in absorbing activities, sports or hobbies, our thinking doesn't become trapped in the endless circles and loops of rumination. We are focusing on external reality, rather than the distressing ruminations in our own heads.

If it isn't practical or possible to be out and about spending time with other people, we can give our attention to books, films, or music.

This distraction technique can be effective but is better used alongside learning the skill of focusing on feelings and dropping the story. If we simply use distraction on its own, the underlying feelings that are causing us to ruminate will not go away.

Dissociation

Dissociation gets you through a brutal experience, letting your basic survival skills operate unimpeded.

—Renee Fredrickson: *Repressed Memories: A Journey to Recovery from Sexual Abuse*

Dissociation is the mind's way of zoning out when situations became too difficult to tolerate. When we were hit, emotionally hurt, or mistreated sexually, we detached ourselves mentally so that we did not have to face the reality of what was happening.

Metaphorically speaking, our mind said to itself, "It's not safe, let's shut down." Like a submarine diving deep into the ocean to hide in the dark silence from the raging battle above and escape from the greatest danger, we similarly subconsciously dissociated to lose touch with our pain.

Dissociation was a strategy that originally helped us to survive a dysfunctional family. It stays with us as adults because it was a helpful tool during our most stressful times.

The amount to which we dissociate varies from individual to individual and within ourselves, depending on what is going on in our lives. It can be mild and harmless. We have all lost ourselves in daydreams on boring bus journeys or "switched off" completely at school or at work.

It may also be so severe that it affects our day-to-day life. Dissociation sometimes evolves into a feeling of emotional numbness. We are fully aware of what we ought to be feeling. On a thinking level, we understand that the wedding, birthday party, or other kind of celebration we're attending is a joyous event. However, we just cannot experience the joy. Similarly, we don't feel sad when sorrowful events occur; we just feel numb.

"Dissociative identity disorder (DID)" describes the situation when dissociation occurs to such an extent that sometimes we go into alternative personality states, known as "alters." These personalities can behave differently to our usual selves and may even have their own body language, tone of voice, emotions, and memories.

It can be helpful to reassure ourselves that dissociation is a common and normal response to childhood trauma. Even adults who haven't had a dysfunctional childhood dissociate to some degree from time to time: about one-third of people describe a mild dissociative state that feels like they are watching themselves in a movie.

If we do find that our dissociation is problematic, here are some of the ways in which it can be treated:

- **EMDR.** The abbreviation stands for "eye movement desensitization and reprocessing." It can be used to help us work through the most difficult memories of our childhood trauma.
- **Dialectical behavior therapy.** This treatment can be helpful especially for those of us who have been diagnosed with borderline personality disorder.
- **Grounding techniques**. Learning grounding techniques may also prove helpful. These are tools that we can use to stay present and connected with our environment during times of stress or dissociation. They are exercises designed to divert our attention away from distressing thoughts or feelings and onto the physical world around us.

Grounding techniques often involve using our five senses—touch, taste, sight, smell, and hearing—to anchor ourselves in the present moment. For instance, it could be as simple as focusing on the feeling of a cool breeze on our skin, tasting a piece of minty gum, or paying attention to the details of a nearby object. These techniques are not a cure, but they can provide temporary relief and help us manage overwhelming moments.

Denial

Denial is enormously common among dysfunctional families. As adults who grew up with toxic parents, we may have used denial as a strategy to minimize the impact of what was happening to us. Abusers also use denial as a way to hide from responsibility.

We usually recognize it when we see it. We all know somebody who refuses to believe that their partner no longer loves them. Perhaps we have friends who are in denial about just how much alcohol they consume or deny that their health problems are exacerbated by their lifestyle.

There are at least four ways in which denial was used in unhealthy families. We may recognize some of these from our own past.

- **The abuse was simply never talked about.** There was a very direct denial about what was happening.

- **The abuse was admitted; however, its effects were minimized.** For example, our neglectful parents might have left us or our siblings alone and vulnerable for long periods, then claimed that such behavior was normal and didn't do any harm.
- **Abuse might have been relabeled as something else.** Parents who physically abused or beat us described what they were doing as strict discipline. Those who constantly criticized us and emotionally abused us might have tried to pretend they were setting high standards and wanted the best for us.
- **If the abuse was discovered, our parents might have claimed it was a one-off incident that would never happen again.** For example, a parent caught screaming obscenities would explain they had been extremely stressed at work and that the abuse had never happened before. But for many of us, it was part of an ongoing pattern of behavior.

Denying our past

As a defense mechanism, denial can be protective and helpful in the early stages of trauma. It buys us time. By denying the existence of something difficult and damaging, we can delay acting until we have the resources to cope.

But once we are out of harm's way and strong enough to begin the process of healing, continued denial can prevent us from accessing the help we need.

Moving forward from denial is a deeply personal journey, but when we feel ready, there are some compassionate steps that we might consider taking:

- **Acknowledgment.** Initially it is helpful to recognize that denial may have played a part in our coping strategy. It served a purpose. At a distressing and vulnerable stage in our life, it protected us.
- **Seek safe spaces.** Non-judgmental spaces or support groups can be places to openly express our feelings and memories. It is beneficial to share and encourage each other.
- **Embrace self-compassion.** We deserve kindness, especially from ourselves. By practicing self-compassion, we can go at our own pace without feeling pressured.
- **Consider professional guidance.** Therapists or counselors, especially those who specialize in trauma, can provide invaluable insights. Their independent point of view can help us to discover paths through our denial that we might not see on our own.

- **Embrace patience.** Overcoming denial is not an overnight process. Some days might be more challenging than others. Healing has its own timeline, and it's okay for us to take all the time we need.

Each of us has our unique path. What works differs between all of us, but the key lies in persistently seeking what's best for our well-being.

Toxic Positivity

We deserve to be happy. Life is richer when we have a positive outlook. That said, there are dangers with too much positivity.

To be emotionally mature and happy, we need to be able to fully feel our emotions, accepting them, understanding them, and processing them. How this works in real life is best illustrated with an example.

Nazia's (an imaginary person, with a very real problem) first serious relationship with someone that she was hopelessly in love with has just ended. There are two ways that she could deal with the situation.

As a strong, warm, intelligent, kind, and successful young woman, Nazia will have plenty of opportunities for great relationships in the future. Nazia can "think positive." She doesn't have to feel the pain of the relationship breakdown. Her energy could be focused on either enjoying her life as a single person or seeking a new partner. Nazia's friends have told her that "everything happens for a reason" and "there are plenty more fish in the sea."

Alternatively, Nazia can feel the sorrow, sense of loss, and sadness at this situation. She may also experience anger and frustration that things did not work out as planned, and maybe even jealousy when in the future she discovers that her former partner is now in love with someone else.

The first approach has advantages in the short term. Nazia can avoid many difficult and uncomfortable emotions. But the emotions that she is avoiding are authentic, normal, and healthy for human beings. Renowned psychologist Carl Jung said that "neurosis is always a substitute for legitimate suffering." If Nazia thinks positively, her feelings won't just disappear: they will be repressed.

Repression

Repression is like storing emotions in a deep vault. At first, it seems like a helpful way to declutter our minds and move forward. Yet these repressed emotions can accumulate and weigh heavily on us. The emotions we push down don't vanish; they lurk beneath the surface. Potentially they lead to unintended outbursts or, over time, manifest as physical illness. By repressing, we risk delaying the inevitable confrontation with our feelings. It's an act of immense courage and self-kindness to face these stored emotions, and it's vital for our well-being. Carl Jung wisely observed that "what we resist persists." In Nazia's case, while it's comforting to think positively, it's equally essential for her to give space to her emotions, acknowledging and understanding them. This self-aware approach ensures that emotions don't become hidden burdens but are pathways to deeper self-understanding and genuine healing.

There are a number of other risks with thinking positively all the time.

- **Ignoring danger.** When we are in abusive situations, it is important to assess them as accurately and objectively as we can. Thinking positively can lead us to the false hope that things will improve.

    The reality is that if our parents have hurt and harmed us for most of our lives, they are likely to carry on doing so. If, for example, we are constantly criticized, belittled, and hurt, it may be better to accept the fact that they will not love and respect us in the way parents ought to and move on. Forgiveness and thinking positively can get in the way of taking action to escape and make our lives happier. There is more about going no-contact in Chapter 17.

- **Not recognizing that we need help or not seeking support.** If we are able to look at our circumstances realistically, we are in a good position to know when we need help.

    Constant optimism and trying to believe the situation is better than it is can lead to real trouble. Sadly, in some circumstances of domestic abuse, people have died after convincing themselves that things will get better, rather than acknowledging how bad they were.

- **We teach ourselves to ignore our own feelings.** Our emotions are there to help us. They give us very valuable information, and we ignore them at our peril.

How to Think Better by Avoiding Trips and Traps

There are several common thinking errors, sometimes known as "cognitive distortions," that everyone tends to make. Even when we are aware of them, it is still easy to fall into thinking traps because they are so customary and familiar.

Cognitive distortions are a familiar feature of life that everybody shares. Perhaps though, we are more likely to have learned them from our parents because it was in their interests for us not to be aware, balanced, and healthy thinkers. Mothers and fathers who abused us protected themselves by stopping us from being able to think straight.

Below is a list of cognitive distortions, with a brief description of how they are likely to have played out in dysfunctional families. There is also a little bit about what we can do if we recognize that we readily fall into the trips and traps of cognitive distortions.

- **Black and white thinking.** Also known as polarized thinking, black and white thinking happens when we are unable to see different shades of gray in situations. We are either a success or a failure, good or bad, right or wrong.

    Toxic parents encourage this sort of thinking. It is helpful to them if their children believe mom and dad are right and they themselves are wrong. It made it easier for them to manipulate us.
- **Mislabeling or global labeling.** Global labeling describes the way in which one or two of our personality traits or behaviors are used to make an all-encompassing, overall judgment about us. We may have been described as thick or stupid because we struggled to understand mathematics. Perhaps we were weak or a loser because we couldn't meet our father's demands to be the best in the class at sport. Some of us live with lifelong insecurities after we were labeled as being ugly or unattractive by cruel parents. Many of us live with toxic shame that grew out of our childhood conditioning.
- **Catastrophizing.** We start catastrophizing when our imagination takes a small problem and turns it into a disaster. In our heads, a minor criticism of our performance at work gradually gets completely out of proportion until it becomes a nightmare about us being sacked. We can go on to see ourselves losing our home and our family because we no longer have the money for our rent or mortgage, and we can't support our loved ones anymore. Or maybe we take ordinary everyday feelings of discomfort or being unwell and let them lead to thoughts of a terrible and incurable disease.

    Although catastrophizing is common among the general population, those of us who had traumatic childhoods may be more vulnerable to it. There is a simple reason for this: the disaster that we really fear has already happened. We have seen and suffered and know how badly things can go wrong.

Compassion and Self-Compassion

Developing compassion toward ourselves and other people is a powerful way to help us grow. This isn't necessarily an easy thing to do. We may find it difficult for three specific reasons.

Firstly, there is a realistic chance that we were shown very little compassion ourselves. Immature parents put their own needs first. We were low down on the priority list and unlikely to have received the love and support that we needed. When we weren't shown compassion, we won't have the experience of having received it. This means that we won't have first-hand knowledge of what it feels like to be regularly comforted and looked after. Compassion then wasn't really part of our world. We didn't become accustomed to it. We didn't expect it for ourselves or from other people.

Secondly, we will have learned from our parents the cruel and unfair lesson that we were not worth showing compassion to. We won't have a model of how to be compassionate, so we don't necessarily have the skills for self-compassion.

Thirdly, some cultures mislabeled compassion as a negative trait. Things that we may wrongly have been taught include:

Self-compassion equals weakness

This is a world view frequently imposed on those of us who were brought up in families where we were physically or emotionally abused. It is also a common feature of many other types of toxic parenting. One reason for this is that all types of child abuse are basically about control. We were easier to control if we lacked self-esteem and self-belief. If we were never shown any compassion, we were more likely to see ourselves as worthless and less likely to defend ourselves.

As adults, we sometimes fall into the trap of judging ourselves harshly and not showing compassion to ourselves. We do not need to repeat the abuse that our parents inflicted on us, and we can be a supportive friend. Perhaps the best way to achieve this is to practice treating ourselves in the same way we would behave toward a valued friend who needs our support.

Self-compassion leads to a lack of motivation

Rebuilding our lives after a difficult and dysfunctional childhood takes motivation. We may believe that if we show ourselves compassion, this somehow means that we will accept our fate and not try to build better lives.

Self-compassion leads to self-indulgence or a lack of self-discipline

Many of us will have been harshly criticized as children and we will have learned that to be tough on ourselves is the only strategy for success. Actually, the opposite is true: the more we criticize and tell ourselves off, the less likely we are to believe in ourselves and our own abilities. When we constantly punish ourselves, we undermine our recovery.

What self-compassion really means

While compassion and self-compassion can be challenging to cultivate, especially for those of us who experienced neglect or emotional harm in our early years, it's important to remember they are not signs of weakness or barriers to motivation.

Self-compassion involves understanding and acknowledging our own pain with a desire to alleviate it, much like we would do for a good friend. It doesn't mean avoiding responsibility; rather, it's about treating ourselves kindly and recognizing our worth.

Self-compassion also increases our resilience. Resilience, or the ability to bounce back from adversity, is not built through self-criticism or harsh judgment. It's fostered through understanding, patience, and a supportive inner dialogue. When we learn to treat ourselves compassionately, we are more likely to pick ourselves up after setbacks, and face challenges with courage and determination.

Self-compassion can be a key component in healing from past traumas, building resilience, and cultivating a positive self-image. It may take time and practice, especially for those of us who weren't shown compassion in our early years, but the benefits are profound. We can unlearn the negative lessons from our past and replace them with self-compassion and kindness, creating a healthier relationship with ourselves and other people.

9

Foundations of Relationships

Secure Bonding and Attachment Styles

> *Love is not the icing on the cake of life. It is a basic primary need, like oxygen or water. Once we understand and accept this, we can more easily get to the heart of relationship problems.*
>
> —Sue Johnson, clinical psychologist and expert on bonding and attachment

Our very first experiences, the amount of love and nurturing that we did or didn't receive as babies and toddlers, continue to affect how we think and feel today.

Each of us carries an internal map of memories and emotions from our childhood. These early encounters shape what's known as our "attachment style": a deeply ingrained set of beliefs and feelings about ourselves and how we relate to others. Think of it as a guiding compass, influencing how we navigate our relationships with partners, lovers, friends, or colleagues.

Our attachment style might have us believing that we need to be constantly on guard, fearing abandonment or rejection, or perhaps it has taught us to prioritize others' needs over our own. Our style might have fostered a sense of independence, maybe to the extent that it's challenging to let others in. These patterns are neither good nor bad; they are simply protective measures we've developed, based on our early life.

But while our past has shaped us, it doesn't define us. As adults, with understanding, patience, and support, we can revisit and reshape our attachment style.

Developmental psychologist and psychiatrist John Bowlby introduced the idea that our feelings of intimacy and security as adults are dependent on the earliest bonds that we formed with our parents, guardians, or primary caregivers. Bowlby described four attachment styles, which were expanded on by Mary Ainsworth in the 1970s. These attachment styles are childhood patterns of interaction that predict adult behavior.

Secure attachment style

The earliest days of our lives were not complicated. As babies, our needs were simple. Attention. Warmth. Love. Sustenance. If these were easily met, we felt secure. The gentle touch of a caregiver's hand mattered. Their soothing voice calmed us when we were upset. We never doubted when our next meal would come. These consistent care signals shaped us. If this was the usual way that we were raised, it's likely we developed a secure attachment style.

With a secure attachment style, we generally have a balanced approach to relationships. Independence and intimacy are feelings that we are comfortable with. We tend to hold positive views of ourselves and others. This leads to healthy, satisfying relationships characterized by trust and open communication. We handle conflict effectively and articulate our needs and feelings with clarity. Our secure attachment style creates emotional resilience that helps us to build enriching interpersonal relationships throughout our adulthood.

Anxious–preoccupied attachment style

When we were babies, consistency was key. But if we sometimes had to scream just to be fed, yet at other times were instantly comforted, this unpredictability likely created an anxious–preoccupied attachment style.

These early uncertainties continue to impact us in our adult life. We crave constant reassurance in our relationships, subconsciously seeking the consistent affection that was missing from our early life. We can be overly sensitive to changes in our relationships and tend to interpret these changes as signs of dwindling affection or possible rejection. This can make us seem "needy" or "clingy" to others.

Dismissive-avoidant attachment style

If as youngsters we hardly ever had our needs met, then the likelihood is that at some stage we simply gave up. Our internal "program" learned that no matter what we did, we would not receive the love that we deserved, so it just was not worth trying.

If this was our early experience, we are likely to have developed a dismissive-avoidant attachment style. This makes it challenging to form close, intimate relationships. We prefer self-reliance and independence. Subconsciously, we may avoid potentially rewarding relationships because, deep down, it feels unfamiliar and uncomfortable. Our mind, influenced by early experiences, may wrongly convince us that we don't deserve to be treated well. We build a wall around ourselves, striving to maintain our independence to avoid the pain of unmet needs that we experienced in our early life.

Fearful-avoidant (also called disorganized) attachment style

Many of us will be familiar with the scenario that, while we were growing up, our parents or caregivers thought that we should look after them, rather than them looking after us. They may also have harmed us, physically, emotionally, or sexually. If this happened, we may have developed a fearful-avoidant attachment style.

We desire close relationships, yet find it difficult to trust others or feel comfortable with emotional closeness. Having been harmed or required to shoulder inappropriate responsibilities in our early life, our subconscious model tells us that people, especially those close to us, are fundamentally unsafe or harmful. This inner conflict can make us seem unpredictable in our relationships, seeking intimacy in one moment and fearing it the next.

Moving forward

Attachment theory can be helpful. Once we recognize our own attachment styles, we can begin to change them. Our mental map does not need to remain the same forever—if we choose to do so, we can change it. We can redraw it to make a more accurate representation of the world. One in which we can leave our past conditioning behind and enjoy fulfilling relationships.

Over time, we can gradually learn to create a secure attachment style for ourselves. We can start to do this by recognizing our own attachment style, by:

- **Reflecting on our past relationships.** By thinking about previous relationships with both friends and lovers, we can begin to discover underlying patterns. Did we tend to cling to others and worry they might leave (anxious–preoccupied)? Perhaps we kept an emotional distance and valued independence more than connection (dismissive–avoidant)? Were we comfortable with closeness and trust (secure)? Or maybe we swayed between wanting closeness and fearing it (fearful–avoidant)?
- **Observing our behavior in current relationships.** We can notice how we respond to conflict, how we communicate, and how we cope with separation in our current relationships. This gives us insight into our attachment style.
- **Journaling our observations and reflections.** Writing about our feelings and behaviors in our relationships with other people can aid our self-reflection and help us identify our attachment style.
- **Reading more about attachment styles.** Popular and helpful books include *Attached: The New Science of Adult Attachment and How It Can Help You Find—and Keep—Love* by Amir Levine and Rachel Heller, and *Insecure in Love: How Anxious Attachment Can Make You Feel Jealous, Needy, and Worried and What You Can Do About It* by Leslie Becker-Phelps.
- **Exploring our inner child.** Once we understand how our attachment style originated, our relationships will make more sense. We can change our ways of relating to people. Inner child work, tools, and strategies for moving forward are covered in the now classic book *Homecoming: Reclaiming and Championing Your Inner Child* by John Bradshaw.

By far the most important aspect of developing a secure attachment style is finding people who are worth being securely attached to. This might be difficult to do at first. We may be more familiar and comfortable in difficult relationships. However, we will become less insecure if we find somebody who is happy within the relationship or friendship and learn by mirroring them.

There is no point in us becoming the most level-headed, confident, and self-assured people that we can possibly be, only to attach ourselves to those who will just hurt us.

REPETITION COMPULSION

History repeats itself, but in such cunning disguise that we never detect the resemblance until the damage is done.
—Sydney J. Harris, journalist

One of the strangest psychological phenomena we may encounter in our journey of healing from childhood abuse or a distressing upbringing is what is known as "repetition compulsion." Our mind plays this trick on us, often without us being aware of it. It can perpetuate past traumas in our lives unless we actively address them.

Repetition compulsion stems from a deep-seated desire to better understand or control our past experiences. This wish makes us unknowingly recreate situations that mirror our past traumas. For instance, if our parents were cold, uncaring, and hostile, we often find ourselves drawn to romantic partners who behave in exactly the same way toward us. Even if we eventually recognize the unhappiness and decide to leave the relationship, we may unknowingly find ourselves entering a new relationship with someone who has the same traits. This pattern is sometimes called "heal or repeat."

The reason we fall into this cycle is because of a deep, subconscious need to change the story of our past. By repeating familiar situations, we hope to take back control and change the outcome of our past traumas—to repeat them to make things right. Sadly, this often just leads to a cycle of pain and distress.

To break free from this cycle and truly start to heal, we need to be aware of it and take action. Here are some action points to consider:

- **Recognize the pattern.** We can take the time to look back on our past relationships and identify any common themes or similarities in the behavior of our partners. Spotting patterns of emotional neglect, abuse, or other harmful dynamics that reflect our upbringing offers a deeper insight into our emotions and responses.
- **Seek therapy or counseling.** Participating in therapy can be vital in unraveling the complex layers of repetition compulsion. A skilled professional can guide us to understand our hidden motivations, to tackle unresolved trauma, and develop healthier ways of coping.
- **Challenge our beliefs.** Often, repetition compulsion is driven by

deep-rooted beliefs and messages from our past that we've internalized. We can question these beliefs and consider if they're good for our well-being. We can replace negative self-perception with positive and empowering thoughts.
- **Embrace self-compassion.** Understanding that repetition compulsion isn't a sign of weakness but a natural reaction to unresolved trauma can help. We can nurture self-compassion by being kind, patient, and understanding with ourselves.
- **Prioritize healthy boundaries.** Familiarizing ourselves with setting and maintaining healthy boundaries can be a key step in breaking the cycle of repetition. It's beneficial to define our limits and communicate them with assertiveness, always keeping our emotional well-being in mind.
- **Venture into new relationship dynamics.** As our awareness deepens and our focus on healing strengthens, we might find ourselves drawn to relationships that foster growth, support, and mutual respect. This journey allows us to gravitate toward healthier dynamics that differ from our past.

Breaking the cycle of repetition compulsion is a process that takes time. It takes effort. And it takes self-reflection. We take control by becoming aware of our patterns and taking steps toward change.

Boundaries

We live in a world where people are fighting for their own needs. Sometimes this is at our expense. Potentially, employers and businesses want to exploit our time and money. They want to make a profit. Families ask for our energy and attention, and lovers and partners have a range of demands.

We are also faced with positive pressures too. Many requests for our attention, support, or resources come from a genuine place of need, love, or desire for connection.

One of the best ways of ensuring that we are not unfairly used or treated badly is to protect our boundaries. We can also shield ourselves against excessive well-intentioned appeals for our resources. This is worth considering in more depth.

Types of boundaries

In the physical world, boundaries are usually clear. Buildings are surrounded by walls or fences. Countries have borders and checkpoints, and social behavior is often guided by defined rules. For instance, we aren't allowed to drink and drive, and speed limits must be observed.

The boundaries within our personal relationships are every bit as important, but less clear. They are unwritten. Especially when we have grown up in families where boundaries were frequently crossed or ignored, it can be difficult for us to set them and stick to them.

In her excellent and insightful book, *The Set Boundaries Workbook: Practical Exercises for Understanding Your Needs and Setting Healthy Limits*, relationship expert Nedra Glover Tawwab lists six types of boundaries.

- **Physical.** This refers to the control we have over our personal space, our bodies, and how and when we are touched. It underlines the importance of our right to physical safety and security, as well as our comfort level with physical closeness or touch in different settings.
- **Sexual.** This defines our comfort and consent with all things related to sexual interaction. It includes not only physical acts and sexual touch, but also discussions about sex, sexual expectations, and comments about our bodies. It protects our right to express our sexual preferences and to say "no."
- **Intellectual.** This boundary emphasizes our right to maintain and express our own thoughts and opinions. It's about respecting our intellectual space, acknowledging our beliefs and thoughts, and accepting our right to have different ideas. It discourages intellectual domination or belittling someone's thoughts and opinions.
- **Emotional.** This protects our emotional health by ensuring that our feelings are not dismissed, belittled, or invalidated. It safeguards our right to experience our emotions authentically and encourages us to express our feelings openly and truthfully without fear of repercussions, ridicule, or dismissal.
- **Material.** This relates to our personal belongings and resources, including money. It's about respecting our right to our possessions and how they are used or treated by others. It establishes control over our material belongings and dictates how we lend or share our possessions and resources.
- **Time.** This refers to how we choose to spend our time, including our work–life balance, personal time, and time spent on specific tasks or with certain people. It ensures we have the space to prioritize our time in a way that aligns with our values, obligations, and personal needs.

We can develop effective boundaries by:

- **Starting as we mean to go on.** It becomes harder to set effective boundaries later in a relationship if we have not agreed on them in the first place.
- **Communicating openly.** Talking about what matters to us helps us understand each other and set boundaries in relationships.
- **Using "I" statements.** We can express ourselves clearly by using "I" statements to talk about our own wants and needs.

To begin with, life can seem lonelier when we set clearer boundaries. Our relationships with colleagues, partners, or friends may seem less rewarding initially, as they become less exploitative. We might miss the positive feedback that comes from pleasing others instead of enjoying the true rewards of being authentic and taking care of ourselves. Or we might find it strange to prioritize our own needs when we're used to having weak or non-existent boundaries.

But in the long run, setting and maintaining healthy boundaries is key to personal well-being and healthier relationships. It may take some time, but the rewards of being true to ourselves and respecting our own needs will eventually become apparent.

People-Pleasing

> *I finally know the difference between pleasing and loving, obeying and respecting. It has taken me so many years to be okay with being different, and with being this alive, this intense.*
>
> —V: *I am an Emotional Creature: The Secret Life of Girls Around the World*

One of the most common defensive mechanisms in response to childhood abuse or a dysfunctional upbringing is people-pleasing. It's the costume we've worn, the mask we've hidden behind, and the shield we've used to protect ourselves from further harm.

People-pleasing is a survival tactic. It's the art of anticipating the needs, expectations, and demands of others to avoid conflict, criticism, or rejection.

In our childhood we discovered that by making ourselves likable, by never stepping on toes, by always being agreeable, we could create a semblance of peace or even win fleeting approval from our caregivers. This was our adaptation to an environment where we didn't feel safe, accepted, or loved unconditionally.

However, as we've come to realize, this armor we've worn for so long has become a burden. The effort we spend maintaining our people-pleasing facade takes energy. We could be investing this in ourselves—in our personal growth, our relationships, and our joy. We've also come to understand that our people-pleasing tendencies often leave us feeling unfulfilled and unrecognized, for we're always performing as someone else, never as our authentic selves.

How the trait of people-pleasing develops

> *No man is an island entire of itself; every man*
> *is a piece of the continent, a part of the main...*
>
> —John Donne

John Donne's poem *No Man is an Island* famously encapsulates the idea that we are all interdependent and intertwined. Published in 1624, it uses the old English term "man" to mean mankind—a now out-of-date way to say "all of us."

As adults, our basic nourishment and needs rely on a complex supply chain that ensures that food, medicine, and the services that we need to survive are available.

As children we had very little ability to meet our own needs. Babies are helpless. They can cry to communicate that they need something or that they are uncomfortable, but they are unable to explain what it is that they need and are completely reliant on other people to provide for them.

As older children there was more that we could do for ourselves. However, we could not, to any realistic degree, show ourselves empathy, compassion, boost our own self-esteem, or give ourselves the necessary, love, guidance, and support to grow into happy adults.

When we endured toxic parents, our needs were not fully met. Yet we needed to survive. We had to find ways to please our parents in the hope that they would treat us kindly. Or simply stop treating us cruelly and hurting us. We had few options. We had no agency. Children can't ring taxis, book into hotels or motels, or find other means of escape. We resorted to people-pleasing to try to stay safe. We became experts at it. If we got it wrong, we risked terrible consequences. Every time that we were criticized, hit, or abused, we learned to do a better job next time.

Over time we grew to be such effective people-pleasers that it affects how we interact with other people and how we deal with life.

Problems caused by people-pleasing

When people-pleasing dominates our actions so much that we consistently neglect our own needs, it becomes an issue. We end up creating a false self, a totally unrealistic picture of who we really are. When this happens there are a number of negative consequences in our adult lives:

- Putting other people's needs first can feel like an easy escape in the short term. In the long term it leads to resentment. Slowly but surely, we begin to lead the lives that other people want us to, rather than choosing what we want ourselves.
- We can end up taking on more tasks and activities than we are realistically able to handle. We feel intense guilt when saying no because we learned our responsibility was to make others feel okay.
- All the best relationships are reciprocal. Whether these are friendships or romantic relationships, we need some give and take. Denying our own needs is destructive and, ultimately, no one is happy.
- Taken to its limits, in the case of romantic relationships we can end up with partners to whom we are totally unsuited.
- We may experience a loss of identity. Constantly trying to please others can make it difficult for us to know our own preferences, desires, and needs.
- We may have difficulty setting boundaries. People-pleasing often leads to an inability to say "no," which can result in us feeling overwhelmed and overcommitted.
- We may have low self-esteem. Our sense of worth becomes tied to others' approval, leaving us vulnerable to criticism and rejection.
- Our relationships may be strained. When we are overly focused on pleasing others, our relationships can become imbalanced and inauthentic.
- Worst of all, if we are still enmeshed with our parents our lives become limited and defined by what we believe they want for us.

People-pleasing can also cause us problems if we are subconsciously using it as a way to try to feel safe. We find ourselves always needing to ensure that everybody likes us so that we don't feel threatened or scared. We risk spending an enormous amount of energy and time with people we do not have anything in common with and who are unlikely to be our friends. Deep down we are still subconsciously trying to secure parental love and approval.

Over-explaining

Over-explaining is when we feel the need to go into long justifications for our actions. It is a common feature of people-pleasing. It chips away at our self-confidence. Over-explaining reinforces the idea that we need approval from others. We are suggesting to ourselves that our own health and our own needs are not valid on their own. Examples of over-explaining include the following:

- **Apologizing for self-care.** We find ourselves over-explaining why we need time for ourselves, justifying our need for space or rest as if it were an indulgence rather than a necessity. For example, "I need to take a break because I've been working for six hours straight without any rest. My body feels tired, and my eyes are starting to strain. Plus, I didn't sleep well last night, so I really need this break…"
- **Explaining decisions that displease others.** We might over-explain why we made a decision that others didn't agree with, like choosing a career path that our parents disapproved of. "I decided to pursue art because I've always been passionate about it. It gives me joy and fulfillment. I understand you think it's not a practical choice, but I've done my research and found several successful artists in this field…"
- **Justifying emotions.** After years of being told our emotions were too much or not valid, we might find ourselves over-explaining our feelings. "I'm upset because when you made that comment, it reminded me of a past experience. Also, I had a long day at work, so I'm more sensitive than usual. Plus, I didn't get much sleep last night…"
- **Over-explaining basic needs.** Sometimes, we might even over-explain our basic needs, as if they require justification. "I'm eating this extra piece of cake because I haven't had much to eat today, and I did a lot of physical work. I know it's not the healthiest choice, but I really need the energy…"
- **Justifying personal preferences.** We might feel the need to over-explain

our preferences, as if they need to be justified or rationalized. "I chose to stay home tonight because I've been out the last four nights, and I feel like I need some time alone. Plus, I have a lot of chores to catch up on, and I think it would be good for me to have some time to myself..."

These instances of over-explaining can serve as self-awareness tools to help us identify when we are seeking external validation for our needs, decisions, or feelings. However, our experiences are valid on their own. They do not need to be justified or approved by anyone else.

What to do about people-pleasing

If people-pleasing has become a damaging and destructive trait, we can take immediate steps to lessen its impact. We can also develop a long-term strategy. Immediate steps include:

- Starting with immediate gentle "no's." We can create a habit of not agreeing to 100% of every request every time. Decide to spend an evening with relatives, rather than staying overnight. Meet friends that we feel ambivalent toward for coffee, rather than dinner. Contribute toward a project at work, rather than being responsible for the whole thing.
- Starting to say "no" with conviction and trying to avoid apologizing too much.
- Setting limits on how much time we are prepared to give to other people.
- Establishing strict red lines—boundaries that will not be crossed. For example, Saturday night is our time and our time only.

A long-term strategy

- Over time we are all much happier when we live life according to our own goals and values. For those of us who had a toxic childhood, this can be challenging. We may have invested so much time and energy in staying safe that we have repressed our true selves. Getting to know ourselves can take time and often a skilled counselor or psychotherapist will prove invaluable here.
- Understand that we have a choice. This may be difficult. Few children from dysfunctional families are encouraged to make healthy choices and rewarded for choosing well. It will take time, practice, and support.
- We can work on removing toxic people from our lives, or at least minimizing their influence.

Codependency

> *Codependency is not a permanent condition. It is a pattern of behavior that can be broken with the right information, practice and instruction.*
>
> —Roberta Sanders: *The Codependency Recovery Workbook: How to Create Healthy Relationships, Stop People Pleasing and Overcome the Fear of Abandonment*

Many of us who have endured childhood abuse or distressing family environments may find ourselves drawn into relationship patterns that can be profoundly damaging. One such pattern is codependency, a complex and often misunderstood behavior that may have been passed down through generations. It's rooted in our efforts to navigate the chaos and instability we once faced. This section explores what codependency is so we can learn to recognize its signs, and discover practical ways to manage and heal from it.

Codependency was originally described within the context of addiction treatment. It was initially used to understand the reactions and behaviors of those close to individuals battling alcoholism or people struggling with legal or illegal drugs. Authors and therapists like Melody Beattie helped bring it to a broader audience, particularly through her influential book *Codependent No More*.

The key feature of codependency is an intense interdependence between two people. This means that the two individuals rely on one another to meet their emotional, psychological, or even physical needs. Sometimes it's difficult for them to function independently or feel complete without the other. This could be in romantic relationships, friendships, family connections, or even with work colleagues.

Unlike healthy relationships, in codependency there is a significant imbalance of power. One partner, often neglecting their own well-being, becomes consumed with catering to the needs of the other. Their self-worth becomes intertwined with their role as a caregiver, a role filled with sacrifice and devotion.

At its core, codependency means we put others' needs before our own. We feel the urge to always be there for those we care about, setting aside our own feelings. Sometimes, the people we support might have serious challenges, like addiction. They lean on us a lot. They might use tactics to make sure we're always there for them. This creates a cycle: we feel important by being needed, while they get used to our constant care. But this cycle can hurt both sides, as we might unintentionally support their harmful habits. Balancing such a relationship can be tough.

How to recognize codependency

By honestly assessing our behaviors, we can identify if we're in a codependent relationship. Here are some signs for us to watch out for:

- Always feeling like we need to take care of others' needs and problems.
- Putting others first to the point where we ignore our own needs and feelings.
- Always trying to avoid arguments or disagreements, even if it means sacrificing our own opinions.
- Constantly seeking approval and validation from others, especially from those we're close to.
- Struggling to say "no" to requests or demands, even if they make us uncomfortable.
- Feeling like we have little or no value unless we are needed by someone else.
- Remaining in relationships that are harmful or one-sided because we feel needed.
- Regularly attempting to help or "fix" people who have problems that are beyond our control.
- Often feeling guilty or apologizing, even when we haven't done anything wrong.
- Feeling like we've lost our own identity or sense of self within a relationship.
- Continuously giving of ourselves to others, even if it harms us in the process.

We may also feel responsible for other people's actions, feelings, choices, and well-being. We may have difficulty identifying our feelings or expressing our needs. We might worry excessively about others and neglect our own self-care. We may also find ourselves in repeated cycles of harmful or abusive relationships which echo our childhood experiences.

Understanding our tendencies toward codependency can be overwhelming and may bring up past traumas and memories. It's essential to remember that these patterns developed as survival strategies during our younger years. They are not our fault. While they served a purpose in childhood, they may not be serving us as adults. The good news is, with commitment and support, we can change these patterns and build healthier relationships.

Action steps to deal with codependency

- **Awareness.** The first step to healing from codependency is recognizing the patterns. Awareness is a potent tool.
- **Seek professional help.** Therapists trained in dealing with codependency can provide much-needed guidance and support.
- **Establish boundaries.** Learning to set healthy boundaries is essential. It allows us to understand where we end and others begin, fostering a sense of self that might have been blurred in the past.
- **Prioritize self-care.** This includes physical, emotional, and mental well-being. Remember, it's not selfish to take care of ourselves.
- **Build a support network.** Joining support groups like Co-Dependents Anonymous can provide a safe space to share experiences and learn from others who are on similar journeys.
- **Work on self-esteem.** Understandably, many of us struggle with low self-esteem. Working on building our self-worth is key. This can be achieved through therapy, self-help books, or practices such as positive affirmations and self-compassion exercises.

Fostering our self-esteem is essential for inner harmony. As we proceed, let's remember the importance of self-kindness.

The next chapter sheds light on a significant aspect of relationships: the recognition and counteraction of abuse. Gaining insight into this can lead us to make better relationship choices.

10

Recognizing and Overcoming Abuse

HOW TO RECOGNIZE ABUSE WHEN IT IS HAPPENING: THE CYCLE OF ABUSE

At first glance, abusive behavior might seem unpredictable or sporadic. However closer observation reveals that it often follows a pattern. Recognizing this cycle helps us to understand the phases an abusive relationship goes through. Typically, the stages are as follows:

1. **Tension.** Communication breaks down. Tension increases. The abused person becomes fearful. Something is about to happen. They try to please the abuser to avoid the imminent abuse.
2. **Incident.** The act of violence, intimidation, or mistreatment takes place.
3. **Reconciliation.** The abuser either:
    - Apologizes.
    - Makes excuses and blames the person he or she has abused.
    - Denies the abuse took place.
    - Minimizes the consequences of the abuse.
4. **Calm.** This is the final phase before the cycle continues. No abuse takes place, nothing happens, and the abusive act is forgotten. The abuse cycle then begins again from stage 1.

After understanding the cycle of abuse, it's important to explore personality traits that might foster abusive behavior. One such dominant trait is narcissism, which can profoundly affect our relationships.

Narcissism

Narcissistic political leaders have done untold damage to the world. We are becoming aware of the destruction caused by narcissists in international relations with cruel and unnecessary wars and suffering. From business boardrooms to our living rooms, narcissists spread chaos.

The myth of Narcissus dates from ancient Greece. Narcissus, the son of the river god Cephissus, fell in love with his own reflection in a tranquil pool. He became obsessed. Unable to pull himself away, Narcissus died by the water, gazing at his own image.

From this story, many people believe that narcissists are in love with themselves. Certainly, they put their own needs first. They can be pathologically selfish. However, there is a depth to narcissism that is not generally understood. It is more about a desperate need for approval and admiration than an excess of self-esteem.

Narcissism exists on a spectrum. At one extreme end, there are people who are diagnosed with narcissistic personality disorder. This is about one percent of the population. At the other extreme, there are those who show very few or no narcissistic personality traits. The majority of people are somewhere in between.

How to spot a narcissist

The American Diagnostic and Statistical Manual of Mental Disorders (5th edition) describes nine characteristics of people with narcissistic personality disorder. These red flags are summarized below.

- **Grandiosity.** Narcissists expect to be treated as being special or superior.
- **Fantasy.** They fantasize about power, success, being super-intelligent or enormously attractive.
- **Admiration.** They need constant admiration from others.
- **Exploitation.** It is common for narcissists to exploit people for their own gain.
- **The absence of empathy.** Narcissists are unwilling or unable to understand other people's feelings.
- **Envy.** They live in a world where they're jealous of others or believe others to be jealous of them.
- **Arrogance.** Frequently narcissists are arrogant and pompous.
- **Sense of entitlement.** They believe that people should be obedient to them or that they deserve special treatment.

- **Superiority**. Narcissists think they deserve to be around high-status people and organizations.

We may be able to recognize some of these traits in our own parents from when we were children. If they are still with us now, the chances are that their behavior is the same. Narcissists seldom change. Perhaps they are unable to accept personal criticism. They become angry when they believe we don't show total admiration and respect for them.

Red flags and green lights: recognizing narcissistic and healthy relationships

Clearly, crashes can be catastrophic. Modern vehicles have a range of safety equipment that make accidents much more survivable: everything from seatbelts to crumple zones, air bags, and collapsible steering wheels. That said, prevention is better than cure. By far the best strategy is to read the road ahead. It is better to avoid smashing and crashing than dealing with it when it happens.

It is the same with narcissists. They are destructive. Narcissists entangle us with their dramas. We become emotionally involved and emotionally damaged by our relationships with them. Recognizing in advance that someone is a narcissist and keeping clear of them works far better than becoming involved and then attempting to disentangle ourselves later on.

Narcissists are charming. At least, they appear to be when we first meet. Sometimes we realize later on in the relationship that this was simply a mask. They are sly and deceitful and cause tremendous harm.

If we suspect that we are in a relationship with a narcissist, there are ways to recognize this. Warning signs include:

- Financial manipulation. Narcissists hate equality. They pay for everything to manipulate us, or exploit us by refusing to pay for anything.
- Isolation from family and friends. Narcissists gradually manipulate situations so that we lose contact with family and friends.
- That we feel afraid to speak.
- That we feel the need to question ourselves.
- That we try enormously hard not to upset them and are overly careful around them.
- That they try to make themselves central and the only person who matters in our lives.

Especially if we grew up with narcissistic influences, we can see the importance of recognizing these traits in other people. Being aware helps us make sense of our past and helps us to make informed decisions about our future relationships.

Gaslighting

When we are tricked or manipulated into questioning our reality, this is known as gaslighting. It is another form of manipulation that can damage our mental health and well-being.

The term comes from *Gas Light*—a thriller set in Victorian times and written in 1938 by novelist Patrick Hamilton. In the story, the husband searches for hidden jewels in the attic each evening, causing the gas lights in the house to dim. When his wife notices and mentions the dimming lights, he denies any change, deliberately trying to make her doubt her perceptions and sanity.

Gaslighting commonly occurs in toxic families. Abusive parents use it as a technique to control us. Most frequently this involves shifting blame for their behavior onto us and making us feel shame and guilt that rightfully belongs to them.

Gaslighting can be deeply disorienting and painful. It's a gradual process that chips away at our confidence and trust in ourselves. It's hard for us to tell reality from manipulation.

We must remember that the feelings of confusion or self-doubt we experience as a result of gaslighting are not reflections of our intelligence, worth, or capabilities. Gaslighting is an external tactic used by someone else to manipulate us. Recognizing and understanding this is the first step toward reclaiming our self-worth and truth.

When we find that we're questioning our reality or constantly second-guessing ourselves, it is beneficial for us to talk to someone we trust. A good friend, or a therapist can provide the perspective and validation we need. We all deserve to be respected and understood in our relationships. Our experiences and feelings are valid.

While gaslighting seeks to undermine our perception of reality, there's another psychological mechanism that can keep us in harmful relationships, often against our better judgment: trauma bonding.

Trauma Bonding

In simple terms, a trauma bond is a psychological trap that keeps us stuck in a damaging relationship.

Many of us experienced trauma bonding as part of our upbringing. It is a technique that is also used by narcissists in unhealthy relationships. It is useful to understand how it works so that we can see more clearly when we are being exploited in relationships.

Psychologists Susan L. Painter and Donald G. Dutton published a research paper back in 1970, looking at why what were described as "battered women"—a terrible, yet realistic phrase that communicates the horror of physical abuse—returned to the relationship in which they had been hurt, after having escaped. As is still the case today, prior to their research there was a great deal of victim blaming. Women were blamed for their own abuse and were seen as being masochistic or having a defective personality trait which led them back to the abusive relationship. Of course, this is wrong.

Trauma bonding theory explains how abusers create a strong emotional bond with the people that they abuse. It helps to explain why we might feel attached to those who have hurt us in the past, or why we feel compelled to stay within destructive relationships now.

As with all forms of abuse, power and control are absolutely central. Trauma bonding occurs when there is a power imbalance. Parents are powerful and we as children were powerless. In institutions, especially when we were young, there was a huge imbalance of power. Frequently, systems of harsh rules and punishments were used to keep us helpless.

If we were simply treated badly all the time, then there would be no bonding. We would see the relationship for what it was: unfair and wrong. What creates the attachment is something known as "intermittent kindness."

Abusers use intermittent kindness as a manipulation tool. Instead of being cruel all the time, they give sudden bursts of warmth and love. This makes us believe there is hope in the relationship. We therefore stay within it, believing that things will change for the better. This is not true. It is just a fantasy. This beautiful, happy place on our map of the future does not exist. Well actually it does exist, but only when we leave the abusive partner who keeps us stuck in a place of unhappiness.

11

Romantic Relationships

The choices we make in partners very often echo the relationship dynamics we've been exposed to in the past. Alain de Botton, Swiss-born British author and philosopher, maintains that instead of choosing love partners who will make us happy, we are out to find ones with whom we will feel familiar. This feeling of familiarity works well and helps us to be successful if it is based on love and generosity that we experienced in our upbringing. We will subconsciously seek out people who give us the same tenderness and warmth.

Unfortunately, the same is also true when we were brought up in a dysfunctional or distressing family or were abused as a child. Without us realizing, our psyche searches for partners who bring out the deep emotions that we are used to. As Alain describes it, we find someone who makes us suffer in a way that we need to suffer to make us feel that love is real. When we are in a relationship, whether this is a long-term commitment or simply a series of short encounters, we may face some challenges:

- **Trust issues.** Due to our past experiences, we may struggle to develop deep relationships. We are afraid of being hurt and are hypervigilant. We are always on the lookout for signs of danger or rejection.
- **Intimacy issues.** We may have difficulty with emotional and physical intimacy. This includes a fear of intimacy, difficulties with vulnerability, and difficulty with sexual arousal. Potentially, we can struggle to connect on an emotional level with a partner.
- **Communication issues.** Communication is vital for every healthy relationship. When our families were poor communicators, it is understandable that we can struggle with communication too. It can be hard

to express our thoughts and feelings. Communication issues lead to misunderstandings and conflict. This damages our relationships and leads to further emotional distress.
- **Sexual challenges.** Experiences from our past can sometimes impact our ability to be fully present and at ease during intimate moments. It's important to remember that we're not alone and it's okay for us to seek help if we find ourselves facing challenges like difficulty in maintaining arousal, navigating intimate moments, or achieving satisfaction. Every one of our journeys is unique, and it's valid for us to feel what we're feeling. And none of this is in any way our fault.

Recognizing these problems can pave the way to a deeper understanding of intimacy and more effective communication. There are actions that we can take to move forward. Some key strategies to help us include:

- **Watching and spotting.** Noticing the massive mountains of nonsense on TV, and in books, films, and adverts that promote misogynistic and unhealthy relationships based on power, money, and control. This helps us to see how some of the wider attitudes in the world reinforce the unhelpful ideas that we may have absorbed from childhood.
- **Creating healthy boundaries.** A solid relationship is built on mutual respect. Setting and respecting boundaries is a fundamental part of this. We have the right to express our limits, and these should be honored by both parties.
- **Building trust.** Trust is the cornerstone of any meaningful relationship. When dealing with past trauma, cultivating trust can be challenging but is essential. This involves consistent efforts, reliability, and showing one another genuine support and understanding.
- **Patience.** Healing and growth are processes. Overcoming challenges with intimacy won't happen overnight, and it's good not to pressure ourselves. Embracing the journey, taking small steps, and remaining patient can lead us toward healthier, more fulfilling relationships.

There's no one-size-fits-all solution to these issues. Some strategies work for some, but not all of us. It might take some time and experimentation to discover what works best. It's natural to seek what feels familiar, but as we become more aware of the patterns we tend to follow, we can recognize and break those that are unhelpful to us.

"Me" Instead of "Us": Transactional Rule-Based Relationships

Rather than experiencing unconditional love—when we are loved and accepted just for being us—we often experienced a childhood where love was conditional. How much we received depended on whether we were judged to be behaving well or badly by our parents. This was completely arbitrary, depending on their own mood. Frequently it was harsh and unfair, with very unrealistic expectations about how children should act.

This model of relationships can influence us as adults. Potentially it leaves us with a tendency toward what are known as transactional relationships. This is where we look at everything as an exchange or transaction. We only ever give things when we expect to get something of equal or higher value back. So rather than being expressions of love or warmth, gifts, special dinners, flowers, and weekends away are given in the expectation we will be rewarded with attention and affection in return. Or perhaps we cook dinner expecting our partner do the dishes. The relationship is measured and judged all the time. We need to know if we are winning or losing or if all seems equal.

This reflects our childhood experience that we were only ever loved by our parents when we did well at school, looked after our siblings, did things for them, or pleased them in some way.

Transactional relationships are more about manipulation and control than equality and partnership. They are not an alliance where both partners support one another.

The first way to begin to change a transactional relationship into a trusting, loving and equal partnership is to recognize that it *is* in fact a transactional relationship. This can be done by asking ourselves the following questions:

- The majority of the time, do we focus mainly on benefits to ourselves? Or is our partner only interested in what is in it for them?
- Are we forever keeping score? Do they appear to be forever keeping score?
- Is our relationship characterized by warmth and support, or resentment?
- Do we tend to view every kind gesture, loving word, or generous act as a debt to be paid off, rather than a simple expression of love?
- Do we feel anxious, unfulfilled, or dissatisfied most of the time?
- Is the relationship mainly about competition or control, instead of mutual respect and understanding?

Once we recognize the transactional nature of our relationship, it's then possible to start challenging this and work toward a better connection.

The transformation from a transactional relationship to a loving partnership is not an overnight process. It requires time. It requires patience. It requires understanding. But the result is a new relationship where both partners feel valued and loved for who they are, not just for what they can offer or give. It is a journey that is often challenging but ultimately deeply rewarding, leading to relationships that thrive on genuine love and mutual respect.

Sexual Identity, Orientation, and Relationships

> *I'm not missing a minute of this. It's the revolution!*
> —The words spoken by Sylvia Rivera, Latina LGBTQ+ activist who inspired a generation to fight for their freedom and celebrate being who they are during the Stonewall riots

Sexual identity, how we express ourselves sexually, and sexual orientation: who we are attracted to is at the core of our being. Progress is being made and hopefully most parts of the world are becoming more open and tolerant. Some of us, though, have scars and psychological injuries after growing up in families where we were pressurized into being something different than we were born to be or chose to be, and having relationships with those that we did not want to.

We may have grown up with the extreme hypocrisy of being sexually abused ourselves, while also being given very strict boundaries around our own relationships.

Often, very authoritarian views were imposed on us. Especially in extreme religious families, we would not have been allowed to explore our own sexuality. This means that if we are heterosexual, the number or type of people that we could date was very limited (or possibly even zero). For those of us who are gay, lesbian, bisexual or have any sexual identity outside the traditional historic model of a heterosexual married couple, we likely met a wall of intolerance. We may have felt the need to keep our sexuality secret.

Keeping our sexuality secret because of intolerance can have lasting effects on our well-being. The experiences of our past, especially during our formative years, significantly influence our thinking and behavior as adults. The memories of being forced to conform to certain norms, the pressure to maintain relationships we didn't desire, and the experience of abuse can affect how we view ourselves and how we relate to others.

Yet it's important to remember that we have the power to reclaim our narrative. Embracing and celebrating our identities through Pride, actively asserting our human rights, and reflecting on our past with a lens of self-compassion and understanding can be deeply empowering.

It can also be part of our gift to the world. The more we empower and celebrate ourselves, the more we help and support others who share our identity.

Characteristics of Healthy Relationships

When we were brought up in dysfunctional families, we may not have a clear model of what a healthy relationship looks like. It is beneficial to be able to spot green lights as well as seeing dangerous red flags. Green lights in a relationship include the following:

- **Emotional intelligence.** Emotionally healthy people are empathic. They show self-awareness and are comfortable sharing their feelings. They can be vulnerable without being needy. A healthy sign is the ability, when appropriate, to laugh at themselves and the absurdity of life.
- **Stability.** When people are kind and treat others with respect, then we can consider the possibility of a long-term relationship with them. A good test of someone's character is how well they treat those who are vulnerable or in less powerful situations than themselves. Are they rude and aggressive or friendly and warm toward serving staff in a restaurant or café? What are they like around children? What is their reaction while watching people in desperate situations, such as those escaping war and disasters seen on the news?
- **Partnership.** We need to look for those who invest their time and effort in making our relationship work. Good people are aware of our needs, while also having independence and knowing what they want from the relationship.
- **Simplicity.** Above all, they need to be easy to spend time with, and time spent with them ought to be enjoyable and sometimes fun.

12

Family Relationships

WHAT HAPPENS IN HEALTHY FAMILIES?

Healthy families possess several key characteristics that help create a supportive, loving environment for all members. Here are a few such traits:

- **Open communication.** Good communication defines a healthy family. Family members should feel comfortable expressing their thoughts, feelings, and concerns with each other, and everyone should be listened to with respect and understanding.
- **Supportive relationships.** Members of a healthy family support each other. Emotionally. Physically. And psychologically. Support includes understanding, love, and care for each other's individual needs and interests.
- **Shared responsibilities.** In a healthy family, work and responsibilities are shared, with everyone contributing to the household. This creates a sense of teamwork.
- **Flexibility.** Healthy families are open to change. They adjust their roles, rules, and behavior when necessary. They handle stress and crises effectively.
- **Time.** Spending time together is a characteristic of healthy families. This creates shared memories, and a sense of belonging and unity.
- **Problem-solving.** A healthy family resolves conflicts. They discuss problems openly, seek solutions, and make decisions together.
- **Respect.** In a healthy family, every member respects each other's space, values, and individuality. They appreciate the differences among them and treat each other with kindness.

- **Strong moral values.** Healthy families often have a set of shared values or principles that guide their decisions and behavior. These can provide a sense of direction and purpose.
- **Love and affection.** Healthy families express love, warmth, and affection toward each other. These expressions reinforce the sense of being cherished within the family.
- **Security and safety.** A healthy family provides an environment where everyone feels safe and secure, both physically and emotionally.

What Happens in Dysfunctional Families?

All families are different. There are, however, general characteristics of dysfunctional families. We may recognize some of them from our own upbringing. Greater awareness of our background gives us deeper insights into our core beliefs. This can help us to change and avoid repeating some of the mistakes (deliberate or accidental) that we endured as children.

- **Poor communication.** Toxic families often have poor communication, which includes a lack of open and respectful discussion. There are constant misunderstandings, secrecy, and dishonesty.
- **Emotions.** Family members are not encouraged to express their feelings, perhaps because they are considered unimportant, or they need to be hidden.
- **There is no such thing as unconditional love.** Love is transactional or manipulative; it is used as a means of control.
- **Denial.** The family outright refuse to admit abuse that is happening. Or if it is not possible to deny the abuse completely then a strategy of minimization is used to suggest that minimal harm has been inflicted.
- **Lack of boundaries.** There may be no respect for family members' personal space. Possessions may be borrowed or destroyed without permission. In some circumstances, physical boundaries are ignored. Physical or sexual assault may happen, a massive breach of both boundaries and trust.
- **Manipulation and control.** At the center of dysfunctional families is the need to control. This is often experienced as having rigid rules. These rules aren't necessarily acknowledged or spoken. They may simply be there in the background all of the time. There is enormous pressure never to break any of these rules. One or more members may manipulate or

control others through guilt, fear, intimidation, or other tactics. This power dynamic creates an unequal and unhealthy family structure.
- **Chronic conflict.** Frequent arguments, hostility, and unresolved conflicts are common traits of toxic families. The environment is often tense, and disagreements escalate quickly into fights. Anger may be the norm and violence between family members common.
- **Unpredictability.** Toxic families often have an unpredictable environment, where family members walk on eggshells for fear of triggering negative reactions.
- **Negativity.** Toxic families often foster an environment filled with negativity, criticism, or cynicism, which can be detrimental to the mental health of family members. They often expect perfection, and if something goes wrong there always has to be someone to blame. The reality of life—that there are accidents and unforced errors—does not exist. It is always someone's fault. This might progress into verbal abuse and harsh and unfair criticism.
- **Lack of empathy and support.** In toxic families, there's often a lack of empathy, leading to members feeling unseen, unheard, or misunderstood.
- **Groupthink.** Damaged families tend to operate as a unit and children within these families are not encouraged to have ideas or opinions of their own.
- **Scapegoating or favoritism.** Some toxic families may place the blame for their problems on one family member (scapegoating), or unduly favor one member over others. These dynamics can lead to feelings of worthlessness or inadequacy in the scapegoated or less-favored members.
- **Isolation.** Frequently outsiders are not welcome within the family.
- **Parents may overshare.** They may tell their children inappropriate information about their relationship: for example, details about one parent who drinks too much or is having an affair. Emotionally immature parents often dump their own problems on their children. Children are expected to take on the role of being a listening and empathic partner, solving problems and providing the support that adults in healthy relationships should give each other.

In addition to these general characteristics, it may have been that our parents had specific roles in our dysfunctional family. One parent may have been responsible for our hurtful upbringing, while the other seemed unaware of what was happening. This is worth considering in further detail, so that we can understand our situation better.

Enablers and passive partners

There are circumstances in which one parent genuinely does not know anything about the other parent's abuse.

Pedophiles groom adults before approaching children. One example is when a man or a woman searches for a partner who already has their own children. They then groom and build a relationship with the adult, gaining their trust in order to access their children. Once they have done this successfully, they groom and abuse the children. The final part of the grooming process is to try and make the child feel responsible for their own abuse so that it is kept secret within the family. When this happens there is a possibility that one parent really does not know what is going on.

Frequently, however, one parent knows, at least on some level, what is going on and chooses not to intervene. They either neglect their responsibility to protect their children or help to create an environment where the abuse can take place. Many of us will have lived in a family with both an active abuser and an enabler or passive partner.

Enablers were those who knowingly or unknowingly enabled our abuser to continue their abusive behavior toward us. They may have covered up the abuse or made excuses for our abuser's behavior, shielding them from consequences of their actions. Enablers also denied abuse or minimized its severity. In doing so, they strengthened the abuser's power and control over us.

Passive partners, on the other hand, were aware of the abuse but chose to remain silent. They took no action to intervene.

There are several possible reasons why parents, or others with a responsibility to protect us, didn't do so.

- They felt powerless or afraid to speak up and challenge our abuser's behavior. They felt threatened themselves.
- Their behavior was motivated by a desire to maintain the status quo, avoid conflict or confrontation, or protect their own interests.
- They may have had their own unresolved psychological issues, low self-esteem, fear, or a sense of helplessness.
- In some circumstances the cruel reality is that they simply didn't care enough to help us.

Triangulation, scapegoats, and the golden child

Triangulation

Triangulation is a powerful means of control within dysfunctional families. As we might guess, triangulation involves three people.

Triangulation is the psychological process where a third person is brought into a relationship between two people. It is an attempt to shift focus away from an underlying problem. It can occur in any type of relationship but is commonly seen in families where communication is poor and there is a low level of problem-solving skills.

If our parents had a strained relationship, then one parent might have used us to communicate with the other parent, rather than talking to the other parent directly. This created a triangle where we became the messenger. Our parents' issues were not directly addressed. This often happened when our parents were separating or involved in an acrimonious divorce.

In some of our families, one parent spoke negatively about the other parent in an attempt to draw us into the conflict by siding with them. This was common if our parents were fighting a custody battle with each other over who we lived with.

Psychological theories suggest that triangulation is a way to reduce anxiety and stress between two people. The third person (us) was handed the toxicity and negativity that should have been resolved by our parents working together.

Or perhaps the triangle involved just one of our parents and one of our brothers or sisters. Frequently our mother or father made an alliance with the "golden" or preferred child against the scapegoated child. We may have been given one of those roles ourselves, or we might have been a witness or accessory to what was happening. In some of our families the roles of scapegoat and golden child were switched between our brothers or sisters. We could be the scapegoat one week and the golden child the next week.

The golden child

The golden child is the favored child, and frequently the most outwardly successful.

Success was judged by many of our parents to be about intelligence, physical appearance, or achievement, for example in sports or drama. It was seldom if ever defined as meeting our personal goals, our values, or being happy. The golden child was frequently the best-behaved child. Our parents decided who was "good." This was usually the one who was most subservient, most easily manipulated, who ignored or was forced into supporting abuse or family dysfunction.

In some families the role of the golden child was to either act as a diversion or a "balance" to abuse. An outwardly successful child drew attention away from wider dysfunction. Or perhaps if our parents felt uncomfortable about mistreating us, they attempted to feel less guilty and persuade themselves that they were good people by behaving well toward one of our brothers or sisters. If this happened, it is usually difficult or sometimes impossible for our siblings to understand or accept that abuse took place, even now that they are adults.

It is often assumed that being a golden child is positive and rewarding. It may be more beneficial than being scapegoated; however, it is also a complex experience. We may have received praise and attention from our parents and have felt special and valued, but it also caused us some difficulties. Pressure to maintain our position within the family and struggling with the fear of disappointing our parents were common. As golden children we may have felt that our accomplishments were expected, and we did not feel truly appreciated for our efforts. Being the golden child also risked the creation of feelings of entitlement, lack of empathy, and difficulty forming healthy relationships later in life.

The scapegoat

The scapegoat has to take responsibility for problems within the family.

When we were scapegoated, we were unfairly blamed and criticized for the dysfunction in the family system. There are several reasons why we may have been scapegoated.

- **Parental incompetence.** One of our parents, unable to manage their own emotions or responsibilities, might have projected their own inadequacies onto us, blaming us for their failures.
- **Jealousy or envy.** A family member, often a sibling or parent, might have felt threatened by our success, talents, or even our personality. In their insecurity, they might have bullied, undermined, or blamed us as a way to regain a sense of control or superiority.
- **To maintain a false narrative.** Our family often had unspoken rules and narratives that everyone was expected to adhere to, such as "we are a happy family," or "we are all high achievers." If our experiences or behaviors challenged this narrative, we might have been scapegoated

and accused of being the problem, rather than the family acknowledging the underlying issues.
- **To uphold a power dynamic.** In our family, with a strict hierarchy or power dynamic often dictated by a controlling or narcissistic parent, any member who challenged the status quo or asserted their independence might have been scapegoated as a way to reinforce the existing power structure.

In her book *Rejected, Shamed, and Blamed*, Rebecca C. Mandeville provides guidance and support for adults who were scapegoated in their families as children. She discusses how being the family scapegoat can lead to feelings of shame, low self-esteem, and a sense of not belonging. Her perspective is that to heal from scapegoating, we need to recognize that the problem was never us. It was the dysfunctional family system itself.

There is some excellent and detailed advice in *Growing Up as the Scapegoat to a Narcissistic Parent: A Guide to Healing*, by psychotherapist Jay Reid. He describes three pillars of recovery:

- Making sense of the narcissistic abuse so we know it was not our fault.
- Creating distance from narcissistic abusers in our life today.
- Living in defiance of the narcissist's rules.

Additionally, recognizing our own worth and practicing self-kindness are key steps in breaking the cycle of scapegoating and moving toward a healthier, more fulfilling life.

Starting Our Own Family

Our family's future

We can be wonderful parents.

After having grown up within toxic families, many of us will make fantastic moms, dads, step-parents and carers. We know how damaging our own childhood was, and we are determined that our own children will grow up happy and free from abuse.

We may have experienced what is known as "generational abuse." This is when abuse is passed down from one generation to another. For example, a child who was physically hurt by her mother goes on to physically assault her own daughter. This happens with 30% of adults who were abused as children, according to statistics from the American Society for the Positive Care of Children. Of course, this abuse is wrong and should not happen. It does, however, show that the majority of us from difficult and dysfunctional families do not continue any sort of cycle of abuse.

Sometimes, hurt people hurt people: what to do if things have gone wrong

It is conceivable that if we have had poor role models and had a difficult or distressing family background ourselves, then we may make or have already made mistakes with our own children. This is understandable. However, it is not an excuse.

Children deserve, and have the right to unconditional love, to have their boundaries respected, and to be supported so that they develop into happy, healthy human beings.

We need to break the cycle of abuse.

If we have harmed our own children then it is important to take action to right the wrongs that we have done. We can do this by:

- Openly and honestly admitting to any wrongdoing, especially to those people who were directly affected by it.
- Taking responsibility for our actions.
- Making amends, for example paying for counseling or psychotherapy to help heal damage that we might have done.
- Growing and developing into the best parents that we can possibly be.
- Learning from our mistakes and becoming the best possible people that we can be.

NAVIGATING SPECIAL OCCASIONS

Christmas (and other big family events)

Not all of us celebrate Christmas. It is a fantastic feature of life that we are all from different racial, religious, and cultural backgrounds. Christmas features in this book, not because the expectation is that everyone is personally involved in the festivities, but rather because the stress, expectations and challenges around Christmas are an example of the dynamics of many large family gatherings and events.

Christmas can be a wonderful time of the year.

For anyone with less than the perfect family (which is everybody—perfection only exists in the movies), Christmas get-togethers can create some tough challenges. Regardless of whether we had a dysfunctional past or not, there are elements of the holiday season that can be stressful for everyone. Expectations about the "perfect" Christmas put pressure on people. In an imperfect world filled with imperfect human beings, things can be great, but they are never perfect. Perfection is a very unrealistic and unhelpful idea that just leads to stress.

Possible problems for us may include:

- **Unresolved conflicts.** The issues from our upbringing may never have been fully addressed, or even spoken about at all.
- **Triggers.** Being with our family may trigger distressing memories. This might retraumatize us. Sometimes, those who hurt or harmed us might be joining us for the celebrations.
- **Loneliness.** Some of us may have gone no-contact or been ostracized by our family. We haven't yet filled the space that was occupied by them.
- **Repetition.** We might see dysfunctional patterns of behavior starting to occur again. This repetition is not just disheartening but can also be deeply triggering. Falling back into old patterns of behavior, despite our best efforts to change, can lead to feelings of failure, helplessness, and despair. It also reinforces the toxic dynamics of the past, making it harder to break free and establish healthier ways of relating to one another. This is why recognizing and addressing these patterns is so crucial for our emotional well-being and the health of our relationships.
- **Fear of missing out.** Regardless of our own personal upbringing, many holidays and events create an almost competitive pressure to be seen to be enjoying ourselves and having a wonderful time. Posts by others on social media make matters worse. They promote the unreal and untrue impression that everyone is having a marvelous time.
- **Alcohol.** For those of us who enjoy a drink, alcohol can be a great way to relax and unwind. Traditionally, beers, wines, and spirits have fueled Christmas celebrations. However, Christmas can be a time when we drink to excess, or other family members drink heavily. This might be a coping strategy: a way of denying and drowning out problems or the way in which the family numbs itself against pain.

- **Manipulative kindness.** Children are usually taught to accept gifts with grace and gratitude. However, many of us know that often presents have a dark side. Gifts may have been used to coerce us to do things that we didn't want to when we were children. They may also have been given to us as an attempt to make us forget what has happened or as a triangulation tactic.

There are some helpful guidelines that we can use to help us spend time at family events, if and when we choose to do so.

- **Managing expectations.** It is helpful to manage our own expectations. The mythical magic of Christmas or any other potentially happy family event—weddings, celebrations, or parties of any kind—has to be balanced with the reality that nothing is perfect.

    Dysfunctional families bring a lot of baggage to these occasions. There is always a potential for arguments and stress. This does not mean that every family event for the rest of our lives will be challenging, just that problems have to be worked through over time. How enjoyable family gatherings are depends on how much we have processed our own emotions and our own past, and how willing our families are to deal with difficult issues. We can control the former but not the latter.
- **Choose.** It is OK to make a decision not to attend. We owe it to ourselves to act in the best interests of our own mental health, no matter what the pressure from our family is. If we decide not to join them for Christmas or any other occasion because it is the best way that we can stay healthy, then this is right and good.
- **Plan ahead.** This means setting clear boundaries and knowing in advance what action we will take if those boundaries are crossed. It's best to have a plan to leave the event at a time of our choosing.

Power and Control: How to Take Charge of Our Own Lives

"I hate this day": dealing with Mother's Day and Father's Day

We can recognize that some people have fantastic loving and supportive parents. That is the way it should have been for all of us. It's great that they can celebrate the warmth and generosity that their moms and dads, step-parents, and grandparents have given to them. This, however, is their reality, not ours. We can both welcome and accept their good fortune while at the same time acknowledging our hurt and loss.

It can be hard to see card shops that are full of the most gushing descriptions of mothers and fathers. Many portray parents as having almost divine qualities. They are about superhuman love, compassion, and self-sacrifice. These traits exist for the benefit of their children. Greetings cards frequently start by saying to the best mother/father in the world. This is usually followed by some sort of statement to the effect that we owe everything to them and that nothing we have achieved could possibly have happened without their selfless love and support. This is in stark contrast to the history that many of us share. Popular books, including *Mothers Who Can't Love: A Healing Guide for Daughters* by Susan Forward, acknowledge that—in her words— "mothers can neglect, betray and batter, as well as be control freaks and severely narcissistic."

There are several ways that we can approach Mother's and Father's Day. Some strategies are more effective than others, although none are actually wrong. Even though we are responsible for how we behave, we are reacting to circumstances that were not caused by us and that we had no control over. So, we need to show ourselves compassion and understanding and accept that we are trying to make the best of a situation that's not our fault.

One common course of action is denial. This has both benefits and drawbacks. In the short term it buys us time until we have the strength to fully face reality. In the long term it holds us back. A frequent form of denial is to minimize the damage that was done to us, rather than blocking it out or pretending that it never happened. We try to convince ourselves that perhaps things weren't that bad after all, or that other people had it much worse than us. Some of us may spend time shopping for cards that we really don't want to buy and disliking ourselves for doing so. Perhaps we might try to find the one card in the shop that's plain or dull and sticks to saying something simple like the bare minimum "Happy Mother's Day."

The first step toward making real progress is to really acknowledge our own feelings, accepting that they are both real and valid. It isn't wrong to feel angry, sad, or jealous about other people's happy relationships, or even just confused and numb.

We can use our emotions as information to guide us. If we are feeling angry, this is likely to be telling us that our boundaries are not solid enough and that we still feel exploited or abused by our parents. We can work toward having clear boundaries.

Sadness can signal the start of grieving the loss of our childhood—the lack of love, respect, or nurturing, or whatever it was that we ought to have had but never did. Grieving can be a difficult process, so it is helpful to have the support of a therapist. We can begin to express our feelings through journaling or writing a letter to our parents. This letter does not necessarily need to be sent and it can be to a parent who has died. It just needs to be an open and honest expression of how we feel.

Celebrating independence: a healthy alternative

If we no longer see our parents, we can use the day to celebrate our independence.

We can decide that Mother's or Father's Day is an opportunity to celebrate our own worth. It may feel strange and against all of society's conditioning; however, we can use the day to treat *ourselves* well. By doing what we love doing and enjoying ourselves, we can remind ourselves that the way we were treated by our parents reflects on them and not us.

We are worth it.

13

Finding Help: Counseling and Psychotherapy

When we set off on a journey, we have a choice of how we're going to travel to our destination. We can take a plane, train, boat, bus, taxi, cycle, walk, or run. It's more than likely that we will use a combination of different modes of transport. We can also choose the route we take. Our decisions will affect how quickly we arrive and how straightforward or difficult our trip will be.

We are heading from one place to another when we start to have counseling or psychotherapy. If everything goes well, we process our past, learn to work with our emotions, and end up far happier and healthier people. Somewhat strangely though, these therapies are usually seen as a process rather than an end result. If we are asked to imagine a psychotherapy session, we are likely to have a vivid picture of two people talking to one another in a small room with a therapist asking questions and their client responding. Or maybe, if we have ever read any books by Freud or watched psychoanalysis depicted in the movies, we will see an old and battered couch. The scene of a contented, smiling client leaving the therapy room for the last time isn't one that we usually imagine. Wider society often has prejudices and myths about therapy that are unhelpful. We may recognize some of these ideas that are listed below.

MYTHS AROUND THERAPY

- **Going to therapy is a sign of weakness.** In reality it takes courage and strength to recognize that there are aspects of our lives that we want to change. Our decision to take action is both positive and empowering.

- **Talking about the past will keep us stuck in the past.** This isn't true. The best way to escape from our past is to acknowledge and accept it, and to learn how to move forward.
- **We tried therapy once before and it didn't work, so there's no point in doing it again.** Often when we appear to fail at something, we have actually learned a great deal that will help us the next time. Few people succeed at giving up smoking or becoming fitter the first time that they try. There is a very good chance that when we start afresh, we will be successful.
- **Therapy takes years and years.** Certainly, traditional psychoanalysis that follows the theories of Sigmund Freud can last an extraordinary length of time. Therapy can be short, however. There is an increasing emphasis on shorter-term interventions such as CBT. These may be helpful as part of an overall strategy for healing.

Maximizing Results: Getting the Most from Psychotherapy and Counseling

Therapy is an investment. It costs us time, money, and emotional energy.

The price that we pay benefits other people as well as ourselves. The Latin phrase *Nemo dat quod non habet* summarizes this very well; it means "you cannot give what you do not have." We can't easily give our family and friends love, compassion, and security when we feel unloved, condemn ourselves, and are anxious and insecure. Going to therapy is not self-centered and selfish. It is a generous act.

Like any investment, it is important to consider the various options, and plan before we choose. Our decisions are made more complex because there are so many therapies available.

The choice feels almost infinite. Existentialist therapy is based on the ideas of French philosopher Jean-Paul Sartre. Laughter therapy, first developed by Dr. Madan Kataria, takes a very different approach. There are creative treatments: art therapy, drama therapy and music therapy. Psychoanalysis can take a notoriously long time, whereas brief interventions such as CBT aim to make a positive difference quickly. Physical therapies include light therapy for seasonal affective disorder (SAD) and aromatherapy. Masseurs and chiropractors claim that some of their treatments can improve mental health. There are group therapies sharing experiences with other people and traditional psychiatric medicine with its focus on pharmaceutical drugs.

This isn't meant to suggest that all therapies are equal or even comparable. They are not. The list simply gives a relatively rough and random view of the landscape.

So how do we choose a therapist? There are several factors to consider before making a decision.

Finding the Right Therapist

There are four key factors that we need to consider when making our choice.

- **Evidence.** What is the evidence that the therapist has the necessary skills to help us to change? Are there independent recommendations to tell us that their work is good? Are they highly regarded by medics or other practitioners? How well or badly are they rated on review websites?
- **Expertise.** Not all qualifications are equal. It is possible with a small amount of money to buy mediocre courses and certificates from the internet. Some practitioners are enormously well qualified. Others are not. It is worth checking the level of the therapist's qualifications. Do they have a university degree, a master's degree, or even a doctorate?
- **Experience.** It is very important that whoever we work with has experience of supporting people like us. Many therapists have very little knowledge or awareness of childhood trauma and of the challenges that we faced being brought up in dysfunctional families.
- **Effective oversight.** Good therapists will belong to some sort of governing body. This helps to ensure that their practice is ethical. It also means that they are supervised and have to keep their training up to date.

Why the relationship matters

> *In my early professional years, I was asking the question: How can I treat, or cure, or change this person? Now I would phrase the question in this way: How can I provide a relationship which this person may use for his own personal growth?*
>
> —Carl R. Rogers, one of the pioneers of psychotherapy

Our relationship with our therapist is crucial to the success of our therapy. In the book *Psychotherapy: A Very Short Introduction,* Oxford University's

Chair of Social Psychiatry and psychotherapist Eva Burns-Lundgren states, "...virtually all psychotherapists now recognize that the quality of the relationship matters in its own right as a major part of the cure."

It is, therefore, worth spending a considerable amount of time finding the right therapist for us before we commit to working with them.

How to find the right relationship

It is a good idea to have our first meeting with a therapist before deciding whether or not we want to work with them. There are a series of questions that we can ask ourselves to see if we are likely to have a healthy, healing relationship.

- How much experience do they have of treating clients from dysfunctional families?
- Do they offer a range of different approaches? If so, are they able to suggest which ones will work best for us and explain why?
- Is the therapist a good listener?
- Are we able to agree on a goal for our therapy?

How to avoid the wrong relationship

There are some red flags to look out for. Warning signs include:

- Feeling that the therapist has an agenda of their own.
- Making us feel worse.
- Making us feel ashamed.
- Making us feel judged.
- Talking too much about themselves.
- Talking about other clients.

Attitude

"Do not adjust your mind, the fault is in reality," stated psychiatrist R.D. Laing. Clearly though, we do want to change the way we think. We want to process our emotions. We want to understand. We want to change. We want to succeed. That said, it is a right and proper part of the healing process to acknowledge that our childhoods were difficult and unfair and that this is not our fault.

R.D. Laing was right. There is a fault in reality. The best therapists will recognize and appreciate this. We need a therapist who is "on our side." It is essential for our therapist to understand our unique experiences. They can then provide more personalized advice and tailored guidance that is most appropriate for us.

Carl Rogers believed that there were three essential elements of a successful therapy relationship. The therapist's attitude toward us should include:

- **Unconditional positive regard:** an unshakable conviction that as clients, we are worthy of respect, no matter what has happened in our lives or how we feel about ourselves.
- **Empathy** is essential so that the therapist can understand our point of view and appreciate our feelings.
- **Congruence** means that the therapist should be genuine. They should express their thoughts and feelings in an open, honest way. Prominent psychiatrist and psychotherapist Irvin D. Yalom (known for his contributions to group therapy and his work on existential psychotherapy) also emphasized the need for genuineness. In his book *The Theory and Practice of Group Psychotherapy*, Dr. Yalom highlighted the importance of genuineness, believing that the therapist's ability to be authentic and genuine is crucial to create a safe and supportive space for us as clients.

A safe and comfortable environment will help to ensure that we progress more quickly. A therapist who has a positive outlook and is open to new ideas can help us to create a positive mindset. This leads to productive conversations and breakthroughs. Ultimately, a therapist's attitude plays a key role in creating a successful psychotherapy experience.

14

Types of Therapy

We are all different. There is no one "right" therapy that will work for all of us and what works at one stage in our life won't necessarily work in another. How effective a therapy is for us as individuals depends on several factors. Personal preference is key. We can experiment and try different approaches until we find a way forward that is helpful for us.

SELF-REPARENTING AND INNER CHILD WORK

Self-reparenting

There are many popular quotes in online forums and Facebook groups which all express the same idea. This is, that we didn't realize as a child that the person who came to rescue us would, in fact, be us as an adult.

In 1974, in her paper *Self-Parenting: Theory and Process*, psychologist Muriel James introduced the idea that if our own parenting had been inadequate, we could "reparent" ourselves to some degree in later life.

Her work was partly based on the theories of another psychologist, Eric Berne, who suggested that we usually behave in a way that is guided by three ego states. These are described in his theories of transactional analysis.

Transactional analysis is a psychological theory of personality and a form of therapy. It describes ego states as habitual patterns of thinking, feeling, and behaving. These all develop in response to our experiences with other people. There are three ego states in transactional analysis: the child ego state, the adult ego state, and the parental ego state.

Child ego state

This is the part of us that thinks, feels, and behaves like a child. At one time when we were growing up it was a real boy or girl. Although we age physically and mentally, our inner child stays locked deep within us. It is built from memories and experiences from our upbringing. It is characterized by emotions such as joy, sadness, anger, and fear. The child ego state can be either adaptive or maladaptive. Examples of the kind of statements we are likely to say while acting from our child ego state include:

- "I hate you! You're so mean!" (Said in response to feeling hurt or angry).
- "I'm bored. There's nothing to do." (Said when feeling restless or disinterested).
- "I want a candy bar! Can we please get one?" (Said when feeling impulsive or wanting immediate gratification).

Adult ego state

Our adult ego state thinks, feels, and behaves like an objective, rational adult. It helps us to process information and make decisions based on reality and reason, rather than emotions or childhood experiences. In similar situations to the above, statements expressed from an adult ego state may include:

- "I understand that we may have different opinions and feelings about the situation, but I would appreciate it if we could approach this in a more respectful and constructive manner."
- "I'm feeling a bit restless and unproductive. Maybe I should find a new project or activity to focus on."
- "I'm craving something sweet, but I know that I should make a healthier choice instead."

Parental ego state

When our mind behaves like a parent or caregiver, we are acting from our parental ego state. It is constructed from the beliefs, attitudes, and behaviors that are based on the values and expectations that were taught to us by our own parents or authority figures. The parental ego state can be either nurturing or critical, helpful or unhelpful. From a critical parental ego state the above examples could be expressed as:

- "I cannot believe you would say something so hurtful. You need to apologize and show some respect."
- "You should find something productive to do instead of complaining. There are plenty of things you could be working on right now."
- "You can't always get what you want, especially when it's not good for you."

We can switch between ego states depending on the situation that we are in. Without necessarily realizing what we are doing, we might act from a child ego state when we are talking with someone senior at work or an authority figure. If we find ourselves becoming judgmental, we are likely to be thinking and acting from our critical parental ego state.

In her book *It's Never Too Late to Be Happy! Reparenting Yourself for Happiness*, lecturer, consultant, and therapist Muriel James states that self-parenting is a theory and procedure for changing the parental ego state.

When we were raised by toxic parents or in a dysfunctional family, our parental ego state is likely to be dominated by unhealthy and unhelpful beliefs and ideas. By using exercises—for example writing out and identifying the characteristics of our parents—we can discover the effects they have on our lives. Ultimately her work helps us to create a new gentle and loving parent within ourselves.

Key concepts of self-parenting include:

- **Self-nurturing.** We learn to give ourselves the kind of emotional support and care that we would give to a child or someone we love deeply. It includes taking care of our physical needs, setting healthy boundaries, and being kind and compassionate with ourselves.
- **Self-discipline.** Self-parenting also necessitates learning to hold ourselves accountable for our actions. This means taking responsibility for our mistakes and committing to making changes when necessary. Muriel James writes about the need for some of us to reparent ourselves with a "firm parent" who can "coach us to set limits and use more self control."
- **Self-awareness.** Self-parenting means developing a strong sense of self-awareness. We can learn to understand our emotional needs and triggers.
- **Self-validation.** As part of self-parenting, we learn to validate our own emotions and experiences. We accept and acknowledge our feelings.

- **Self-soothing.** Finally, self-parenting involves learning to soothe ourselves when we are feeling anxious, overwhelmed, or distressed. This involves practicing relaxation techniques, engaging in self-care and seeking support from others.

Inner child work

John Bradshaw's book *Home Coming: Reclaiming and Championing Your Inner Child* is a seminal work in the field of psychology that examines how understanding our inner child helps us to heal. It explores the concept of the inner child and how it relates to recovery and personal growth. Bradshaw believes that the inner child represents our core emotional self. Many of our emotional wounds and negative patterns of behavior are rooted in unresolved childhood traumas. He argues that by connecting with our wounded inner child, we discover a wealth of hidden emotions and healing potential. By reclaiming our lost or forgotten childhood experiences, feelings, and relationships we develop deeper insights into our adult selves.

The concepts introduced by John Bradshaw relate to Muriel James's theory of "ego state therapy" which also focuses on helping people access their inner child so they can come to terms with past traumas and create a healthier, happier life for themselves. Both Bradshaw's and James's work place empathic and compassionate understanding at the center of their approaches to help us heal.

We can use the following approaches to inner child work on our journey to better health.

- **Learn to listen to our inner child.** We can pay attention to our emotions and inner voice and learn to communicate with our inner child in a kind and compassionate way.
- **Practice self-care.** Taking care of ourselves physically and emotionally by prioritizing our own needs and well-being is crucial both to inner child work and most other therapies.
- **Explore our family of origin.** Consider the impact of our childhood experiences and family dynamics on our emotional development, and work to heal any unresolved wounds. This is best achieved with a therapist.
- **Release repressed emotions.** We can use techniques including guided imagery, writing exercises, or group therapy to access and release repressed emotions and energy.

Safety

Above all, reparenting means ensuring that we are safe.

Many of us grew up in environments where we were not safe. Our inner child may feel vulnerable and scared.

To be safe, we need financial security, somewhere healthy to live, and supportive relationships.

Self-care

It isn't selfish to make self-care a priority. The more we look after ourselves, the more we will be able to give generously and warmly to other people. Self-care means learning to focus on our physical, mental, and spiritual needs. At its most basic level we can ensure that we are eating as healthy a diet as we can, exercising, and having whatever regular medical and dental check-ups and treatments we need. It also means getting enough sleep.

There are misconceptions about self-care, as well as traps that we can fall into. It basically means doing the best we possibly can in the circumstances where we are at the moment. It doesn't mean comparing ourselves to unachievable perfection. This is portrayed in magazines and media, whose goal is to increase our feelings of inadequacy to sell us products. It is compounded by social media and the false reality of other people's posts.

It is helpful to approach self-care from a compassionate perspective. If we currently do not look after ourselves well enough, this shouldn't be a source of shame, guilt, or self-loathing, but rather a positive realization that we deserve to look after ourselves and to make ourselves our top priority.

Self-care can also mean changing our environment. This may mean moving on from an unsatisfactory relationship or job, finding new friends, or moving somewhere new.

EYE MOVEMENT DESENSITIZATION AND REPROCESSING (EMDR)

Dr. Francine Shapiro, American psychologist and educator, had a fascinating experience, some aspects of which many of us will have shared. While strolling through the park she found that her mind overflowed with stressful thoughts and memories. This was distressing; however, something surprising and very positive happened to her next. Dr. Shapiro noticed that her eyes had started moving rapidly from one side to the other, and the more that this happened, the greater relief that she felt. Somehow eye movements were connected to processing trauma. This discovery became the starting point for developing a new therapy.

EMDR is an abbreviation for "eye movement desensitization and reprocessing."

There is controversy around how much research evidence supports the technique. It remains popular, however, and many people who have experienced trauma have found it effective.

Some of us who have used EMDR to heal childhood trauma warn that it is a difficult process and that it involves going deeply into previous suffering. It is, therefore, not recommended for the early stages of recovery. Choosing a therapist who we trust a great deal and are very comfortable with is essential.

The therapy uses left-to-right eye movements, and it has been suggested that these rhythmical movements reduce the brain's fear response. They are also believed to replicate systems in the brain that allow memories to be processed. It has been described as "rewiring" the brain so that when we have a traumatic memory it creates a new neural pathway from that memory to a safer place.

EMDR is a way to process traumatic memories. This is best illustrated with an example.

If we have a distressing memory of being physically hit when we were younger, then we will be asked what beliefs this is associated with now. Often, we will feel worthless. In EMDR therapy the therapist will ask us to formulate a positive belief about ourselves, for example that we are worthy of love and respect, while asking us to watch their finger move from side to side. They then ask us how we feel about the memory and continue this process until it is no longer upsetting.

This technique can appear strange, but is very popular and seems to be effective for those of us who have tried it.

Internal Family Systems (IFS)

"Effective and weird." Many of us share the same experience of IFS therapy. It is strange but appears to work.

IFS therapy is unique. It's an innovative form of psychotherapy that is unconventional and often feels "wacky." There are several reasons why we perceive IFS as being unusual:

- **The concept of "parts."** One of the central beliefs in IFS therapy is the

idea that individuals have "internal parts." These sub-personalities have their own thoughts, emotions, and behaviors. This is very different from traditional forms of therapy, which view us as having one single, unified sense of self.
- **Working with the imagination.** Using our imagination, IFS therapy involves visualizing and working with our internal parts. This feels strange or unfamiliar to begin with, especially if we are more used to traditional "talking" therapies.
- **Emphasis on self-compassion.** IFS therapy places a strong emphasis on developing self-compassion and understanding. This contrasts with traditional forms of therapy that focus on problem-solving and behavior change.

How IFS works

IFS was developed by psychologist Richard Schwartz in the 1980s. In 2000, he established the Center for Self Leadership as the IFS's training organization. He has also popularized the concept through his books, including *No Bad Parts: Healing Trauma and Restoring Wholeness with the Internal Family Systems Model.*

Instead of viewing our mind from an external, collective perspective, IFS takes a holistic view. It suggests our internal "parts" or sub-personalities often have conflicting needs and desires. This can cause mental health issues if left unresolved. By engaging in IFS therapy, we learn to recognize and communicate with these parts. This gives us insight into the root of our problems. We can then develop strategies for resolving them.

When we attend IFS sessions, we work with our therapist to explore our internal parts. These include "protectors" (parts of ourselves that work to keep us safe, but may also cause harm), "exiles" (parts of ourselves that have been hurt or traumatized), and a central "self" that serves as a compassionate and wise guide. The goal of therapy is to help us integrate these parts into a cohesive and functional whole. Perhaps a simple way to understand this is to picture different parts of our mind having different objectives. Although they are trying to help us, they don't always work well together. IFS helps to create a much better functioning team.

Advantages and disadvantages of IFS therapy

As with any therapy or healing system, IFS has both advantages and disadvantages. Some of the positive elements of IFS include:

- **Healing from past trauma.** IFS therapy can provide a safe and structured environment for us to process and heal from past trauma. By working with our sub-personalities and developing a compassionate relationship with the self, we can make sense of our past experiences.
- **Development of self-compassion.** Frequently our childhood has left us with internalized messages of self-blame, shame, and criticism. IFS therapy helps us to build a more accepting relationship with ourselves. It promotes self-compassion and a sense of worthiness.
- **Clarity from confusion.** The internal "parts" that we developed in response to childhood trauma or abuse can feel overwhelming and confusing. Through IFS therapy, we can learn to identify and work with these parts in a way that promotes greater understanding and integration.
- **Enhanced self-awareness.** IFS therapy places a strong emphasis on developing self-awareness and mindfulness. This is particularly helpful if we have learned to disconnect from our emotions or physical sensations as a coping mechanism.
- **Increased resilience.** Sometimes we may struggle with feelings of powerlessness and helplessness. Through working with internal parts, we can create a greater sense of control.

IFS therapy may have some limitations, depending on our needs and circumstances. Here are a few potential disadvantages to consider:

- **The wrong fit.** IFS may not be right for us. While IFS therapy can be highly effective for many people, it might not work for us as individuals. The concept of "parts" can be confusing or unhelpful. We may prefer a more traditional, structured, or directive approach to therapy.
- **It can be time-consuming.** Working with internal parts in IFS therapy can be a complex and time-consuming process. We will need to invest significant time and energy in the therapy process to succeed in our healing.
- **Lack of experienced and qualified therapists.** Because IFS therapy is a specialized form of treatment, in some countries it may be difficult to find a therapist trained in IFS.
- **Emotional demands.** Perhaps we just aren't ready for this type of therapy yet. The process of working through past trauma or difficult emotions in IFS therapy can be emotionally challenging. We need to be prepared to confront difficult emotions and experiences as part of the process.

GROUP WORK

Group therapy provides us with additional benefits above and beyond individual counseling. There are some fantastic counselors for one-to-one work; however, being part of a group of our peers helps us to:

- **Feel less isolated and more validated.** When we hear other people's experiences it becomes much clearer that we are not alone.
- **Enjoy greater support.** Groups act like a supportive team and the more people that we have "on our side," the better.
- **Learn from the wisdom of the crowd.** The most insightful and helpful individual therapists are relying on their own experience and expertise within a counseling session. They will receive supervision so they can check and take advice on their relationship with us, but this takes place when we are not there. With group therapy, there are several other people who also had difficult and distressing childhoods available to talk through what has happened and is happening to us.
- **Identify commonalities.** In group work it soon becomes apparent that many of us blame ourselves for what happened to us. Being part of the group helps us to realize that many of these ways of thinking are not natural. They were inflicted on us as a way to make us more controllable.
- **Feel normal.** Any sort of abuse is abnormal and wrong. We have done nothing wrong, and we are normal and right.
- **Increase our self-acceptance.** Group work makes us more aware of the context in which we grew up. It helps us to accept that there was nothing that we could have done about the distress and dysfunction in our environment. In turn, we can learn to see ourselves as innocent rather than blameworthy.
- **We develop a language of recovery.** Distressing and dysfunctional families manipulate and prevent children from talking about their abuse. This means that as adults, we do not have the words to describe our past and our feelings now. By being part of the group and listening to what other participants say we can learn to express ourselves more deeply.

There are limitations to group work:

- In group work, support needs to be spread among all the group's members, compared with the more in-depth and focused attention we receive during individual one-to-one work with a counselor.

- Sometimes the group's rules may prevent us from fully exploring issues. For example, one possible scenario is that we might find it helpful to describe our trauma in detail; however, we are not allowed to do this in case it triggers other people.

Depending on our time and resources it might not actually be necessary to choose between group or individual therapy. Perhaps we can combine the two and this will progress our recovery more quickly.

Narrative Therapy

The fascinating book *The Stories We Live By: Personal Myths and the Making of the Self* by Dan P. McAdams, PhD, (Professor of Human Development and Social Policy and Professor of Psychology at Northwestern University) contains many insights. Dr. McAdams suggests that we all create personal myths: stories that we tell ourselves about ourselves.

Being raised by toxic parents or in a dysfunctional environment often robbed us of our sense of identity. We had other people's views of the world imposed on us. Their priority was to meet their own interests. Constant criticism from emotional abusers would have prevented us from having a balanced view of reality. We would have accepted their version of us and concluded that we were bad people. Those of us who were physically abused may well have grown to believe that we deserved to be hit. If we were sexually abused, deep down we may have concluded that even our own bodies existed for the purpose of gratifying other people.

We had stories to tell; however, we did not write these stories ourselves. In these circumstances, narrative therapy can be a powerful tool for recovery. It helps us to write our own story, a story that gives us strength, dignity, self-worth, and optimism for our future.

As with all therapies, it is best undertaken by spending time with a skilled and qualified practitioner. However, there are elements of this approach that might prove useful on their own or as an addition to other therapies.

Developed during the 1970s and 1980s, by Australian social worker Michael White and psychotherapist David Epston of New Zealand, narrative therapy has several attractive underlying ideas, tools, and techniques.

- Writing our own story ensures that we can be fully clear that the abuse

was something that happened to us and is in no way our fault. It therefore helps us to rid ourselves of shame and guilt that rightfully belong to someone else.
- We can also begin to destroy any self-blame that haunts us.
- It can be helpful to accept and truly see that, as children, we were powerless. By acknowledging our helplessness when we were young, we can begin to see ourselves as powerful adults.
- All good stories have a beginning, a middle and an end. We can start to write our difficult traumatic childhood as the beginning. We can start to leave it in the past. We can see the healing work that we're doing now as the middle of the story. Finally, we can project and build a positive, happy, and healthy future for ourselves as the end of our story.
- Challenging though it may prove to be initially, we can eventually write ourselves as heroes rather than victims.

There are three main steps to writing our own story.

1. First, we write our story exactly as it is usually written in our own head. We don't try to edit or interpret it; we simply tell it as it is. Of course, how it is isn't necessarily reality. It is simply a story that we have told ourselves about ourselves so many times that we have come to accept it as true. It is worth ensuring that we have some sort of emotional support system in place before we tell our story, as seeing it in writing can trigger challenging emotions.
2. Next, we rewrite our story from the perspective of a wise, compassionate, and educated friend. It is important to do this as diligently as possible. It might sound strange; however, it is useful to imagine that we're not us anymore. For the purpose of the exercise, we temporarily believe that we are that kind and compassionate friend. We should not hesitate to challenge negative descriptions of ourselves in our first story. We tackle assumptions and ideas where we blame ourselves with all the vigor of a skilled attorney or lawyer.
3. The most empowering and hopeful part of our stories is yet to be written. In this exercise, we imagine and outline future chapters where we take decisive, healing steps toward crafting a life filled with joy, purpose, and fulfillment. Through this creative process, we envision and actively shape an optimistic future for ourselves. In doing so, we lay a strong foundation for a life story where resilience, growth, and happiness take center stage.

This gives us the exhilarating opportunity to script a future where we are not just survivors, but thriving, content individuals.

There are some important points to consider.

The journey from victim to hero does not mean in any way denying or minimizing the abuse that we suffered. Quite the contrary. In films, literature, and TV, heroes have always overcome some great adversity to seize the prize. The greater the challenges were, the more heroic the hero or heroine was to succeed. We can rewrite our story as many times as we want to. No author ever wrote a brilliant novel at the first attempt. Most stories are recrafted again and again until they come close to where the novelist wants them to be.

It may feel awkward and difficult changing our initial story. This is to be expected. We have grown to believe that our story is true and, in some ways, it may well have been helpful to us. However, if we can change the narrative to one that is helpful and supportive to us, full of compassion and wisdom, this will be tremendously beneficial in moving forward.

Finally, of course, we should keep our story somewhere safe. We have the right to be proud of our heroism and to be optimistic about our futures; however, it is good to ensure that we share our stories with the people that we want to share them with, when we want to share them, rather than having others discover them by accident.

All of our stories will be different; however, there may be some more frequent themes on our journeys from victims to heroes (summarized in the table opposite).

Using externalization in narrative therapy

A further helpful technique from narrative therapy is known as externalization.

Wise words from narrative therapy are that *we* are not the problem. The *problem* is the problem.

By externalizing our difficulties, rather than making them part of us, they can be dealt with more easily. This can be a tricky concept to understand. It is best illustrated by an example.

Rather than stating that we are "an anxious person," we can tell ourselves that we have difficulties with anxiety. This means that we do not identify with anxiety. We do not make it a core part of our personality. Instead, we look at anxiety as being a problem that is external to us.

Similarly, we can view ourselves as having problems with low self-esteem,

Victim	Progress Stage	Hero
Lives a life of endless problems and difficulties	More self-aware; understanding motivations and patterns of behavior and repetition compulsion	Successfully controlling own destiny with new insight and a range of knowledge, tools, and skills
A people-pleaser who puts everyone else's needs first	Able to draw and stay within clear boundaries	Happy to place own needs first, while, on occasion, choosing to put other people's needs first when appropriate, e.g., own child's needs
Self-medicates with drugs, alcohol, or destructive behaviors	Can tolerate emotional pain	Has a new understanding of emotional pain and inner world, and can use insights and learning for a better future
Feels overwhelming guilt and shame	Able to place blame where it belongs: with toxic parents or traumatic childhood	Feels pride
Denies and hides their past	Feels OK to share personal history with others, if chooses to do so	Accepts the past can't be changed and has written their own liberating story

as against stating that we have low self-esteem. There is a subtle difference. Having low self-esteem makes it more of a permanent and fixed part of "us," whereas having problems with low self-esteem changes it into a behavior and keeps it a distance away. Low self-esteem then becomes something that we are able to manage and change, rather than being an unchangeable characteristic of who we are.

The practical way to externalize problems is to change the language that we use. We can say "the anger problem" rather than "I am an angry person." Sometimes it is helpful to describe the problem as "it." This means that as an alternative to stating "I am an angry person when I am tired," we say "it" bothers me most when I am tired. This makes a problem into a behavior that can be tackled rather than a way of being.

Cognitive Behavioral Therapy (CBT)

CBT is an enormously popular treatment worldwide. It was developed in the 1960s by Dr. Aaron T. Beck, an American psychiatrist and professor at the University of Pennsylvania. He noticed that his patients had negative automatic thought patterns that affected their mood and behavior. Dr. Beck developed a range of techniques to help his patients think in a more helpful way.

CBT has been extensively researched and appears to be effective for a wide range of mental health issues. These include depression, anxiety disorders, and CPTSD.

The theory behind CBT is that our thoughts, emotions, and behaviors are all interconnected. They work together. CBT proposes that unhelpful thoughts and beliefs contribute to emotional distress and problematic behaviors. By changing our thought patterns, we can improve our emotional health.

The ABC model is a key concept in CBT. It describes the sequence from an event that happens to us, how we interpret this, and the consequences of our interpretation as follows:

- A: Activating event or situation.
- B: Beliefs or thoughts about the event/situation.
- C: Consequences or emotional and behavioral responses.

A simple example of this model is:

- Activating event: A close friend cancels plans for a night out.
- Belief: My friend doesn't value our friendship anymore and prefers to spend time with other people.
- Consequence: We feel upset and withdraw from our friendship.

CBT emphasizes that it isn't the event itself that is the problem. Our belief that we are no longer valued causes our distress. We then make the situation worse by avoiding our friend. CBT therapists, among other techniques, train us to add an extra step to the ABC model:

- D: Disputing. Our therapist helps us to challenge the belief by asking questions: "Could there be other reasons why your friend canceled?" or "Have there been other times when your friend has shown that they value your friendship?" This helps us to see the situation objectively. By identifying and challenging negative automatic thoughts and beliefs, and replacing them with more realistic and helpful ones, we can improve our mental health.

One of the advantages of CBT is that it is a structured and goal-oriented therapy. We work collaboratively with our therapist to set specific treatment goals and develop a treatment plan to achieve those goals. This may involve completing assignments, such as keeping a thought diary, to help identify patterns in our thinking. Our therapist may also use techniques including cognitive restructuring, behavioral experiments, and exposure therapy.

Techniques from CBT that can be particularly helpful include:

- **Cognitive restructuring.** This means identifying and challenging negative thought patterns that can lead to emotional distress. We may have developed negative beliefs about ourselves or the world around us, such as "I'm worthless," or "The world is a dangerous place." Through cognitive restructuring, we can learn to recognize these negative thoughts and replace them with positive and realistic ones.
- **Exposure therapy.** Exposure therapy involves gradually exposing ourselves to situations or stimuli that trigger anxiety or distress. This takes place in a safe and controlled environment. It may involve revisiting past memories or situations that are associated with the trauma, with the guidance and support of a therapist. It can help us to confront and process our traumatic experiences, and reduce the emotional distress associated with them.
- **Mindfulness.** Put simply, mindfulness means bringing our attention to the present moment, without judgment or distraction. Mindfulness can be a useful tool for managing overwhelming emotions and reducing stress. Mindfulness techniques, such as deep breathing or body scan exercises, help us to stay grounded in the present, rather than being captured by past memories or future worries.
- **Behavioral activation.** This means finding ways to enjoy ourselves, even when we are in difficult circumstances. Behavioral activation can be an effective way to improve mood and increase feelings of self-worth. By setting small, achievable goals and rewarding ourselves for accomplishing them, we build confidence and resilience.

- **Graded task assignments.** Graded task assignments involve breaking down larger tasks into smaller, more manageable steps, then gradually building up to more challenging tasks over time. Graded task assignments help to overcome feelings of being overwhelmed. They create and build a sense of mastery. By starting with smaller, more manageable tasks and gradually working up to larger ones, we feel a sense of accomplishment. This is an important part of the healing process.

There are some disadvantages to CBT. One of the criticisms of it is that it is a relatively brief and structured therapy. It may not provide enough time and space to fully process and work through our traumatic experiences. CBT focuses on the present moment and helping us to identify and change unhelpful patterns of thinking and behavior. This approach may not adequately address the underlying emotional and psychological wounds that resulted from our dysfunctional childhood.

CBT requires a high degree of collaboration and engagement with a therapist. This is challenging if we have difficulty trusting others and forming healthy relationships. It may be more effective to work with a therapist who specializes in trauma-informed care, which emphasizes safety, trust, and empowerment.

There are many psychologists and trauma survivors who believe that it isn't possible to out-think trauma, as it is stored in our body. CBT may, therefore, not be fully effective on its own. They believe that movement-based therapies are most effective in tackling trauma (See Chapter 16: Whole Body Healing).

Dialectical Behavior Therapy

Dialectical behavior therapy, often referred to as DBT, is a type of CBT that was initially developed to treat people with borderline personality disorder. It is now also used for a range of other issues, including problems with dissociation. The "dialectical" part of DBT refers to balancing opposing forces, such as acceptance and change.

DBT borrows ideas from ancient Buddhism. These are combined with modern skills and tools from CBT. It emphasizes development in four key areas: mindfulness, relationships, emotional processing, and resilience.

For us, as survivors of childhood trauma who may struggle with dissociation, DBT can be particularly beneficial. The mindfulness skills help us stay present in the moment, which is a direct counter to dissociation. It helps us to learn to tolerate distress, manage our emotions, and improve our relationships.

DBT doesn't just focus on the problems we are currently facing, but also aims to build a life that we find fulfilling and meaningful. It equips us with practical skills and strategies that we can use in our daily lives, contributing to a greater sense of control and personal agency.

15

Additional Means of Support

COACHING

Coaching and life coaching have become increasingly popular in recent years. Many of us will have used or considered using the services of a life coach to help us to reach our goals. They can help us to make the most of our strengths, overcome obstacles that are holding us back, and support us in improving our relationships, careers, health, and happiness.

Coaches work differently from therapists and it is sensible to consider using them either alongside counseling or psychotherapy or after we have finished seeing a counselor or psychotherapist. It is helpful to be aware of the differences between coaching and psychotherapy.

Life coaches:
- Do not treat mental health problems.
- Are often unregulated.
- May have a range of qualifications from simple certificates to master's degrees. It is less likely, but possible, for some coaches to hold a doctorate in coaching.
- Usually behave ethically.
- Are likely to focus on measurable results.
- Generally, do not need a license to work.

Psychotherapists and counselors:
- Treat mental health conditions.
- Are usually highly regulated.

- Can have basic qualifications, but tend to have higher qualifications: a degree, a master's degree, or sometimes a doctorate.
- Have strict ethical codes.
- Are less likely to focus on measurable results.
- Must have a license to work in many countries.

Regulations vary in different countries and there are often exceptions to the general rules. It is, therefore, best to thoroughly investigate how well qualified and experienced the people that we consider working with are. It is good to check what codes of conduct they adhere to, and which professional bodies they belong to. Most importantly, we need to know how much expertise they have in working with people like us.

How we might benefit from life coaching

Life coaches can help us to see things from a new perspective. They are particularly good at keeping us motivated and working toward measurable goals. Coaches support us where we want to improve our lives and help us to have, for example:

- Stronger relationships.
- A better work–life balance.
- Financial security.
- More creativity.
- A more rewarding career.

Some of these examples demonstrate other areas where the work of a life coach is different from that of a psychotherapist. We might gain promotion at work if our self-confidence and self-efficacy improves after having seen a psychotherapist; however, this is usually more of a secondary benefit rather than a deliberate plan.

How to choose a life coach

Erik de Haan (Director of the Ashridge Center for Coaching at Hult International Business School) suggested that the greatest factor affecting how successful coaching would be was how good the relationship between the coach and the client was. It is therefore essential that we find the right coach for us.

We are more likely to succeed when we choose a life coach who understands people like us. Trauma-informed life coaches should have a greater appreciation of our background and be able to work with us most effectively.

To find the right coach it is worth checking a few out. We can have an initial session (virtually or in person) with several potential coaches to get a feel about who is likely to be able to help us most.

After an initial session we can ask ourselves questions if we want to be clearer about who will be best. Questions include: did they seem open, reliable, honest, and trustworthy? Did they focus on us and our goals?

AI Chatbots, Supportive Social Media, Self-Help Books, and Journaling

The possibilities for future advancements are endless. Outside traditional one-to-one human therapy, there is a growing worldwide business to improve our well-being provided by artificial intelligence (AI) and chatbots.

We can also connect with healing communities and online support groups 24/7, any and every day of the year.

For decades we have been offered information and advice from a multibillion-dollar self-help book industry.

All of the resources create both opportunities and risks. Used wisely, however, they can all be valuable guides on our journey.

AI chatbots

Artificial intelligence is usually presented in two forms:

- There is an increasing number of mobile phone apps that can be extremely helpful. They variously describe themselves as offering mental health support, being self-care experts, therapy assistants, and being able to guide us through stress, anxiety, anger, shyness, self-esteem, and more. At the time of publication, these included Wysa, Woebot, Limbic, and Rise Up. Undoubtedly many more are on their way.
- Desktop chatbots including ChatGPT can give us information and insights. ChatGPT is, however, clear that it isn't a licensed therapist or mental health professional and shouldn't be seen as a substitute for professional therapy or medical advice.

AI chatbots offer accessibility, affordability, and personalized feedback.

They can be accessed anywhere, at any time. AI chatbots have the potential to provide even more personalized support as technology advances. Proponents argue that these technologies create an anonymous, low-pressure space to discuss topics that we find difficult. Anonymity ensures that we do not fear judgment or stigma from in-person counseling sessions. Many chatbot programs are designed to provide comforting conversation companions. This may help reduce feelings of loneliness and isolation. AI-driven conversations can also increase our access to mental health support when we live in remote areas where professional resources may not be available.

Each chatbot is constantly developing and improving. It is impossible to give specific guidance and each one has its own terms and conditions that we need to check and evaluate ourselves. At the time of going to print:

- Most appear to be based around a cognitive behavioral therapy (CBT) model.
- Dialogue between a client and therapist is highly nuanced and complex. AI-driven conversations may struggle to recognize subtle emotional cues or respond in an emotionally attuned way.
- Those of us who are survivors of trauma and abuse may have difficulty forming trusting relationships. When conversations are with a robot instead of a professional counselor, this means that they may not be effective.

Supportive social media

Online forums on social media provide us with a sense of community and connection. This can be difficult to find elsewhere. Peer support can be validating and empowering. Online forums can make it easier for us to share our experiences and feelings and we can usually choose to be anonymous. Online support groups are often available 24/7. They can be accessed from anywhere with a good internet connection.

There are some risks:

- **Misinformation.** Some may provide inaccurate or potentially harmful advice or information.
- **Cyberbullying and harassment.** Potentially we might experience cyberbullying, harassment, or trolling from other users who do not share our beliefs or opinions.
- **Dependence and addiction.** It is important to be mindful of the potential for dependence and addiction to social media or other online platforms.

This isn't necessarily a real addiction, just that we may find ourselves spending more time than we want to on the Internet.
- **Privacy.** There are concerns that our most private thoughts and emotions may be shared or used against us if the technology is abused.

Self-help books

Self-help books provide a self-directed approach to our recovery. They offer information, advice, exercises, and insights from other people's experiences. They can encourage self-reflection and help us to grow our self-awareness. They can provide a sense of empowerment and hope. By offering practical tools and strategies for healing, self-help books can help us to take control of our recovery journey and feel more optimistic about our future.

One disadvantage is that they are often very focused on one particular aspect of our personality and healing. For example, they promote the idea that self-confidence or self-esteem, or maybe grit and tenacity are the key to our recovery. The reality is that growth and change are complex and require a range of skills and techniques that can be applied to different aspects of our lives.

Journaling

> *Write what disturbs you, what you fear, what you have not been willing to speak about. Be willing to be split open.*
> —Natalie Goldberg

Long before journaling was invented as a therapeutic technique, writers expressed their innermost desires, fears, thoughts, and feelings on paper. The greatest works of literature, novels, poems, and plays would not exist if we weren't able to be in touch with our inner selves and share this through writing. Leading twentieth century novelist Graham Greene wrote in his second volume of autobiography, "Writing is a form of therapy; sometimes I wonder how all those who do not write, compose, or paint can manage to escape the madness, melancholia, the panic and fear which is inherent in a human situation."

Perhaps it was a natural progression to take something that was already being used informally as a therapy and expand it into a more formal healing approach. American psychotherapist Ira Progoff first developed journaling as a psychological tool for clients in New York in the 1960s.

Journaling can be a powerful tool in our recovery. It provides an opportunity to:

- **Express ourselves openly and honestly without concerns about what other people may think.** This is particularly helpful because often in our dysfunctional families we weren't allowed to communicate. The needs of our toxic parents took precedence. So as adults, it is important to build our own identity.
- **Share our thoughts and feelings more accurately if we are working with a therapist.**
- **Validate our feelings.** The act of writing down emotions helps to make them solid and real.
- **Clarify and give structure to how we feel.** Even in the best of times our thoughts are a messy jumble, jumping up, down, and generally all over the place. Journaling helps us to straighten, sort, and store information.
- **Understand ourselves better.** The phrase "name it to tame it" expresses how accurately describing an emotion can help take away its power. For example, labeling a constant feeling of restlessness and irritability and wanting to explode as "anger," and identifying this as being rooted in our past, can help us to begin to deal with it.
- **Begin to describe the future.** We can start to use our creative imagination to build success on the road ahead.

Although journaling can be positive, there are nevertheless some inherent risks. These can be managed effectively if we know what they are in advance and act if we notice that problems are happening. One potential challenge is rumination, where we get stuck in a pattern of thinking distressing thoughts over and over again, and getting nowhere. Or perhaps our journal will connect us with deep emotions that we find too difficult to handle. Both these situations suggest that we would benefit from some professional help to support us on our journey.

Of course, there is one final step that is wise to take. It is sensible to ensure that anything we write is private, safe, and secure. This can be easily achieved on our laptop or computer by downloading software that creates high-security password-protected files that only we have access to. Alternatively, we can use similar secure online storage systems.

If we prefer to use pen and paper, we need a lockable space to keep our journal. There is some online advice that recommends writing our contact details alongside a notice on the first page instructing anybody who finds the journal not to read it. Unfortunately, this almost guarantees to spark the curiosity of any casual stranger who might stumble across our journal if it has accidentally been left on the train, in a taxi, or at our favorite café. Perhaps the best advice is to restrict our journal writing to when we are at home. We can then choose a time when we will not be disturbed and the journal will not be lost.

16

Whole Body Healing

MEMORY MACHINES: HOW OUR BODIES STORE TRAUMA

In her best-selling book *Why Has Nobody Told Me This Before?*, Dr. Julie Smith suggests that "everything we think and feel happens within the body."

Our everyday language shows that we have never lost an understanding of how our bodies and minds are connected. We describe trembling with fear, having butterflies in our stomachs, and our hearts missing a beat.

There is a thorough account of how we store trauma within our bodies in the widely acclaimed book *The Body Keeps the Score* by psychiatrist Bessel van der Kolk.

Healing is not confined to the realm of thoughts and emotions. To truly heal, we must engage our whole being—mind, body, and spirit. This chapter considers a holistic approach to our health and development.

We explore the transformative power of movement. We breathe life back into our bodies that have been stifled for far too long. We venture into yoga and tai chi to help us establish a deeper connection with ourselves. To find a sense of balance and inner peace.

We learn about empowerment through fighting techniques, boxing, kickboxing, and mixed martial arts. These physical disciplines provide an outlet for our emotions. They also help us reclaim our power, our boundaries, and our self-confidence.

We embrace the chill of cold water immersion and outdoor swimming. This reminds us of our resilience and capacity to endure, to feel alive amidst the icy embrace of nature. We learn to shake off the numbness, to feel again, to re-establish the connection with our bodies.

And then we step onto the stage of drama, theater, and therapy. We give ourselves the freedom to express, to be seen and to be heard. We can explore our stories, play out different roles, and step into the shoes of the person we aspire to be.

We move with the rhythm of life in dance. We shed pain and fear with each step, each twirl, each beat. As we dance, we are reminded of our inherent ability to find joy. To express. And to connect.

To begin, we look at the ultimate practice that engages our thoughts, feelings, and our body together: mindfulness.

Mindfulness in Daily Life

Mindfulness, in essence, is the practice of being fully present in the moment, intentionally and non-judgmentally. This means focusing on our thoughts, feelings, sensations, and the world around us, without getting caught up in them. It's about experiencing the world in real time, rather than being preoccupied with the past or future. With mindfulness, we learn to navigate our inner and outer experiences with greater calm, clarity, and acceptance, fostering a deeper connection with ourselves and our lives.

Mindfulness misinterpreted: a cautionary note

While mindfulness encourages us to be present and accepting of our circumstances, it's important to note that this practice is sometimes misused as a tool for complacency or ignorance. Mindfulness is not about dismissing the reality of suffering or injustice, nor is it about convincing ourselves that all problems reside solely within our minds. Instead, it's about acknowledging these challenges and understanding our reactions to them. It's about fostering resilience and clarity, not escaping responsibility.

Mindfulness is occasionally abused by persuading us to zone out rather than engage with the world. As progressive author and newspaper editor William Allen White (1868–1944) noted, "peace without justice is tyranny." In other words, ignoring the need for justice and focusing solely on internal peace can be a form of self-imposed tyranny.

Mindfulness, therefore, should empower us to be present, self-aware, and ready to contribute to a better world, rather than push us toward indifference or inaction.

Developing mindfulness

When we are being mindful, we focus on awareness of what we're feeling in the moment. We try not to interpret or judge this. We simply allow our thoughts "to be." They are not good, bad, right, or wrong; they simply are.

Here are some ways we can develop the skill of being mindful:

- **Practice mindful breathing.** This is one of the simplest forms of mindfulness meditation. It involves focusing on our breath, observing each inhalation and exhalation without trying to change them. It can be done anywhere, at any time.
- **Mindful eating.** Each taste, sight, aroma, and texture of our food matters. We totally immerse ourselves in the enjoyment and experience of our meal.
- **Mindful walking.** This involves focusing on the sensation of walking, feeling the ground beneath our feet, and noting the rhythm of our steps. It can be a great way to connect with our environment and the present moment.
- **Body scan meditation.** From our toes to our head, we observe all of our sensations. Pain. Tension. Warmth. Relaxation. We notice and feel everything.
- **Mindful listening.** When we fully focus on what is being said to us, rather than planning what we're going to say next, we are listening mindfully. This helps improve our relationships as other people feel valued and validated.

Like any other skill, mindfulness takes practice. We can start with a few minutes each day and gradually increase the time we spend. We can also use apps or guided meditations to help us stay focused.

THE POWER OF MOVEMENT: YOGA AND TAI CHI

Yoga

In the later stages of recovery, mindfulness and meditation can be helpful. However, early on when our experiences are locked into our bodies, then bodily healing including yoga may be more effective.

It is best to find a trauma-informed yoga practitioner. This is because if our yoga instructor is unaware of the risk inherent in treating trauma survivors, they might make our situation worse. For example, some yoga poses, in particular the happy baby pose, are known to be triggering for those of us who experienced sexual abuse. Additionally, it is easy to become triggered or simply feel extreme discomfort if a teacher touches us or moves our body without first asking our permission and explaining what is happening to us. Holding positions for a considerable amount of time can cause stress.

Trauma-informed yoga aims to increase our own body awareness, in a way that helps us to feel safe. It can also help with some of the symptoms of what is known as nervous system dysregulation. This is when our emotions are poorly regulated, and we may experience angry outbursts, anxiety, depression, and mood swings.

Yoga moves our bodies from a dysfunctional, dysregulated state to a more relaxed and healthy way of being.

Tai chi

Tai chi, often described as "meditation in motion," is a gentle approach to reconnecting with our bodies. It cultivates a sense of peace and stability. This ancient Chinese martial art is a series of slow, flowing movements paired with deep breathing. There is a helpful balance, both building strength and promoting relaxation.

For survivors of trauma, the practice of tai chi can be an invaluable tool. It allows us to regain control over our bodies. This feels empowering without being overpowering. Movements are designed to create physical and emotional balance, alleviating the symptoms of anxiety and depression that frequently accompany trauma.

When we start tai chi, it's important to find an instructor who understands trauma and its nuanced effects on the body and mind. A knowledgeable and empathic teacher will create a safe, supportive space where we can explore the practice at our own pace, without fear of judgement or further harm.

Tai chi can be adapted to meet our needs, whatever our level of physical fitness and mobility. The fluid, mindful movements of tai chi serve as a gentle reminder that healing is not a destination but a process, one that we can approach with patience, compassion, and a commitment to ourselves.

Fighting: Boxing, Kickboxing and Mixed Martial Arts

Fighting trauma becomes much more literal when we train in the martial arts. There are good reasons why this intense action can help us to heal.

- **Feelings of safety.** Many of us struggle with hypervigilance. We are constantly on the lookout for real and imagined threats. The world can be unsafe; however, we can worry too much about events that are unlikely to happen. Training in martial arts can help us to build confidence knowing that we have real skills to handle genuinely threatening situations.
- **Belonging.** Good sports clubs are supportive places to be. Members train together, bolster one another's confidence, and encourage each other.
- **Trust.** When we are sparring or learning new techniques with a partner, we need to trust one another to train responsibly within boundaries. This is especially helpful if we were brought up in a family where there were few or no boundaries and we could not trust our parents. Learning to trust is an essential part of our recovery.
- **Power.** Punching and kicking punch bags or other people in a safe and controlled way helps us to feel powerful. This in turn makes us feel strong and enhances our sense of control.
- **Achievement.** Learning any new skill makes us feel that we have achieved something. This increases our self-efficacy and self-belief.
- **Focus.** Especially when we were hit or sexually abused as children, we may have learned to dissociate. We mentally distanced ourselves from the world and so, as adults, we struggle to connect. Taking part in intense sparring sessions necessitates total concentration and focus. Over time, we gradually become more connected with the world around us.
- **Endorphins.** The feel-good chemicals released during vigorous exercise help to combat anxiety and depression.

How to choose somewhere to train

Starting any new activity involves risk. This needs to be a sensible and managed risk and above all we should put our own safety first.

Many gyms, dojos, and boxing and kickboxing clubs are friendly and welcoming places. Not all are though, so it is a good idea to try several different venues to get a feel of them. Most good places will give us a week or at least a day's free trial.

One way to judge whether a place is going to be helpful, and whether we are going to be happy there, is to look how much attention and support is given to us as new learners. There is a phenomenon within the martial arts world where some clubs exist to build the ego of the instructors or owners. We should run as far and as fast as we can away from places that exist only to inflate someone else's feelings of self-worth.

Other training places are only focused on elite or competition-winning practitioners. We may be among them one day; however, we do not want to experience a difficult and unpleasant time until we are considered to be one of the best.

Misogyny is a red flag. Not only is prejudice against women wrong in its own right, but it is also symptomatic of somewhere with backward attitudes and an outdated view of the world.

Freezing: Outdoor Swimming and Cold Water Immersion

> *No matter how cold it is, nor how grim the weather, simply anticipating that amazing feeling never fails to get me into the water in the dark depths of winter. No matter how bad I feel when I get in, I always feel better when I get out.*
>
> —Mark Harper MD PhD: *Chill: The Cold Water Swim Cure*

There is a strange paradox at the heart of modern life. Frequently we suffer from too little stress. This seems bizarre, especially when we are struggling with anxiety, depression, and many other difficult problems derived from our childhoods. The problem is that this is internally generated stress. It is real and can be tremendously unpleasant.

Our bodies were built to battle a tough environment. Evolution designed us to fight external threats more than internal stressors. Pictures in history books depict ancient tribes using spears to fight off saber-toothed tigers. There is archaeological evidence that these ferocious predators were a genuine threat to our ancestors. The environment itself was hostile, and primitive people had few resources to protect themselves. Today, there are central heating systems, air conditioning, and quality clothing to protect us from nature. We spend more time watching the weather than being exposed to it. Rain, snowstorms, and gales are more likely to be viewed from office windows, or from the comfort and safety of a taxi, train, or bus, rather than being felt or immediately experienced.

Swimming outdoors in the cold is becoming increasingly popular everywhere in the world where there is a suitable climate. Variously known as winter swimming or ice swimming, it is popular in North America, North and Western Europe, China, Russia, Eastern Europe, and Australia.

Cold water swimming is believed to reset our body's internal "stress clock." The shock to our physiology triggers a stress reaction. Over time, our body adapts and gradually becomes better at dealing with this stress. Although this is environmental stress caused by things outside us, the ability to regulate stress also helps with the type of stress that comes from within us. This means that by swimming outdoors in the cold we can become better at dealing with all sorts of stress, including the stress that has its origins in our childhood abuse.

Cold water swimming can have other positive effects on both physical and mental health. Internal inflammation, which contributes toward cancer, diabetes, and heart disease, is reduced. This means that our bodies are stronger and less vulnerable to illness. It is especially helpful if we were raised by neglectful or emotionally abusive parents to learn to truly value ourselves and look after our health. We deserve to be well.

The vagus nerve, which—among other functions—helps to slow down our heart rate, is stimulated by cold water adaptation. It begins to act more quickly which combats stress. The parasympathetic nervous system, the part that is responsible for keeping us calm, also learns to react more quickly to stress. This explains why we are likely to be less anxious when we swim regularly in cold water.

There are further benefits for our mental well-being if we join a community of outdoor swimmers. Camaraderie develops, everyone looks after each other, and there is a sense of purpose. Members battle and beat the elements together. We may be fortunate enough to have a network of people close to where we live. If not, there are some fantastic and supportive groups online.

The activity does have some risks in addition to its many benefits though. Before deciding it is right for us, it is worth reading up on what these risks are and taking sensible precautions.

Swimming won't be right for all of us, but we can still get the benefits that cold water offers. Icelandic extreme athlete Wim Hof includes having regular cold water showers as part of his "method." There is certainly some scientific evidence that cold water immersion, be it in showers or baths, produces health benefits, although they obviously lack the extra rewards of being outdoors in nature.

If the thought of chilly outdoor swims leaves us cold, then there are ways that we can fight against our childhood traumas from the relative safety and warmth of the indoors.

Drama, Theater and Therapy: How They Give Us Unique Tools for Insight and Recovery

> *Acting was my classroom in many ways and I always believed and I still do that acting is not just about pretending to be someone else, it's also about discovering yourself and reaching deeper inside yourself.*
>
> —Kristen Stewart

Drama: why acting has unique benefits

Most of the time we are "stuck" being us. And of course, there will only ever be one of us.

Drama helps us experience other ways of being. When we are acting, we embody and portray characters with different backgrounds, beliefs, and experiences. As we step into these roles, we can temporarily suspend our own identity. We can be someone else. Just for a short time we stop being us. We immerse ourselves in the life of the character we are playing. We can be a hero, villain, introvert, extrovert, famous historical or fictional character. The possibilities are almost endless. This creates a sense of liberation from our usual self. We can explore alternative ways of thinking, feeling, and behaving.

Acting not only allows us to experience the thoughts and feelings of the character we are playing, but it also gives us the opportunity to experience new and challenging situations.

For example, we might play the role of a police officer and experience the rush of adrenaline that comes with responding to a high-pressure situation. We could be a doctor and explore the challenges and emotional toll of delivering difficult news to a patient. Playing the role of a violent mobster creates the opportunity to explore the darker aspects of human nature and the consequences of criminal behavior.

Stepping outside of ourselves from time to time is very helpful because:

- We gain an insight into the thoughts and feelings of other people. By inhabiting a character's perspective, we develop a deeper understanding of their motivations, fears, and desires. This can help us empathize with and relate to others more effectively.
- The act of stepping outside ourselves and taking on different roles can widen our view of ourselves and our own potential. As award-winning actress Kristen Stewart states, "we are reaching deeper inside ourselves." By doing this, we recognize aspects of ourselves that we weren't previously aware of. We can explore different ways of being that we might not have otherwise considered. This is very valuable for our personal growth and self-discovery.

Being part of a drama group has a range of psychological and social benefits, including:

- **Improved self-confidence.** When we act, we are often outside our personal comfort zone. If the experience is new to us, then it takes courage to perform in front of other people. This gives us a greater sense of self-confidence and self-esteem, which seeps into other areas of our lives.
- **Enhanced communication skills.** Body language, the way we move, our tone of voice, and our facial expressions are all essential to acting. By developing these, we improve our communication skills. This helps us in our relationships, professional and social lives.
- **Improved creativity.** When we are developing a character, improvising a scene, or working with limited resources, acting requires us to be imaginative and think outside the box. This can help us to cultivate a creative and innovative mindset.
- **Greater social connection.** Being part of a drama group, class, or course provides a sense of belonging and community. We are surrounded by supportive people. Performances need collaboration and teamwork. And it's fun! This can help us to beat any feelings of isolation and loneliness that we all feel sometimes.
- **Stress relief.** Physical, mental, and emotional activities like acting can be a great way to relieve stress and help us to relax. Acting can provide a

much-needed outlet for our emotions and can help us to manage difficult emotions like anxiety or depression.

Drama: why acting has specific benefits for us

When we were raised in dysfunctional families or abused as children, acting may have definitive benefits for us. Here are some specific ways in which acting helps:

- **Emotional expression.** When we were taught to suppress or deny our emotions in an abusive family, it is most helpful to have a safe and supportive environment for us to express our emotions. By expressing our feelings through acting, we develop our self-awareness. We become better at experiencing, understanding, and communicating our emotions. This effectively promotes healing and growth.
- **Cognitive restructuring.** When we have experienced abuse or trauma, we often develop negative and distorted beliefs about ourselves and the world around us. Acting can help to challenge and reframe these beliefs. It provides a new perspective so that we can explore new ways of thinking and feeling.
- **Role-playing.** If we are stuck in a behavior pattern as a result of our past experiences, participating in drama groups can give us the opportunity to role-play and experiment with different behaviors.
- **Secure attachment.** Our early attachment experiences shape our ability to form healthy relationships later in life. Drama provides a new and positive attachment experience after we have experienced insecure or disorganized attachment in our past. Acting gives us the chance to form secure attachments in a safe and controlled environment. Through the process of acting and engaging in drama, we develop new relationships and connections that are rooted in trust, support, and collaboration. These experiences help to counteract the negative attachment patterns that we developed in early life. This can help us to develop greater emotional regulation. In turn this helps us to enjoy better interpersonal functioning, meaning of course that we can experience happier relationships, especially closer and more rewarding romantic relationships.

Drama therapy

Beyond the personal growth and development that we can create through drama, there are further gains that we can discover by undergoing drama therapy. In his comprehensive and insightful work, *Drama as Therapy Volume 1: Theory, Practice and Research,* Phil Jones emphasizes that drama therapy isn't simply psychotherapy with drama added on. He states, "The drama does not serve the therapy. The drama process contains the therapy."

The North American Drama Therapy Association describes drama therapy as "an active, experiential approach to facilitating change. Through storytelling, projective play, purposeful improvisation, and performance, participants are invited to rehearse desired behaviors, practice being in a relationship, expand and find flexibility between life roles, and perform the change they wish to be and see in the world."

Drama therapy was developed by Dr. Augusto Boal in the mid-twentieth century. It has been found to be an effective treatment for psychological issues, including PTSD, anxiety, depression, behavioral difficulties, relationship issues, and loss and grief.

Through improvisation, role-playing, and script writing, drama therapy techniques help us to freely express ourselves. We can learn to do this without fear of judgment or stigma. Drama therapy can be used alongside traditional therapies to create a holistic treatment plan that is tailored to our needs.

For those of us who want to participate in drama therapy we can take the following steps:

1. Research and find a qualified practitioner somewhere close and convenient to where we live or work.
2. Develop a level of comfort and trust with the therapist.
3. Be open to exploring and expressing our emotions through movement, role-playing, and creative expression.
4. Engage in regular therapy (as agreed with our therapist).
5. Be patient with ourselves and the process of drama therapy.

We can have a challenging therapeutic experience which helps us to grow, while also at times being fun and liberating. Drama therapy can provide a fresh perspective on our challenges, and it can help us practice new ways of thinking, feeling, and behaving. By stepping into different roles and scenarios, we can gain insights into ourselves and others, and explore and rehearse different strategies for handling difficult situations.

Drama therapy, like any therapy, requires commitment, but the potential rewards are immense. It can assist us in building self-confidence, improving our communication skills, and increasing our emotional intelligence. It can also help to foster empathy and understanding as we experience different perspectives through role-playing.

In addition, drama therapy can be empowering. It allows us to take control of our narratives, altering or reframing them in ways that can provide relief or even profound transformations. This creative process can be especially beneficial for those of us who find verbal communication challenging or limiting.

Overall, drama therapy is a versatile and effective therapeutic tool that can be customized to address a wide range of psychological issues and emotional needs. Whether we are struggling with personal issues, relationship challenges, or even societal pressures, drama therapy provides a safe and supportive space for exploration, expression, and evolution.

Dance

> *Along with language, dancing, marching, and singing are uniquely human ways to install a sense of hope and courage.*
>
> —Bessel Van Der Kolk: *The Body Keeps the Score: Mind, Brain and Body in the Transformation of Trauma*

There is something distinctly primeval about dance. It has been part of our world since the beginning of time. Ancient cultures placed dancing at the center of life.

- For centuries in temples throughout India's Tamil Nadu region, the graceful Bharatanatyam has been practiced. This classical dance combines intricate hand gestures with coordinated footwork and intricate stylized movements. These weave and spin stories describing Hindu mythology and culture.
- The Haka dance from New Zealand is a powerful, intimidating display of strength and skill. Performed as a ceremonial war dance by the indigenous Māori people, it is composed of facial expressions, body movements, and foot-stamping, creating a captivating performance. The Haka symbolizes courage in the face of danger.

- The traditional Ballet Folklórico is a vibrant dance celebrating the history and culture of Mexico. Spanish, African, and indigenous influences inspire a powerful performance of colorful costumes, rhythmic music, and intricate choreography.
- Turkish whirling dervishes practice dance as a form of physical meditation. Steadily spinning in circles while wearing long, white robes, they enter a mesmerizing trance. Ritual is based on the teachings of Sufism, a mystical branch of Islam focusing on asceticism and spiritual transformation.

Dance is a key component in building and strengthening communities. It is an expression of who we are, and it can bring us together in ways that no other activity can. It is also fun. Great fun! Celebrations including weddings, New Year get-togethers, and parties, from small family events through to enormous festivals, all have dancing at their core.

Dr. Peter Lovatt, a former professional dancer who became a dance psychologist, believes that we are "born to dance." Author of *The Dance Cure: The Surprising Science to Being Smarter, Stronger, Happier* and *Dance Psychology*, Peter's perspective is that it doesn't matter how skillful we are or what styles we use, dancing transforms us.

Dancing with other people is incredibly beneficial. It helps build trust. For those of us who were physically or sexually hurt, we relearn healthy bodily boundaries. We touch others and are touched by them in a boundaried and supportive way.

When we dance, we forget our day-to-day worries and escape into a world of music and movement. Through dance, we can express ourselves in ways that words cannot.

We can join dance groups and classes. If we are not yet ready to join others, we can dance alone. We will still benefit from our mind and body working together, synchronizing with a beat and rhythm outside of ourselves.

Beyond dance as an enjoyable and rewarding activity (with its many advantages), we might choose to explore dance therapy. This is much more than dance. As the words suggest it is a specific therapeutic tool.

Dance therapy

The American Dance Therapy Association defines dance/movement therapy as "the psychotherapeutic use of movement to promote emotional, social, cognitive, and physical integration of the individual."

It helps us to explore and understand our emotions and feelings. With our dance therapist we can begin to process our past, use this to interpret our present, and create a more joyful future.

Dance therapy is based on the theory that emotions are embodied and expressed through movement. Underlying principles include:

- Our mind and bodies are deeply connected and work with each other. This means that movement can affect our thinking and feeling in a profound way.
- We can express our personality through dance.
- The way in which we move can show our emotions.
- By experimenting with dance, we can learn new ways of thinking and behaving.
- Dance is by its nature gratifying, healing, and fun.

Dance therapists (sometimes called dance/movement therapists) are usually well qualified. Often, they have obtained specialist master's degree qualifications. Most larger countries have a professional association with a list of qualified, experienced, and supervised and regulated therapists. Checking these databases for someone close to where we live or work is an excellent way to find someone good to help us.

When we take part in dance or dance therapy, we often develop and grow beyond traditional healing techniques. Wherever and however we dance, we can rebuild our spirit. We can find the freedom of the innocent child who remains within us and of the adult that we were meant to be. This is elegantly expressed in the words of American dance pioneer and choreographer Isadora Duncan: "You were once wild here. Don't let them tame you."

New Frontiers: Cannabis and the Science of Psychedelics

Almost since the beginning of time, humankind has used plants and herbs to heal. Traditional and folk medicine make widespread use of an abundance of available natural medicines. Some of these medicines have strong effects on the way that we think and feel.

Over time, different countries in different parts of the world have changed, unchanged, then changed again their drug laws. Often these have not been based on scientific evidence of relative harm and benefits to those who use them, but on a mixture of cultural, religious, and political ideas as well as personal prejudices of people in positions of power and privilege. That said, we would not want our recovery to be complicated by legal issues and criminal convictions, so it is wise to stay within the law.

If we are living in an area where drugs such as cannabis are legal, and we can use them medicinally, this might be something that we want to consider. It is important to recognize that substances with powerful therapeutic effects can also have side effects. If considering taking any of them, it's best to do so under medical supervision.

Cannabis

Those of us who have been actively involved in forums or recovery groups for people with CPTSD will be familiar with positive reports of the beneficial effects of medicinal cannabis.

There is now some scientific evidence that cannabis works. Research that was carried out by the University of Pennsylvania, University of California San Diego, Johns Hopkins School of Medicine, and the University of Colorado showed that patients using cannabis were more likely to recover from PTSD than those who were not using cannabis. The cannabis users had less severe symptoms than the non-users and were 2.5 times less likely to have PTSD after one year.

However, there also appears to be evidence that cannabis use can be harmful and may increase the risk of developing psychosis. This emphasizes the need to educate ourselves about potential risks and benefits, and to be guided and monitored by appropriate medical experts.

Psychedelics

> *Although many of us think of psychedelics as dangerous drugs, it's time for a rethink. They are non-toxic, non-addictive, have very few side effects, and could potentially offer relief for people suffering from a range of psychological difficulties.*
>
> —Dr. Rosalind Watts, Clinical Lead for Imperial College London's psilocybin trial.

Other academics, researchers, and practitioners are thinking similar thoughts. In his paper (published on the Royal College of Psychiatrists website) *From Sacred Plants to Psychotherapy: The History and Re-Emergence of Psychedelics in Medicine*, Dr. Ben Sessa invites readers to consider that psychedelics may be defined as "useful and safe medical treatments. Tools that, as adjuncts to psychotherapy, can be used to alleviate the symptoms and course of many mental illnesses…"

Psychedelics were used in traditional cultures as a medicine and a means for spiritual exploration. Indigenous communities in the Amazon Basin took ayahuasca, a powerful psychedelic brew made from the *Banisteriopsis caapi* vine. DMT, the active ingredient in ayahuasca, has been shown to have profound effects on the brain, promoting new cell growth and reducing inflammation.

In ancient Mesoamerican times, psilocybin mushrooms were consumed. The Aztecs and Maya used psilocybin mushrooms in sacred ceremonies, and many modern-day indigenous communities in Mexico continue to use them for healing and spiritual practices. Psilocybin appears to possess potent healing potential. It may be an effective antidote to depression and anxiety.

Many researchers now believe that psychedelics will become increasingly popular in modern medicine. Dr. Rick Doblin, founder of the Multidisciplinary Association for Psychedelic Studies (MAPS), champions the study of psychedelics. MAPS is a non-profit organization that is dedicated to researching the therapeutic potential of psychedelics, including psilocybin and ayahuasca.

There is an excellent history and glimpse into the future use of psychedelic drugs in Michael Pollan's book *How to Change Your Mind*.

How do psychedelics work?

Scientists believe that psychedelics work to improve our mental health by promoting neuroplasticity and increasing the flexibility of our brains. Unlike conventional psychiatric drugs, which work by suppressing or enhancing certain neurotransmitters, psychedelics have a more profound and long-lasting effect. They temporarily disrupt the "default mode network," brain regions that are fully operational when we are introspective or daydreaming. In this way, psychedelics can create new connections between different parts of our brains. This means that we can experience a new perspective on our thoughts, emotions, and behavior. We can look at life in a new way. Many of us who have undergone psychedelic therapy report significant improvements in symptoms and quality of life.

What does the experience of taking psychedelics feel like?

Those of us who have used psychedelics describe the experience as profound, transformative, and even mystical. They create intense and unique sensory and perceptual experiences, vivid and colorful visuals, an altered sense of time and space, and a sense of connectedness with others and the universe. This may be accompanied by a sense of "ego dissolution." The loss of our sense of self helps us to build empathy and connection. Psychedelics have helped some of us to gain powerful insights into our thoughts, emotions, and behavior. They have helped us to have a deeper understanding of ourselves and our world.

Additionally, many of us who have used psychedelics report that the experience has helped to address underlying emotional issues and past traumas. This can be transformative. It can have a positive and long-lasting impact on our thoughts, feelings, and well-being.

Risks

It is important, however, to be aware of the risks associated with using psychedelics therapeutically. These risks increase if they are not used under proper medical supervision. Psychedelics can produce intense and potentially distressing experiences. They may exacerbate some mental health conditions including psychosis and bipolar disorder.

How to minimize risks

- It is important when using psychedelics therapeutically to do so under the guidance of a trained medical professional.
- As with every type of therapy we should thoroughly research the potential risks and benefits.
- We should check our own personal risk with a doctor who has a complete knowledge of our medical history and any specific vulnerabilities that we might have.
- We should only take psychedelics in parts of the world where we can take them legally.

Legality

Depending on the country and the specific substance in question, the legality of psychedelic drugs varies. In many countries, including the United States, psychedelics such as psilocybin and LSD are considered to have a high potential for abuse and no recognized medical use.

It would be a mistake to take psychedelics in places where they are illegal. There may be severe criminal sanctions: we could lose our liberty and, in some countries, risk losing our lives.

However, there is a growing movement to re-examine the legal status of psychedelic drugs, particularly in light of recent research showing promising results for their therapeutic potential.

17

Confronting our Parents

It is the most frightening and at the same time the most empowering act that you will ever perform.

—Susan Forward: *Toxic Parents: Overcoming Their Hurtful Legacy and Reclaiming Your Life*

In the bestseller *Toxic Parents: Overcoming Their Hurtful Legacy and Reclaiming Your Life*, Susan Forward provides comprehensive advice on confronting our parents in the chapter entitled "Confrontation: The Road to Independence."

Confrontation may indeed lead to independence. However, the decision of whether and how to confront our parents is a complex and deeply personal one. It requires careful consideration. It may have both immediate and long-term consequences.

Our journey toward confronting our parents is a courageous act of self-discovery and reclaiming our own narrative. As we look into the issues in greater detail, we will explore the potential impacts of our decision and consider the complexities of forgiveness. By understanding the motivations behind forgiveness, the risks it entails, and the societal pressures associated with it, we can make informed choices that align with our individual needs and aspirations.

Whether we choose forgiveness or not, it is vital to remember that we are not responsible for the abuse inflicted on us. The consequences of childhood abuse rest solely with the abusers. Neither need our journey toward healing and self-empowerment be burdened by guilt or self-blame. They, too, belong to our abusers, not us.

Deciding to Confront Our Parents

The aftermath of our decision

If we do confront our parents, we need to recognize that we cannot force them to react in a way that we want. We cannot change anyone's behavior. It is also helpful to understand that their initial reaction may change over time.

They could deny our truth. They may become angry or aggressive. After a while, however, some parents begin to admit what happened. What was secret can no longer be kept secret.

Conversely, they might initially own up to what they have done and apologize. Afterwards though, they slowly begin to rebuild the dishonesty. They may accuse us of making it up. Or they may promise to change their behavior, but continue behaving as before.

No matter how they respond, we need to reassure ourselves that we acted with honesty and integrity. We have taken back our own power.

Brothers and sisters

Our families are systems that try to preserve themselves. In the process of confronting our parents, we may encounter resistance from our brothers and sisters. Other family members might side with our parents. This is hard. Especially when we have been honest about a truth that we have kept secret for years, it is tough to see others fight against us. While honesty may not always be welcomed, it is good to prioritize our well-being and the well-being of future generations by facing reality.

Fences and fortresses: building unbreachable boundaries

> *What we can do is set limits on our own exposure to people who are behaving poorly; we can't change them or make them behave right.*
>
> —Dr. Henry Cloud and Dr. John Townsend

Henry Cloud and John Townsend, co-authors of the New York Times bestseller *Boundaries: When to Say Yes, How to Say No to Take Control of Your Life*, eloquently express the reality that we simply cannot change other people. Their book details helpful techniques for managing boundaries.

As people who were raised in dysfunctional families, we are likely to have lived our lives in a world where boundaries were either non-existent or frequently broken. When our parents hit or hurt us, they crossed the invisible line that loving, kind and supportive people should never cross.

We are all at different ages and stages in our lives. The guidance below covers a range of possible scenarios. Not all of them will apply to us personally. It is meant as a map of the territory where we are all in different places. What matters is being safe on our journey.

Safety First, Second, and Third

In all relationships, from casual acquaintances through to romantic partnerships, our first priority is safety. Not just our own safety, but the safety of any vulnerable people who rely on us for their security. This includes children. Naturally, we wouldn't want our own childhood experiences to be inflicted on anyone else. But it also encompasses those who need us for physical or emotional support.

- **Physical safety is our number one priority.** Those of us who were physically or sexually abused as children know the extent to which parents and families can break boundaries. We can also remain vulnerable as adults. At one extreme, some societies and cultures countenance and condone "honor killings." Family members are killed because they are deemed to have offended rigid and authoritarian views of the world. When our physical safety is at risk, we need to escape, now.
- **Emotional safety.** From our own childhoods, we may not have learned to value our own emotional needs. Perhaps it is something that we are still working on. If we haven't already developed it, we need to build an inherent sense of our own self-worth. We must remove ourselves from relationships where we are being coercively controlled, in any way degraded, are subject to online abuse, or are being emotionally hurt.
- **Spiritual safety.** This doesn't necessarily refer to something religious. Rather it references the impact poor or breached boundaries can have on our "core being." The long-term drag on our personality caused by dysfunctional relationships can ultimately be soul-destroying.

To stay safe, it is essential to have a plan. It is helpful to create this with professional support. When this isn't obtainable, there is guidance available from multiple support agencies online.

The basics of a plan include:

- Being able to escape undetected and remain hidden if necessary.
- Having the resources and networks to survive away from whoever is hurting us.

Gray Rock

"Gray rock" is a strategy we can use in the short term to deal with abusive or manipulative people.

If we have ever walked through hills and mountains, passed by rivers or streams, or meandered by the coast, we will have seen hundreds, if not thousands, of gray rocks. We are extremely unlikely, however, to have talked about them to our friends or enthusiastically shared pictures of them on Instagram, Facebook, WhatsApp, or TikTok.

Gray rocks are boring. They're just something that is not worth paying attention to, so they are ignored.

This is the basis for the technique called going gray rock. The idea is that we make ourselves so dull and uninteresting that we are ignored by those who are making our lives difficult. This may be one or both of our parents. If we are in a pattern of repetition compulsion, it could be an ex-partner or someone whom we are currently in a relationship with that we are planning to leave.

For example, we might have a mother who consistently criticizes us to undermine our self-esteem. When she starts to tell us that we would have had a much better job or partner and be much more successful if only we had been reasonable enough to listen to her advice, we don't react. Or if a narcissistic partner or ex-partner is trying to manipulate us into attending an event we don't want to go to, or spending money on something they want and we don't, we avoid getting into a dramatic fight.

The theory is that going gray rock works because narcissists and manipulative people need chaos and conflict in their lives. We are much less interesting to them if we are not supplying these for them. A good analogy is to think of a boxer who needs an opponent. Without an adversary, the boxer would just dance around the ring punching the air. When we stop being the person that the narcissist in our life fights with, then he or she has to look elsewhere for drama and destruction.

Gray rock or the silent treatment?

It is easy to confuse the two; however, there are real and clear differences between gray rock and the silent treatment.

Gray rock is for our protection. The silent treatment is about punishment.

We live in a world where it is natural to want to communicate with one another. When we refuse to talk to someone, this is likely to be psychologically difficult for them. Although there may be occasions when it is justified, if this is the case then it may be better to go no-contact. No-contact has clarity about it. It means not having someone in our lives anymore, so we don't see them, talk together, send messages on Facebook or WhatsApp, or communicate in any way. The silent treatment is, however, confusing and ambiguous; we can be physically quite close to someone, even perhaps sharing a house, while refusing to actually say anything to them. We are then choosing to stay within a relationship of sorts. This keeps the opportunity open for more and more conflict, without really resolving anything.

The gray rock strategy is different because we aren't trying to punish or get into fights; in fact, quite the opposite—we are melting into the background to avoid problems.

How to go gray rock

Safety first

Most importantly, if we are afraid for our own safety then this is a time when going gray rock will not work. We need to inform the authorities, remove ourselves from the situation, and seek legal advice.

Don't give them what they need

Narcissists, including narcissistic parents, need what is termed by psychologists "narcissistic supply." This is basically wanting attention and admiration.

We should not:

- Give them compliments or praise.
- Help them to feel power over us.
- Let them feel that they are controlling us in some way.
- Give them any sort of emotional energy, whether that's positive or negative.

It can be really tempting not to do this. For example, if they suddenly start being kind or generous it feels very natural to want to reward and encourage this sort of behavior. However, realistically this is just manipulation and there will be consequences later on. It is unlikely to be genuine—it is just a way to gain control over us.

"Hmm, uh-huh, I see"

It's best if we can keep our conversations as short as possible. Words and phrases like "hmm, uh-huh, I see" are neutral. They also need to be spoken without any strong emphasis so that they don't sound sarcastic or forceful.

Stay detached

If possible, try to avoid prolonged eye contact. This is because eye contact is essential for building and maintaining relationships and emotionally connecting with people. These are all things we wish to avoid with a narcissist. It helps to focus our attention elsewhere, by gently gazing into another area of the room or the space ahead.

Don't tell them about gray rock

There is a legendary line in the 1999 movie *Fight Club* when Tyler Durden (played by Brad Pitt) says, "The first rule of Fight Club is: you do not talk about Fight Club." Of course, gray rock is a strategy to avoid fights and drama, but the same rules still apply. When narcissistic people know what we're doing, they will be much better at using manipulation in an attempt to once again exert control over us.

Backlash, baiting, and biting

Often narcissists react to the gray rock technique with more attempts at manipulation and control.

We can expect some of the following responses:

- After all I've done for you!
- How could you? How can you?
- Why don't you ever…?
- You are so rude, ungrateful, selfish, spoiled, cruel, etc.
- Listen to me!

The trick is to stick to the plan. We will be most successful if we can manage not to be provoked into reactions that will help our narcissistic parents, partners, or ex-partners have their needs for drama and conflict met.

It may help to remember the acronym "JADE": do not justify, argue, defend, or explain yourself.

Advantages and disadvantages of the gray rock technique

Within our community of adults who had difficult childhoods, there are mixed feelings. Not everyone thinks that gray rock is a helpful strategy.

Some people believe that it is better to sever ties completely and go no-contact. This isn't always possible though. Or it might be possible, but now isn't the right time.

Going gray rock might be:

- **A helpful short-term measure, while we build the necessary resources before we go no-contact.** For example, we might be living with toxic parents who constantly row and criticize us. It makes sense then to tolerate and minimize the situation until we have saved enough money to rent or buy a place of our own, or until we have built a supportive community of friends to help us.
- **Part of a strategy when we are working things through with a counselor or psychotherapist and need space before making decisions about our future.** Maybe it's a stage of our journey when we are beginning to see our parents for what they are and we need help and support handling the situation, while at the same time not suffering from some of their most toxic behaviors.
- **A sensible decision when we decide that it is in our best interests to stay in touch with our parents, but we are not prepared to tolerate their abuse anymore.** We may have shared business interests, financial arrangements, or contracts that are difficult to break free from. In this case, we may choose to have minimal contact and clear boundaries created by going gray rock.

Risks of going gray rock

One of the risks of going gray rock is that we might actually become too good at it.

It is meant to be a technique for dealing with specific troublesome narcissists. Sometimes, though, we find it so helpful that it gradually begins to creep into other parts of our lives. This means that we adapt to not showing or expressing our true feelings. Slowly but surely, we lose touch with our true selves as we become super-competent at dulling our emotions. It is important to remember that we have the right to be angry, sad, happy, frustrated, and feel the full range of human emotions. It is helpful to constantly remind ourselves that going gray rock is just a skill that might be necessary for some limited circumstances.

There is also a danger we can begin to "regress" (as psychologists call it). We start to take on the characteristics and behaviors from a much earlier part of our lives. Especially if we were physically, emotionally, or sexually abused, we may have adopted strategies similar to gray rock. We hoped that by doing this we would be left alone. Now that we're adults, however, we deserve to enjoy being assertive and confident, and live life the way we want to.

Moving on from gray rock

Gray rock is a helpful technique but ultimately, we may choose to go full no-contact.

Going No-Contact

Going no-contact is tough. We are all different, however. And the challenges that we face partly depend on how emotionally and financially independent we are already.

We may have some emotional ambivalence. Perhaps we still have feelings or a connection for the person that we are trying to get away from. Or we might have brothers or sisters whom we are very fond of in the home that we are trying to leave. Maybe, among the chaos and stress, the only rock that we could rely on was a much-loved cat or dog that we may now have to see less often.

Practically we might need to sort out belongings, books, video games, or treasured possessions.

Timing might be a challenge too. There are events that prompt us to leave; for example, we have a baby on the way and don't want our parents to be part of our new family. Having experienced what they inflicted on us, we have decided to break the cycle and no longer want to see, hear, or speak to them. Frequently we find a new perspective on life when we first meet a new romantic partner. We want to keep them as far away as possible from the environment that we were brought up in. Equally, there might be things that are happening that simply coincide with our wanting to go no-contact but nevertheless might make the situation more complicated. These sorts of situations include family illness, accidents, and bereavement.

Depending on our circumstances there could be financial ties that we need to untangle.

Even if we are financially independent, already live away from our parents, and are in an emotionally strong place, there is a good chance that we have family members or friends in common with our parents. We may want to remain in close relationships with these people while going no-contact with our mom or dad or both of them.

We might feel confused. We might feel ambivalent. We might crave the freedom and opportunity to escape, while also being scared, experiencing guilt and shame, anger, or simply being hopelessly stressed. All of this is normal.

We can also experience a loss of hope. Finally, we understand and accept the brutal truth that our parents will never change.

Loss of hope

The desire to "one day get it right" and fix the relationship is a powerful force that keeps us locked in toxic relationships. This is because:

- **We believe in our parents' capacity to change.** We want to believe that they can change and become loving, supportive people. We keep trying to fix the relationship, even in the face of repeated failure and disappointment.
- **We have a sense of obligation or duty.** We feel a strong sense of obligation to maintain our relationship with our parents, regardless of how toxic or abusive this is. Our sense of obligation may be rooted in societal or cultural expectations around family loyalty.
- **We fear abandonment or rejection.** As adult children of toxic parents, we are afraid of abandonment or rejection when we have been conditioned to believe that our worth and value as a person are tied to our relationship with our parent.
- **We experience trauma bonding.** Trauma bonding refers to the development of a strong emotional attachment to an abuser as a result of the intermittent reinforcement of rewards and punishments. We may experience trauma bonding as a result of the unpredictable and inconsistent nature of our parents' behavior.

To break free from the compulsion to fix the relationship, we need to address these underlying beliefs and fears. It helps to work through our traumatic childhood, develop self-compassion and self-worth, set boundaries, and seek support from a therapist or support group.

Practical steps to going no-contact

The reality of going no-contact becomes clearer when we take practical steps to enforce our boundaries. These include:

- **Blocking our parents' phone numbers and email addresses.**
- **Blocking our parents on social media.** This can be done through settings or by unfriending and blocking our parents' accounts.
- **Blocking mutual contacts.** When we share mutual contacts with our parent, it may be necessary to block them as well, to prevent them from passing on messages or information.
- **Avoiding family events or gatherings where our toxic parent may be present.** It can be helpful to communicate with other family members beforehand to let them know about the decision to go no-contact and to avoid any situations where contact with the toxic parent may be likely.
- **Avoiding places or activities that the toxic parent may frequent.** This may involve changing routines or finding new places to go to avoid any chance encounters.
- **Screening phone calls or messages.** When our toxic parent continues to attempt contact, it may be necessary to screen phone calls and messages to avoid any unwanted contact.

We may also have to deal with what are known as enablers and flying monkeys.

Enablers and flying monkeys

Enablers and flying monkeys are individuals who support abusive and dysfunctional parents and enable their behavior. Enablers may be other family members, friends, or even therapists who support our parents' version of events. They will minimize or deny the abuse.

Flying monkeys are individuals who are recruited by our toxic parents. They may spy on us, pressure us to reconcile, or carry out smear campaigns on our parents' behalf.

Broadly speaking, we need to use the same tactics with enablers and flying monkeys as we use with our parents.

If our brothers or sisters or other close family members act as enablers or flying monkeys, it is helpful to prepare some responses to them. These should be statements that respect our boundaries without becoming confrontational. For example.

- "I appreciate your concern, thank you, but I have made the decision to go no-contact with [toxic parent's name] for my own well-being. I need you to respect my decision."
- "I understand that [toxic parent's name] may have a different version of events. But I have experienced abuse and toxicity in our relationship. I need to prioritize my own healing and well-being, and that means going no-contact. I hope you understand."

Grief

We know from attachment theory that it is normal and natural to form close relationships with others. Children need their parents' love and support to survive. Even as adults who choose to go no-contact, we may experience grief when our parents are no longer in our lives.

Grief for the loss of what didn't happen

It may seem strange. We tend to think of grief as the intense emotion we feel when someone we love dies. Perhaps our thinking extends to grieving the loss of a relationship. Grief for something that didn't happen might seem odd, but it is very real.

This loss can be difficult to cope with, especially if we had hopes of repairing the relationship. The loss of hope for a better relationship can be a significant source of grief, as we mourn the loss of what might have been.

When we stop having contact with our parents, we may mourn the loss of the relationship that we didn't have as children. And the relationship that we will never have as adults.

One theory—the Kübler-Ross model of grief—helps to explain the emotions we may experience when we go no-contact. There are five stages of grief: denial, anger, bargaining, depression, and acceptance.

1. We may at first try to ignore or minimize the abuse or neglect we experienced.
2. Anger grows when we recognize the extent of the harm done to us.

3. Bargaining happens when we attempt to negotiate with our toxic parents to change their behavior.
4. Depression arises when we understand that our toxic parents are unlikely to change and that we must cut off contact.
5. Acceptance comes when we accept that the relationship with our parents is over and we begin to move on.

To eventually reach the acceptance stage it is helpful to be able to process our grief.

Processing grief

Processing means working through intense emotions and changes that arise after a significant loss or life transition. To do this we can:

- **Acknowledge and express our feelings.**
- **Practice self-compassion.** Be kind and gentle with ourselves during the grieving process. Recognize that grief is a natural response to loss and that everyone processes it in their own way. We mustn't judge ourselves for how we feel or how long it takes to work through our grief.
- **Seek support.** Surround ourselves with people who can provide emotional support and guidance. This may include friends, family members, a therapist, or a support group. Having someone to talk to helps us to process our grief and feel less alone.

Finding meaning in our loss

We can start by acknowledging the reality that the relationship with our toxic parents was not loving or supportive, and accept that the potential for a great relationship was never there. It can help to focus on personal growth and healing: we can work on self-compassion, self-care, and personal boundaries to prevent future harm from toxic relationships. Reflecting on the experience of being in a toxic relationship with our parents can provide important insights and lessons for future relationships. It can help us develop self-awareness, recognize patterns of behavior, and learn to set healthy boundaries and expectations in relationships. Creating a new narrative can help us to find meaning in the loss by reframing the experience in a way that is empowering and transformative. This may involve focusing on our personal strengths and resilience, or recognizing the opportunity for growth and change that comes from letting go of toxic relationships.

Should We Forgive Our Parents?

Forgiveness is often seen as a bridge to a better place. If we don't forgive, we are viewed as being "stuck" in a world of self-pity, anger, and frustration; by crossing the "forgiveness bridge" we can enter a new world of peace and acceptance.

There are books written on the power of forgiveness and some that even suggest that it is the greatest healer of all. There are endless quotes that claim that we are prisoners until we can forgive and that we only hurt ourselves by not forgiving. There is a consensus that forgiveness is a necessary part of healing. This is not true.

That's not to say there are no advantages to forgiveness. It can, under the right circumstances, be helpful to us. However, forgiveness is complex. When we are considering the possibility of reconciling with our parents, it is best to have a thorough understanding of our ideas of forgiveness. Where did they come from? How will our decisions about whether or not to forgive impact on our lives?

When we know what is motivating us, we are in a stronger position to decide whether to forgive or not and if it would be helpful to reconcile.

Where does the desire to forgive come from?

The desire to forgive is instinctive. A powerful need to forgive comes from a place of powerlessness. Our total reliance on our parents when we were children meant that we had an incredibly strong instinct to bond with them. No matter how badly they treated us, our tiny brains were hard-wired to forgive. We tried to make them love us for the simple reason that we wanted to stay alive.

The idea of forgiving our parents began with this biological imprint. It then stayed with us long after it was no longer necessary. Even if we are fully independent adults who are completely able to look after ourselves, we may still have something locked deep inside us telling us to forgive.

As adults we can recognize where this need to forgive has come from. We can choose to act on it, or not. We can see it as it really is. It was a strategy that was vital to our early childhood survival but is now redundant. It can serve as a memory, not a motivator.

We may also be exposed to strong external pressure to forgive our parents. This makes evolutionary sense. Ancient tribes had to work together. Societies relied on everyone getting along. People holding grudges and taking part in unnecessary arguments stopped work being done. It was counterproductive. A strong moral pressure for people to forgive developed to protect the community. Many of the world's religions include forgiveness as a core concept.

There can, however, be a difference between general rules that are good for society, and the decisions that we take that relate to our own circumstances.

It probably is helpful to forgive a work colleague who was rude to us, or our partner whom we got into an argument with. We can also forgive ourselves for the mistakes and errors that everyone makes on a daily basis. They are part of life. However, this does not mean that it is necessarily right to forgive parents who abused us.

The hidden dangers of forgiveness

When we consider forgiving our parents, it is important to have a complete picture of what might happen. This includes understanding possible risks of forgiveness as well as potential advantages.

There are hidden dangers when we forgive those who have hurt us deeply. These are as follows:

- **It can actually prevent us from healing.** Many self-help books and social media influencers suggest that forgiveness is essential to healing. This is untrue. In fact, if we forgive, especially if we forgive too early, it can slow down or even stop us becoming healthy and whole. This is because it can take hard work to learn to accept that what happened to us was wrong. We need time to process our emotions. We have to grieve the loss of the childhood we could and should have had. We deserved better. If we jump straight to forgiveness without these steps, we lose an essential element necessary for us to grow and develop.
- **It can be a sort of denial.** Sometimes forgiveness is a way of minimizing the hurt and damage that was done to us. At times we forgive because it is too painful to face the truth: that the very people who should have protected us injured us physically, emotionally, or psychologically.
- **It can leave us feeling worse.** It can be a tremendous disappointment when we make a huge effort to forgive and don't feel any better for it. Realistically, many of the challenges that we face—low self-esteem, guilt, and shame—don't go away. We can end up feeling life is depressing and hopeless because we made what we believed was going to be a big and important step, and nothing changed. We forgave and it made no difference.

- **It can increase self-blame.** Often blame, guilt, and responsibility become confused. We are responsible for our own lives, but we are not responsible for what happened to us. It was not our fault. It is absolutely OK to put all the blame, shame, and guilt firmly where they should be. They belong to our abusers. It is also normal, and sometimes healthy, to feel angry about our past. Sometimes when we forgive, we don't actually let go of the anger. We stop blaming our parents for what they did to us. Instead, because we have forgiven our parents, we begin to direct the blame back on ourselves.
- **It can let our abusers get away with it.** When we forgive people without first ensuring that they have taken responsibility for their actions and made amends, it allows the cycle of abuse to continue. We owe it to ourselves, our families, future generations, and other people not to let this happen. None of us would want our children and grandchildren to share the same experiences we had in our childhoods.
- **It can keep our families toxic.** It is possible that when we forgive, the dynamic within the family simply remains the same. Forgiveness allows the dysfunctional system within the family to stay the same because there is nobody to challenge it.

When it might be healthy to forgive

We must and should do what is right for us. Other people who haven't experienced what we have don't have the right to pressure us into forgiveness. There might, however, be times when it is healthy for us to forgive.

If our parents or people who have hurt us have taken full responsibility for their actions and the consequences of their actions, and have taken steps to compensate for the damage that they have done, then we can consider forgiveness.

Will we regret not forgiving and reconciling?

There are a number of times in our lives that provoke us to think more about whether we should try to find a way to reconcile with our parents. The list below is incomplete, but it highlights the main occasions when we are likely to be thinking about these things more.

- If we are going to get married or commit to a long-term relationship with a new partner.
- When we are about to start our own family and have children of our own.

- If we are starting a new life in a different country or far away from our parental home.
- During the final phase of our parents' lives, when it is clear that soon they will no longer be with us and, should we choose not to forgive now, we will never be able to forgive them in person.

The last point on this list is likely to be the one time where we feel most pressure to act. It is real and honest to accept that our parents are not immortal. There will come a time when we cannot either confront them or forgive them in person.

Yes, we may regret not forgiving them. But if we do forgive them, we may equally regret that decision. There is no risk-free option. We must be clear though that we did not create these risks. We can try our best to heal and repair; however, we are not responsible for what happened to us. The consequences of childhood abuse belong to the abuser. And always will do.

18

Beyond Recovery

Would it make sense to take a battered, bruised, and broken vintage car, lovingly restore it, then only ever use it to sit in traffic jams? Or perhaps stop a beautiful sailing boat from sinking, simply to spend time in stormy seas under sullen skies?

Arguably, this is how many of us end up after psychotherapy and counseling. Instead of being prepared for a fulfilling and fun-filled future, we are taught to be normal. And normal just isn't that great. For millions of people all over our planet, being normal means being bored, frustrated, sad, lonely, and spending time daydreaming of a better life.

The famous quotation from philosopher Henry David Thoreau states, "The mass of men lead lives of quiet desperation." The concept of *Dukkha* within Hinduism and Buddhism describes the general unsatisfactoriness of living a mundane life. Modern psychologists would use the term "mild dysphoria." However we express this situation, it is clear that ordinary life is unhappy for many people.

This means that whenever we are seeking professional help or working through our issues ourselves, it is best to see recovery as a stepping stone. It is somewhere that we pass through on our journey, but we really need to travel beyond it on our road to recovery.

Radical Scottish psychiatrist, R.D. Laing. stated that "Our 'normal' 'adjusted' state is too often the abdication of ecstasy, the betrayal of our true potentialities." This is interesting for two reasons. Firstly, R.D Laing introduces the idea of ecstasy. Nowadays this is associated more with the recreational drug MDMA; however, he was using it to describe feelings of euphoria. Secondly, Laing mentions our true potentialities. This introduces the idea that we are not being as brilliant, happy, and fulfilled as we could be. Perhaps this also alludes to the fact that many of us end up living to false potentialities: we meet the limited goals and ideals of what other people think we should be, or we stay forever restrained by our own conditioning.

After having grown up with trauma and distress, it is easy to have low expectations of life. But it simply is not enough to recover from our childhood wounds and spend our time in varying degrees of boredom and unhappiness. There is an incredible world of excitement, bliss and what psychologist Abraham Maslow called "peak experiences" that we can discover beyond our recovery. We owe it to ourselves to find and spend time there.

This section explores how we can reach the end of our journey and the start of a truly happy life.

Gratitude

Gratitude is not only the greatest of virtues, but the parent of all the others.

—Cicero

Gratitude is fascinating. It is counterintuitive.

Depending on our own personal experience, we might feel that there is not that much in our lives so far that we feel grateful for. As adults who were brought up in dysfunctional families, we have a right to feel angry. We are also justified in grieving the loss of our childhood. Our lives so far may have been dogged by depression and crushed by anxiety. It is perfectly reasonable to conclude that developing gratitude should be low down on our list of priorities.

There is, however, a catch. Gratitude works.

Grateful people are happier and enjoy better mental health than those who don't practice gratitude, with decreased anxiety and depression. Not only this, but studies have also shown that feeling thankful can improve sleep, mood, and immunity. Why, then, should we allow the benefits of gratitude to go only to those who enjoyed a happy childhood? We have been punished enough. We are entitled to, and deserve to profit from the development of an attitude of gratitude ourselves. Additionally, of course, the more we recover, the more positive people and experiences we will attract in our lives as they change for the better.

Practicing gratitude involves making a conscious effort to appreciate what is good in our lives, the things that are valuable and have meaning to us. It's about acknowledging the positive things, events, and people around us and expressing appreciation for them.

It doesn't mean invalidating or ignoring the challenges we've faced, but rather introducing a new lens to view our life through, a lens of gratitude. This lens doesn't sugarcoat our reality but gently reminds us of the silver linings that exist, even in stormy weather.

There are various ways of practicing gratitude. One of the simplest and most popular is to keep a gratitude journal, where we can note things that we are grateful for each day. These can be big things, like a promotion at work, or simpler things, like the taste of our morning coffee or a kind gesture by another person. An alternative to a gratitude journal is a gratitude jar, where we write down something we are grateful for each day on a piece of paper and put it in the jar. Over time, we have a jar full of positive things to look back on when we need a lift. Similarly, we could write a note of appreciation to people who have a positive impact on our life; we could choose to send the letters, or not—it's our choice.

Gratitude doesn't have to be written down. It can be expressed in our thoughts. For example, during a walk, we can practice mindfulness of our surroundings, expressing gratitude for any positive aspects we observe—the beauty of a flower or a view, the sound of birdsong, or the feeling of the breeze on our face or the warmth of the sun on our back.

Or gratitude can be expressed verbally, with a kind word or a simple "thank you."

Some people find it helpful to set up reminders throughout the day to pause and consider something they're grateful for. This could be done through alarm reminders, gratitude apps, or visual cues around the home or workspace. Psychologist Martin Seligman, known for his work on positive psychology, and a leader in research into gratitude, suggests a simple practice: "Every night for the next week, set aside ten minutes before you go to sleep. Write down three things that went well today and why they went well. This simple practice can help you focus on the positive aspects of your life and cultivate gratitude."

The key to practicing gratitude is consistency. It's about making it a habit to focus on the good, regardless of how small or simple it might seem. Over time, this practice can shift our mindset and have a positive impact on our overall outlook and well-being.

In the words of Melody Beattie, author and self-help advocate: "Gratitude makes sense of our past, brings peace for today, and creates a vision for tomorrow."

As we embark on this journey, let us remember that gratitude is not a product of our circumstances, but a choice we make. The poet Rumi beautifully encapsulates this sentiment: "Wear gratitude like a cloak, and it will feed every corner of your life."

Kintsugi

Kintsugi is the Japanese art of repairing broken pottery by gluing pieces back together with gold. The theory is that by embracing flaws and imperfections, a stronger, more beautiful piece of art can be created.

Of course, we would not choose to break a vase to make it better. It is more than likely that we would look at it and think that it was perfectly fine the way it was originally designed to be.

We were also fantastic little human beings. We should not have been treated the way we were treated. It was wrong. Yet no matter how much we may want to, we cannot change what has already happened. Irvin David Yalom, American existential psychiatrist and emeritus professor of psychiatry at Stanford University, gives some excellent advice for therapists; he states, "Sometimes I simply remind patients that sooner or later they will have to relinquish the goal of having a better past." Given then that we cannot "unbreak" ourselves, our best option now is to put ourselves back together with gold.

We can also embrace our own history using the parts of our lives that once kept us weak to make us strong. Dr. Richard Tedeschi, psychology professor and expert on resilience, describes the process by which this happens as "post-traumatic growth." There are several areas in our lives where trauma or a dysfunctional upbringing can, in the long term, be used to improve our future.

- **Compassion.** We understand what it is like to be hurt, which means in turn that we can more easily understand other people who have been hurt.
- **Better relationships.** Sometimes, having seen the worst sort of relationships,

we are so determined to do better that we put an enormous effort into understanding ourselves and our partners. Knowing what things look like when they're wrong can help us to see the opposite; in other words, what they're like when they are fantastically right.

- **Waking up.** Our own personal horrible histories can help us to think, "There must be more to life than this." We can therefore see opportunities and possibilities. We are motivated to achieve, rather than living an unfulfilled life of mediocrity.
- **Appreciating life more.** Warmth, love, affection, meaning, happiness, trust, and so many other aspects of our lives feel much more valuable when we experienced very little love as children. We do not take these things for granted; we appreciate them much more as adults because of the deficit we had as children.
- **Spiritual growth.** Through our experience we have learned to question. And this questioning brings us a deeper, more meaningful reality.

Thinking Like a Mountain

Ecologist Aldo Leopold first expressed the idea of "thinking like a mountain" in his book *A Sand County Almanac*. He described the way in which nature is an interconnected system and how people's interference with it causes damage. In his essay, he tells how hunters kill wolves so that there are more deer for them to hunt. The increase in the deer population begins to destroy the habitat as they eat more and more vegetation; flowers, plants, and trees are all harmed and begin to disappear. In the end there is not enough for the deer to eat, and they cannot survive themselves. Aldo's idea is that hunters are not old and mature enough to understand what they're doing; however, the mountain itself has wisdom and understands what the environment needs to thrive.

We can use thinking like a mountain as a metaphor for our own connectedness to our own communities. German American developmental psychologist Erik Erikson summarized our longing for unity with his words "Life doesn't make any sense without interdependence. We need each other, and the sooner we learn that, it is better for us all."

In the same way that the environment around the mountain was destroyed, our own personal ecosystems may well have been damaged by things that went beyond our control. So, as the early sections of this book acknowledge, we are in a position of rebuilding, or even building for the first time, a healthy and nurturing environment for ourselves. This means creating our own healthy and happy social support network. We need to find people and develop relationships that help us on our journey.

Justice

Justice is righting wrongs.

By securing justice for ourselves, we also improve the lives of future generations. We may wish to consider finding out from a lawyer if we can seek compensation for the wrongdoing that was done to us. The chances of our success vary depending on where in the world we are, available evidence, the relative harm that was done to us, and other factors that are beyond the scope of this book.

Sometimes we cannot receive the personal justice we deserve. It is possible, though, to help to ensure that the world becomes a kinder and fairer place. Children who follow us do not have to share our experiences. We can draw inspiration from the words of civil rights activist Rosa Parks who said, "I believe we are here on the planet Earth to live, grow up and do what we can to make this world a better place for all people to enjoy freedom."

We can:

- **Make our voices heard.** This does not necessarily mean sharing our own personal experience, although if we are supported and feel safe enough to do this we may choose to do so. The "Me Too" movement is an incredible example of how individual people working together can seek and find justice. If we do not want to share our own experience, we can still add our weight to petitions, and support changes in legislation.
- **Campaign.** We can join campaigns to raise awareness of the damage done to people who, like us, were brought up in dysfunctional families.
- **Donate.** If we have the resources, we can give to not-for-profit organizations or charities who have the same goals as we do.
- **Take on powerful positions ourselves.** Russian writer Fyodor Dostoevsky suggested that "Power is given only to those who dare to lower themselves and pick it up. Only one thing matters, one thing; to be able to dare."
- **Securing justice will help us to make sense of what happened to us**. Even if this is not possible, we can still find fulfillment through exploring ideas around a greater meaning to life.

Spirituality, Meaning, and Purpose

As we embark on our journey toward recovery, wellness, and joy, we may often find ourselves contemplating life's deeper questions. Growing up in challenging environments, our focus was primarily on day-to-day survival, leaving little space for existential musings. As adults carrying the weight of our past, our primary goal often revolves around creating a safe, stress-free, and depression-free existence.

It is natural as we become healthier and happier to ask deeper and more meaningful questions. This can be both intimidating and rewarding. We need to be able to explore from a place of personal safety and avoid being exploited. To do this we should avoid simplistic and dogmatic explanations about the meaning of life, especially when these involve spending our money.

There are a multitude of ways to seek understanding—spiritual, religious, metaphysical, paranormal, scientific, and more. While all of these perspectives can offer insights, none of them hold the definitive answer. We are still in the early stages of our collective human journey, barely scratching the surface of the knowledge available to us.

In the words of philosopher, psychologist, and historian William James, "We may be in the Universe as dogs and cats are in our libraries, seeing the books and hearing the conversation, but having no inkling of the meaning of it all." As we evolve as a species, we may begin to grasp at least a fragment of the universe's mysteries. For now, we can acknowledge that humankind is at the very start of its journey toward understanding.

Even the question "What is the meaning of life?" is to some extent meaningless. Who is it that says that life has only one meaning? There may be multiple meanings, much like there might potentially be multiple universes. Perhaps as we evolve and change, so does the universe, and meaning itself might change with this evolution. It's plausible that the universe is constantly creating its own meaning, in the same way as we carve out our personal meanings.

The lack of a definitive answer can be frightening or daunting, or it can be seen as an incredible opportunity. We have the power to choose to create our own personal meanings, to seek purpose in our daily lives, in our relationships, and in our actions. We can choose to approach life with benevolence and curiosity, striving to make ourselves and our world a better place, while also taking time to simply observe and enjoy.

Our journey toward greater wisdom and peace can be taken alone, or with other people. It doesn't have to be an arduous learning process, though some of us may find joy in the rigorous challenge of academic pursuits or independent study. Exploring nature, discovering ourselves through sport, or learning new skills can provide meaning and insight. Equally, blissful and peak experiences, or a feeling of oneness achieved through meditation, yoga, dance, singing, or creative arts, gift us with experience, understanding, and fulfillment.

This is our journey, our opportunity. Let us embrace it with open hearts and curious minds.

Together.

A Word from Jackie Poet

Thank you for reading and joining us on our journey.

Throughout this book I have been very careful to use the words "us" and "we," because we all share similar backgrounds, experiences, and challenges. It is about us, not me. Understandably though, readers sometimes want to know more about a book's writer. If you don't, that is absolutely fine—I am not offended. If you do, here is some further information.

Jackie Poet is my pen name; it's not the name I use in my everyday life. While fully acknowledging the destruction and devastation of my past, I want to be able to have choices for the future. My pen name gives me safe and effective boundaries. It enables me to discuss what happened to me when and if I choose to do so.

I have had the privilege of learning from many of you who shared your own stories with me. My first degree was in psychology, and I have studied CPTSD, trauma, abuse, and resilience from specialist institutions and experts located in different parts of the world. I have worked as both a paid professional and volunteer in mental health services. I have had the pleasure of meeting some truly inspirational people, both those who were using these services and dedicated staff.

Being raised in a dysfunctional family and being abused myself means that I have direct lived experience. Years of psychotherapy helped me to develop insight and understanding.

I am not an expert. I am working hard to develop expertise by reading, studying, and listening each day to gain further knowledge and wisdom.

I am definitely not a role model. I am an imperfect person living in in an imperfect world.

I do have a passion for change. I want to become a better person.

Within the bounds of what I can realistically achieve, I want in some small way to make the world a better place. This book is a beginning. There is a long road ahead.

If this book resonated with you, I ask if you would kindly consider leaving a review—just a line or two would mean a lot to me. Your feedback not only helps me to improve my work in the future but also really does make this book more visible and aids others who would find it helpful to discover it.

If you want to join me on my mission, it would be wonderful to have you as a fellow traveler. Please take a look at jackiepoet.com.

Many thanks again,

Jackie

Further Reading and Resources

Books

Agassi, Andre. *Open: An Autobiography*. Random House, New York, 2009.

Alberti, Robert and Michael Emmons. *Your Perfect Right: Assertiveness and Equality in Your Life and Relationships*. Impact, Oakland, 2017.

Barry, Nicola. *Mother's Ruin: The Extraordinary True Story of How Alcohol Destroys a Family*. Headline Review, London, 2018.

Becker-Phelps Leslie. *Insecure in Love: How Anxious Attachment Can Make You Feel Jealous, Needy, and Worried and What You Can Do About It*. New Harbinger, Oakland, 2014.

Bradshaw, John. *Homecoming: Reclaiming and Championing Your Inner Child*. Bantam Books, New York, 1990.

Burns, Tom and Eva Burns-Lundgren. *Psychotherapy: A Very Short Introduction*. Oxford University Press, Oxford, 2015.

Christakis, Erika. *The Importance of Being Little: What Young Children Really Need from Grownups*. Penguin Books, New York, 2017.

Cloud, Henry and John Townsend. *Boundaries: When to Say Yes, How to Say No To Take Control of Your Life (Updated and Expanded Edition)*, Zondervan, Grand Rapids, 1992.

Coleman, John. *HBR Guide to Crafting Your Purpose*. Harvard Business School Publishing, Boston, 2022.

Covey, Stephen. *The 7 Habits of Highly Effective People: Powerful Lessons in Personal Change*. Free Press, New York, 2004.

Engel, Beverly. *It Wasn't Your Fault: Freeing Yourself from the Shame of Childhood Abuse with the Power of Self-Compassion*. New Harbinger, Oakland, 2015.

Ewart, Heyward Bruce III. *Am I Bad? Recovering from Abuse*. Loving Healing Press, Ann Arbor, 2007.

Forward, Susan. *Mothers Who Can't Love: A Healing Guide for Daughters*. HarperCollins, New York, 2013.

Forward, Susan. *Toxic Parents: Overcoming Their Hurtful Legacy and Reclaiming Your Life*. Bantam Books, New York, 2002.

Fredrickson, Renee. *Repressed Memories: A Journey to Recovery from Sexual Abuse*. Fireside, New York, 1992.

Gibson, Lindsay C. *Adult Children of Emotionally Immature Parents: How to Heal from Distant, Rejecting, or Self-Involved Parents*. New Harbinger, Oakland, 2015.

Gillihan, Seth. *Cognitive Behavioral Therapy Made Simple: 10 Strategies for Managing Anxiety, Depression, Anger, Panic, and Worry*. Althea Press, Emeryville, 2018.

Greenberg, Elinor. *Borderline, Narcissistic, and Schizoid Adaptations: The Pursuit of Love, Admiration, and Safety.* Greenbrooke Press, New York, 2016.

Halvorson, Heidi Grant. *Nine Things Successful People Do Differently.* Harvard Business School Publishing, Boston, 2012.

Harris, Nadine Burke. *Toxic Childhood Stress: The Legacy of Early Trauma and How to Heal.* Bluebird, Englewood, 2020.

Herman, Judith Lewis. *Trauma and Recovery: The Aftermath of Violence—From Domestic Abuse to Political Terror.* Basic Books, New York, 1997.

James, Muriel. *It's Never Too Late to Be Happy! Reparenting Yourself for Happiness.* Quill Driver, Sanger, 1992.

Jones, Phil. *Drama as Therapy Volume 1: Theory, Practice and Research.* Routledge, London, 2007.

Klein, Linda Kay. *Pure: Inside the Evangelical Movement That Shamed a Generation of Young Women and How I Broke Free.* Atria, New York, 2019.

Leach, Penelope. *Putting the Children First When You Divorce: How to Parent Together When You're Apart.* Robinson, London, 2018.

LePera, Nicole. *How to Do the Work.* Orion Spring, London, 2021.

Levine, Amir and Rachel Heller. *Attached: The New Science of Adult Attachment and How It Can Help You Find—and Keep—Love.* TarcherPerigee, New York, 2011.

Lovatt, Peter. *Dance Psychology.* Dr Dance Presents, Norwich, 2018.

Lovatt, Peter. *The Dance Cure: The Surprising Science to Being Smarter, Stronger, Happier.* HarperOne, New York, 2021.

Mandeville, Rebecca C. *Rejected, Shamed, and Blamed: Help and Hope for Adults in the Family Scapegoat Role.* [place of publication not identified], 2020.

Manson, Mark. *The Subtle Art of Not Giving a F*ck: A Counterintuitive Approach to Living a Good Life.* Harper Paperbacks, New York, 2019.

Maté, Gabor. *In the Realm of Hungry Ghosts: Close Encounters with Addiction.* Vermilion, London, 2018.

Maté, Gabor. *The Myth of Normal: Trauma, Illness and Healing in a Toxic Culture.* Vermilion, London, 2022.

McAdams, Dan P. *The Stories We Live By: Personal Myths and the Making of the Self.* The Guilford Press, New York, 1997.

McCurdy, Jennette. *I'm Glad My Mom Died.* Simon & Schuster, New York, 2022.

McKay, Matthew, Michael Jason Greenberg and Patrick Fanning. *The ACT Workbook for Depression and Shame: Overcome Thoughts of Defectiveness and Increase Well-Being Using Acceptance and Commitment Therapy.* New Harbinger, Oakland, 2020.

Mitchell, Charlie. *The Nipper. The Heartbreaking True Story of a Little Boy and his Violent Childhood in Working-Class Dundee.* HarperElement, London, 2008.

Neff, Kristin. *Self-Compassion: The Proven Power of Being Kind to Yourself.* Yellow Kite, London, 2021.

Palazzi, Lily. *My Daddy the Pedophile: A Memoir.* [place of publication not identified], 2018.

Parris, Matthew. *Fracture: How Great Lives Take Root in Trauma.* Prospect Books, London, 2020.

Pollan, Michael. *How to Change Your Mind: The New Science of Psychedelics.* Penguin, London, 2019.

Remes, Olivia. *The Instant Mood Fix: Emergency Remedies to Beat Anxiety, Panic or Stress.* Ebury Press, London, 2021.

Renton, Alex. *Stiff Upper Lip: Secrets, Crimes and the Schooling of a Ruling Class.* Weidenfeld & Nicolson, London, 2017.

Schwartz, Richard. *No Bad Parts: Healing Trauma and Restoring Wholeness with the Internal Family Systems Model.* Sounds True, Boulder, 2021.

Smith, Julie. *Why Has Nobody Told Me This Before?* Michael Joseph Ltd, London, 2022.

Tawwab, Nedra Glover. *The Set Boundaries Workbook: Practical Exercises For Understanding Your Needs And Setting Healthy Limits.* TarcherPerigee, New York, 2021.

Thomas, Shannon. *Healing from Hidden Abuse: A Journey Through the Stages of Recovery from Psychological Abuse.* [place of publication not identified], 2016.

van der Kolk, Bessel. *The Body Keeps the Score: Mind, Brain and Body in the Transformation of Trauma.* Penguin Books, London, 2014.

Webb, Jonice. *Running On Empty No More: Transform Your Relationships With Your Partner, Your Parents and Your Children.* Morgan James Publishing, New York, 2018.

Webb, Jonice. *Running on Empty: Overcome Your Childhood Emotional Neglect.* Morgan James Publishing, New York, 2012.

Yalom, Irvin D. *The Theory and Practice of Group Psychotherapy*, 6th edn. Basic Books, New York, 2020.

REPORTS AND ARTICLES REFERRED TO IN THIS BOOK

CHAPTER 2

Page 13. CDC-Kaiser Permanente Adverse Childhood Experiences (ACE) Study

- **Summary:** https://www.cdc.gov/violenceprevention/aces/about.html
- **Full article:** Felitti, Vincent J., Robert F Anda, Dale Nordenberg, David F. Williamson, Alison M. Spitz, Valerie Edwards, Mary P. Koss and James S. Marks. Relationship of Childhood Abuse and Household Dysfunction to Many of the Leading Causes of Death in Adults. The Adverse Childhood Experiences (ACE) Study. American Journal of Preventive Medicine (1998) Vol 14 No 4, 245–258. https://doi.org/10.1016/S0749-3797(98)00017-8

CHAPTER 3

Page 21. National Society for the Prevention of Cruelty to Children. Emotional Abuse. https://www.nspcc.org.uk/what-is-child-abuse/types-of-abuse/emotional-abuse/

Page 27. The Report of the Independent Inquiry into Child Sexual Abuse for England and Wales (2022). https://www.iicsa.org.uk/

Page 29. UK Government. Evidence on the Impact of Parental Conflict on Children (2021). https://www.gov.uk/guidance/reducing-parental-conflict-the-impact-on-children#evidence-on-the-impact-of-parental-conflict-on-children

Page 41. American Academy of Child and Adolescent Psychiatry. Gangs and Children, Facts for Families No. 98 (2017). https://www.aacap.org/AACAP/Families_and_Youth/Facts_for_Families/FFF-Guide/Children-and-Gangs-098.aspx

CHAPTER 5

Page 65. Women's Aid. Myths About Domestic Abuse. https://www.womensaid.org.uk/information-support/what-is-domestic-abuse/myths/

Page 66. Allnock, Debbie and Pam Miller. No One Noticed, No One Heard: A Study of Disclosures of Childhood Abuse. NSPCC (2013). https://learning.nspcc.org.uk/research-resources/2013/no-one-noticed-no-one-heard

Page 67. Oxfam. Ten Harmful Beliefs that Perpetuate Violence Against Women and Girls. https://www.oxfam.org/en/ten-harmful-beliefs-perpetuate-violence-against-women-and-girls

CHAPTER 7

Page 89. Seltzer, Leon F. What Your Anger May Be Hiding. Psychology Today (2008). https://www.psychologytoday.com/intl/blog/evolution-of-the-self/200807/what-your-anger-may-be-hiding

Page 89. Spring, Carolyn. Working With Shame Online Training. https://www.carolynspring.com/shop/wws-online-training/

Page 103. CPTSD Foundation. What is Post-Traumatic Stress Disorder? https://cptsdfoundation.org/what-is-complex-post-traumatic-stress-disorder-cptsd/

CHAPTER 10

Page 141. Painter, Susan and Donald Dutton. Patterns of Emotional Bonding in Battered Women: Traumatic Bonding. International Journal of Women's Studies (1970), Vol 8, 363–375. https://www.researchgate.net/publication/232584113_Patterns_of_emotional_bonding_in_battered_women_Traumatic_bonding

CHAPTER 14

Page 167. James, Muriel. Self Reparenting: Theory and Process. Transactional Analysis Bulletin (1974), Vol 4 No 3, 32–39. https://doi.org/10.1177/036215377400400307

CHAPTER 16

Page 207. Bonn-Miller, Marcel O., Megan Brunstetter, Alex Simonian, Mallory J. Loflin, Ryan Vandrey, Kimberly A. Babson and Hal Wortzel. The Long-Term, Prospective, Therapeutic Impact of Cannabis on Post Traumatic Stress Disorder. Cannabis and Cannabinoid Research (2022) Vol 7 No 2, 214–223. http://doi.org/10.1089/can.2020.0056

Page 208. Sessa, Ben. From Sacred Plants to Psychotherapy: The History and Re-Emergence of Psychedelics in Medicine (2007) https://www.rcpsych.ac.uk/docs/default-source/members/sigs/spirituality-spsig/ben-sessa-from-sacred-plants-to-psychotherapy.pdf?sfvrsn=d1bd0269_2

CHAPTER 18

Page 231. Leopold, Aldo. Thinking Like a Mountain. In: *A Sand County Almanac and Sketches* (1949) https://trainingcenter.fws.gov/resources/knowledge-resources/wildread/thinking-like-a-mountain.pdf

www.ingramcontent.com/pod-product-compliance
Lightning Source LLC
Chambersburg PA
CBHW060353080526
44583CB00012B/291